ADVANCING CULTURALLY RESPONSIVE RESEARCH AND RESEARCHERS

Advancing Culturally Responsive Research and Researchers: Qualitative, Quantitative, and Mixed Methods encourages readers to design and engage in methodologies and methods that place cultural relevancy at the center of inquiry. In doing so, it highlights the need to uplift voices and needs of people who have been historically marginalized in the environments that we both inhabit and engage in as part of knowledge construction.

The scholars whose work is featured in this volume take up research from different paradigmatic, ontological, epistemological, axiological, and methodological approaches – yet, with adherence to centering cultural responsiveness in all research decisions. Each chapter seeks to extend understandings of social inequities, methodologies, and/or methods – and to contribute to meaningful and evolving social change through innovative and cutting-edge research strategies. While doing this work, the authors illustrate and highlight the importance of researcher positions and reflexivity in supporting the expansion of culturally responsive approaches; they also do so while considering global sociopolitical conditions of this moment in time. The contributions to this volume were initially presented at the first biennial Advanced Methods Institute in 2021. The Institute was hosted by QualLab in The Ohio State University's College of Education and Human Ecology and shared this volume's thematic focus.

As a handbook, the volume can help faculty and advanced researchers with interest in doing culturally responsive projects to better understand frameworks, approaches, and considerations for doing so. It includes activities to support readers in developing said understandings.

Penny A. Pasque is a Professor in Educational Studies, Director of Qualitative Methods, and Director of the QualLab in the Office of Research, Innovation and Collaboration (ORIC) in College of Education and Human Ecology at The Ohio State University. She is editor of the *Review of Higher Education* (with Nelson Laird).

e alexander is an Assistant Professor at the University of Kansas, and qualitative-leaning mixed methodologist who enjoys learning with others about tailoring research to be grounded in community and place.

ADVANCING CULTURALLY RESPONSIVE RESEARCH AND RESEARCHERS

Qualitative, Quantitative, and Mixed Methods

Edited by Penny A. Pasque and e alexander

Routledge
Taylor & Francis Group

LONDON AND NEW YORK

Cover image: Artwork by Suzanne Margaret (Agnello) Haberstroh (–2021)

First published 2023
by Routledge
4 Park Square, Milton Park, Abingdon, Oxon OX14 4RN

and by Routledge
605 Third Avenue, New York, NY 10158

Routledge is an imprint of the Taylor & Francis Group, an informa business

British Library Cataloguing-in-Publication Data
A catalogue record for this book is available from the British Library

Library of Congress Cataloging-in-Publication Data
A catalog record has been requested for this book

ISBN: 9780367648596 (hbk)
ISBN: 9780367648626 (pbk)
ISBN: 9781003126621 (ebk)

DOI: 10.4324/9781003126621

Typeset in Bembo
by KnowledgeWorks Global Ltd.

CONTENTS

SECTION IV
The Future of Culturally Responsive Research   237

ABOUT THE AUTHORS

Bryant Keith Alexander (he/him) is Dean, College of Communication and Fine Arts, and Interim Dean, School of Film and Television at Loyola Marymount University. He is an active scholar with nearly 200 scholarly publications that appear in leading journals and major handbooks that evidence the broad interdisciplinary and intellectual curiosity of his engagement, including: *The Handbook of Qualitative Inquiry, The Oxford Research Encyclopedia of Communication, The Handbook of Autoethnography, The Blackwell Handbook of Critical Intercultural Communication, The Handbook of Communication and Instruction, The Handbook of Critical and Indigenous Methodologies, The Handbook of Qualitative Research, The Handbook of Performance Studies,* and *Men and Masculinities: Critical Concepts in Sociology.* He is co-editor of *Performance Theories in Education: Power, Pedagogy, and the Politics of Identity* (Erlbaum, 2005); author of *Performing Black Masculinity: Race, Culture, and Queer Identity* (Alta Mira, 2006), author of *The Performative Sustainability of Race: Reflections on Black Culture and the Politics of Identity* (Peter Lang, 2012), co-editor of the *Routledge Handbook of Gender and Communication* (2021), co-author of *Still Hanging: Using Performance Texts to Deconstruct Racism* (Brill|Sense, 2021), and co-author of *Collaborative Spirit-Writing Performance in Everyday Black Lives,* (Routledge, 2021). He holds an earned Ph.D. from Southern Illinois University Carbondale. At LMU he is tenured faculty in the Department of Communication Studies and serves as Affiliate Faculty in the Educational Leadership for Social Justice Doctoral Program in LMU's School of Education.

e alexander is an Assistant Professor at the University of Kansas, and qualitative-leaning mixed methodologist. They enjoy learning with others about tailoring research to be grounded in the communities, geographies, ancestries, and spiritualities of feminine BIPOC. Dr. alexander's work draws on many fields and approaches in service to dismantling neocolonialist logics, structures, and operations in both scholarship and the postsecondary industry. Dr. alexander is particularly interested in how researchers' and practitioners' epistemic, axiological, ontological, and praxeology constructs converge to inform their conceptualizations of and inter/actions with environments in which they work. They are also interested in these convergences' impacts on organizational cultures across the postsecondary industry, industries that claim to champion social mobility, and industries that are known to uphold western, white, and masculine supremacy.

Kakali Bhattacharya is a Professor at the University of Florida working as a qualitative methodologist serving the College of Education and other related humanities and social science disciplines. Trained by the University of Georgia, since 200, her research interests are interdisciplinary, exploring transnational issues of race, class, gender in higher education in the U.S. and de/colonizing qualitative and educational research. Dr. Bhattacharya's work has made spaces in interdisciplinary de/colonizing and qualitative research where creativity and contemplative approaches are legitimized and seen as gateways for cultivating depth, criticality, integrity, and expansive inquiry. With over 90 publications with critical, de/colonial, and anti-oppressive work, Dr. Bhattacharya has been recognized via various professional organizations. She is the 2018 winner of AERA's *Mid-Career Scholar of Color Award* and the 2018 winner of AERA's *Mentoring Award* from Division G: Social Context of Education. Her co-authored text with Kent Gillen, *Power, Race, and Higher Education: A Cross-Cultural Parallel Narrative,* has won a 2017 *Outstanding Publication Award* from AERA (SIG 168) and a *2018 Outstanding Book Award* from the International Congress of Qualitative Research. She is also the 2020 winner of the Mary Frances Early College of Education Distinguished Alumni Award for research from the University of Georgia.

Jamilia J. Blake (she/her) is a Professor at Texas A&M University. Dr. Blake's research examines the developmental trajectory of peer-directed aggression, bullying, and victimization in socially marginalized youth and racial/ethnic disparities in school discipline. She has authored more than 40 publications and is a fellow of the American Psychological Association. Dr. Blake has published studies examining the social and psychological consequences of aggression and victimization for African-American girls and students with disabilities and the disparate impact of school discipline for African-American girls.

Siqi Chen (she/her) is a Psychometrician in Pearson Clinical group. She earned her Ph.D. in Research, Measurement, and Statistics from Texas A&M University. Dr. Chen's research interest lies in the area of applying quantitative and machine learning methods to improve educational evaluations and assessments.

Jessica T. DeCuir-Gunby (she/her/hers) is a Professor of Educational Psychology at the University of Southern California. She currently serves on the editorial board for *Educational Psychologist, Contemporary Educational Psychology*, and the *American Educational Research Journal*, where she was a former associate editor. DeCuir-Gunby's research interests include race and racial identity development, critical race theory, mixed methods research, and emotions in education. Her work has been featured in top-tier journals such as *Contemporary Educational Psychology, Educational Psychologist, Educational Researcher, and Review of Educational Research*, among others. DeCuir-Gunby has also co-authored/co-edited four books. She has served as Co-PI on two National Science Foundation funded grants, totaling over $4.3 million: Nurturing Mathematics Dreamkeepers (NSF DRK-12 Grant) and Peer Mentoring Summits for Women Engineering Faculty of Color (NSF ADVANCE Leadership Award Grant). Her most recent grant, funded by the Spencer Foundation, explores Black essential worker mothers and their experiences with distance learning during COVID-19. DeCuir-Gunby is an American Psychological Association Fellow for Division 15 (Educational Psychology). She was awarded the University of Georgia's College of Education Outstanding Educator Award for alumni (2015–2016).

Antonio Duran (he/him/él) is an Assistant Professor in the Higher Education program at Florida International University. Dr. Duran received his B.A. in English and American Literature from New York University, his M.S. in Student Affairs in Higher Education from Miami University, and his Ph.D. in Higher Education and Student Affairs from The Ohio State University. His research explores how historical and contemporary legacies of oppression inform college student development and experiences. He is often interested in how systems such as racism, heterosexism, and trans oppression shape how those with multiple minoritized identities navigate college campuses. Namely, Dr. Duran leverages theoretical frameworks (e.g., intersectionality, queer of color critique) originating outside of educational disciplines to engage in this critical work. As a qualitative researcher, he seeks to understand the potential of these frameworks to inform research and practice within higher education settings. Dr. Duran has written, alongside other scholars, about how to engage with critical and poststructural schools of thought in educational scholarship, as well as in practice. His research has been published in venues such as the *International Journal of Qualitative Studies in Education, Journal of Diversity in Higher Education,* and *Journal of College Student Development*.

Stephen M. Gibson (he/him/his) is a third-year doctoral student in the Developmental Psychology program at Virginia Commonwealth University. Stephen holds a Master of Science in Teacher Education and Learning Sciences with a concentration in Educational Psychology from North Carolina State University and received his Bachelor of Arts degree in Psychology from North Carolina Central University. Broadly, Stephen's research examines how cultural and contextual factors (schools; communities) contribute to family processes and youth development among Black families. Specifically, his research interests included critical race theory, racial and academic socialization, racial identity development, sense of belonging, and mental health symptomatology. As a fully funded doctoral student, he was a recipient of the prestigious National Science Foundation Graduate Research Fellowship.

Sylvia Hurtado (she/her) is a Professor of Education and was Director of the Higher Education Research Institute at the University of California, Los Angeles for over a decade. Previous to that, she was Director of the Center for Higher Education and Postsecondary Education at the University of Michigan. She has written extensively on student development and college experiences, campus racial climate, STEM education, and diversity in higher education. She received the 2018 Social Justice in Education Award from the American Educational Research Association (AERA), served as President of the Association for the Study of Higher Education (ASHE) in 2005 and is a member of the National Academy of Education. She is co-editor of two recent books that won awards from the International Latino Book Awards: *The Magic Key: The Educational Journey of Mexican Americans from K-12 to College and Beyond* (2015, University of Texas Press); and *Hispanic-Serving Institutions: Advancing Research and Transformative Practice* (2015, Routledge Press). Her current national projects focus on diverse learning environments and student retention, STEM education interventions and diversification of the scientific workforce, institutional transformation, and innovation in undergraduate education. She employs mixed methods research and case studies of institutions that contextualize the experiences and success of underrepresented and marginalized groups.

Jason Jabbari (he/him) is an Assistant Professor of research in the Brown School at Washington University in St. Louis, where leads the education research portfolio at the Social Policy Institute. A former classroom teacher, school leader, and basketball coach, Jabbari continues to partner with a variety of community organizations and education institutions to help them understand and solve pressing social problems. In doing so, Jabbari uses sociological theories and advanced quantitative methodologies to explore education programs, policies, and practices related to equitable outcomes in urban communities. One of Jabbari's most recent projects involves understanding the impact of a novel coding and apprenticeship program – LaunchCode – on currently incarcerated individuals' long-term social and economic circumstances. His work has been supported by a variety of foundations, including Ascendium and Mastercard. His research has appeared in places like *Urban Education, Brookings,* and *Forbes.*

Lyric Jackson (she/her) is currently a fourth-year doctoral student in the School Psychology Ph.D. program at Texas A&M University. She is a member of Dr. Blake's Peer Relations and Adjustment Lab. Her current focuses on parent and peer racial/ethnic socialization and Black girls school discipline experiences.

Odis Johnson, Jr. (he/him) is a Bloomberg Distinguished Professor at Johns Hopkins University, where he has faculty appointments in the Department of Health Policy and Management at the Bloomberg School of Public Health, the School of Education as Executive Director of the Center for Safe and Healthy Schools, and in the Department of Sociology at the Krieger School of Arts and Sciences. He also directs the Institute in Critical Quantitative, Computational, and Mixed Methodologies (ICQCM), and is editor of the journal, *Sociology of Education*. Odis Johnson previously served as a faculty member at Washington University in St. Louis, and chaired the African American Studies Department at the University of Maryland. His work on the interrelated topics of neighborhoods, social policy, and race have been funded by the National Science Foundation, National Institutes of Health, William T. Grant Foundation, and the Spencer Foundation. Odis Johnson's work and ideas about social change have been featured in prominent media outlets, including the *Oprah Magazine, Christian Science Monitor, CNN, The Washington Post, MSNBC, NPR, Teen Vogue, The Associated Press, Vox, The New Yorker, The New York Times, NBC News, The Chicago Tribune, SiriusXM,* and a variety of international and local news outlets.

Susan R. Jones, (she/her) is Professor Emerita in the Higher Education and Student Affairs program at The Ohio State University. Prior to re-joining the faculty at Ohio State in 2010, she was an Associate Professor and Director of the College Student Personnel program at the University of Maryland-College Park (2005–2010). She has published six books, more than 28 book chapters and more than 25 journal articles, mostly in top-tier journals, including the Journal of College Student Development and the Journal of Higher Education. She is the co-author (with Dr. Elisa S. Abes) titled *Identity Development of College Students* (Jossey-Bass, 2013). She and two colleagues (Drs. Vasti Torres and Jan Arminio) published a book entitled *Negotiating the Complexities of Qualitative Research: Fundamental Elements and Issues* (Routledge, 2006; 2nd edition, 2014). Jones is one of the co-editors (Schuh, Jones, and Harper) of the 5th edition of *Student Services: A Handbook for the Profession* (Jossey-Bass, 2011), referred to as "the Green Book" and arguably the leading textbook for graduate programs in higher education and student affairs.

Minjung Kim (she/her) is an Assistant Professor in the Quantitative Research, Evaluation, and Measurement (QREM) program in the Department of Educational Studies, College of Education and Human Ecology, at The Ohio State University. Dr. Kim received her Ph.D. in 2012 from Texas A&M University. Her research interests include examining methodological issues in the use of the advanced quantitative methods under the framework of multilevel modeling and structural equation modeling. She is also interested in applying those models in different educational and psychological research and providing the easy-to-use guidelines for substantive researchers. Dr. Kim was recently awarded an EHE Emerging Scholar Seed Grant for *Assessing Causal*

Mechanisms in Complex Educational Data: A New Approach of Multilevel Mediation Analysis. She has also served as the chair of the American Educational Research Association (AERA) Multilevel Modeling Special Interest Group (MLM-SIG) from 2017 to 2018.

Patti Lather (she/her) is Professor Emerita in the Department of Educational Studies, College of Education and Human Ecology, at The Ohio State University where she taught qualitative research, feminist methodology and gender and education from 1988 to 2014. She is the author of numerous articles and five books, the latest being *(Post)Critical Methodologies: The Science Possible After the Critiques: The Selected Writings of Patti Lather*, 2017. She has lectured around the world, including a 1989 Fulbright to New Zealand, and is a 2009 inductee of the AERA Fellows, a 2010 recipient of the AERA Division B Lifetime Achievement Award, and a 2015 recipient of the International Congress of Qualitative Inquiry (ICQI) Lifetime Achievement Award.

Whitney N. McCoy (she/her) is a Research Scientist focusing on Equity and Inclusion for the Center for Child and Family Policy at Duke University. Prior to her role at Duke, she was a postdoctoral researcher associate in STEM education at the School of Education and Human Development at the University of Virginia. Whitney earned her Ph.D. in Teacher Education and Learning Sciences with a concentration in Educational Psychology from North Carolina State University. She holds a Master of Arts in Teaching from the University of North Carolina at Charlotte and received her Bachelor of Science in Biology from Winston-Salem State University. McCoy's research explores identity development for Black girls in educational settings. Her research interests include critical race theory, racial identity development, self-efficacy, and STEM education. Her dissertation, *Black Girls Accepting the Grand Challenge: A Qualitative Exploration of a Summer Engineering Program's Influence on Black Girls' Racial Identity, Engineering Identity, and STEM Self-Efficacy* was awarded Outstanding Dissertation of the Year in the Department of Teacher Education and Learning Sciences at North Carolina State University. As a fully funded doctoral student, she was a Southern Regional Education Board Doctoral Scholar and a recipient of the prestigious National Science Foundation Graduate Research Fellowship.

Penny A. Pasque (she/her) is a Professor in Educational Studies, Director of Qualitative Methods, and Director of the QualLab in the Office of Research, Innovation and Collaboration (ORIC) in College of Education and Human Ecology at The Ohio State University. In addition, she is editor of the *Review of Higher Education* (with Nelson Laird), which is considered one of the leading research journals in the field. Her research addresses complexities in qualitative inquiry and dis/connections between higher education and society, as she works toward socially just critical and (post)qualitative paradigms, methodologies, and methods. Dr. Pasque's research has appeared in over 100 journal articles and books, including in *The Journal of Higher Education, Qualitative Inquiry, Diversity in Higher Education, Critical Studies ↔ Critical Methodologies, The Review of Higher Education*, among others. Her qualitative books include *Qualitative Inquiry in Higher Education Organization and Policy Research* (with Lechuga, Routledge), *Qualitative Inquiry for Equity in Higher Education: Methodological Innovations, Implications, and Interventions* (with Carducci, Kuntz & Gildersleeve, Jossey-Bass), and *Critical Qualitative Inquiry: Foundations and Futures* (with Cannella & Salazar Pérez, Left Coast Press). She is also author of *American Higher Education Leadership and Policy: Critical Issues and the Public Good* (Palgrave Macmillan), *Empowering Women in Higher Education and Student Affairs* (with Shelley Errington Nicholson, Stylus), *Transforming Understandings of Diversity in Higher Education* (with Ortega, Burkhardt & Ting, Stylus), and *Engaged Research and Practice* (with Overton & Burkhardt, Stylus).

Naomi Ruffin (she/her) is currently a third-year doctoral student in the School Psychology Ph.D. program at Texas A&M University. Her current research interests revolve broadly around the School-to-Prison Pipeline, Zero-tolerance Policies, Discipline Disparities in Schools, and Restorative Justice practices. She is a member of the Peer Relations and Adjustment Lab led by Dr. Blake.

Winston C. Thompson (he/him) is an Associate Professor of Philosophy of Education within the College of Education and Human Ecology at The Ohio State University (and an Associate Professor of Philosophy by courtesy). An internationally regarded philosopher of education, Thompson has been a faculty member at New York University, Hofstra University, and the University of New Hampshire. In 2016–17, Dr. Thompson was a Fellow-in-Residence at the Edmond J. Safra Center for Ethics at Harvard University. Thompson's scholarship focuses upon normative ethical and social/political questions of justice, education, and the public good, with recent efforts analyzing dilemmas of educational policy. Additionally, Thompson's work has given special attention to ethical dilemmas of identity related to race, immigration, and citizenship. His publications have appeared *in Harvard Educational Review*, the *Journal of Moral Education, Educational Theory, Philosophy of Education, Teachers College Record, The Journal of Philosophy of Education, Educational Philosophy and Theory, and Studies in Philosophy and Education*. Thompson received his Ph.D. (with distinction) in Philosophy and Education from Teachers College, Columbia University.

Verónica N. Vélez (she/her) is an Associate Professor in the Woodring College of Education at Western Washington University (WWU). Her research focuses on Latinx im/migrant mother activism, popular education, and (re)imagining cartographic tools for movement building. Each of these areas is informed by expertise in Critical Race Theory (CRT), Latinx Critical Theory (LatCrit), Radical and Tactical Cartography, and Chicana Feminist Epistemologies. Influenced and inspired by these varied, but interrelated frameworks, she developed Critical Race Spatial Analysis (CRSA), a framework and methodological approach that seeks to deepen a spatial consciousness and expand the use of geographic information systems (GIS) in critical race research in education. Connected to her work on advancing geospatial and computational methodologies, Dr. Vélez recently co-edited a special issue in *Race, Ethnicity, and Education* on "QuantCrit," a methodological subfield of CRT that troubles the decontextualized and color-evasive nature of quantitative research in education. In addition to her scholarly work, Dr. Vélez worked as a grassroots organizer with Latinx im/migrant families for over 15 years on local school reform efforts and adult literacy campaigns. She is currently collaborating with teachers, administrators, and community members to develop an Ethnic Studies framework for use in K-12 public schools in Washington State. Dr. Vélez is the proud daughter of im/migrant parents, whose journey to provide her with a quality education fundamentally inspires her work for social and racial justice.

Casey Philip Wong, (he/him) holds a Ph.D. and is an Assistant Professor of Social Foundations of Education in the Department of Educational Policy Studies at Georgia State University, and an affiliated scholar in the University of California, Los Angeles (UCLA) Department of Anthropology. Recently recognized with the *2021 UCLA Chancellor's Award for Postdoctoral Research*, Dr. Wong's interdisciplinary research examines social justice in educational theory, policy, and practice. He elucidates this perspective within an article that he published in 2021 within the *Review of Research in Education*, "The Wretched of the Research: Disenchanting Man2-as-Educational Researcher and Entering the 36th Chamber of Education Research." Dr. Wong was most recently an invited panelist for a Presidential Session at the American Educational Research Association on creating expansive and equitable learning environments (virtual), an invited presenter for a Presidential Session on Hip Hop Pedagogies at the American Association of Applied Linguistics (Chicago), and a speaker at the International James Baldwin Conference (Paris). He has worked with scholars and activists in Hip Hop Education to organize four Think Tank gatherings, as well as a Culturally Sustaining Pedagogy conference that brought together leaders working for educational justice. Dr. Wong has been working inside and outside of schools to heal, cultivate critical thinking, and educate for collective freedom with K-16 youth and young adults, from Oakland to NYC, for over 15 years.

Junyeong Yang (he/his) is currently a doctoral student in the Quantitative Research, Evaluation and Measurement (QREM) program in the Department of Educational Studies, College of Education and Human Ecology at The Ohio State University. His current research interests are the various advanced research methodologies such as structural equation model (SEM), hierarchical linear model (HLM), mixture models, and Monte Carlo simulation study. Through research on these methodologies and applying them to actual data, he wants to give practical guidance and inspiration to various fields of social-behavioral science.

ACKNOWLEDGMENTS

We dedicate this book to those who create and construct knowledge to uplift and empower their communities – past, present, and future. These scholars – whether ever acknowledged as such – include researchers, practitioners, practitioner-scholars, activists, advocates, people carrying out justice work across non-profits and industries, and community members who exercise agency in creating positive changes for themselves. Thank you for employing research, theory, and practice that is driven by, responsive to, and sustains the cultures in the communities that you serve (and perhaps belong to, as well). You are engaging in this labor while attending to the world's ever-changing socio-political-economic-cultural milieu; we salute you. Thank you to the scholars who came before us – in and beyond the academy – who worked harder than we may ever know to make important changes regarding what is considered research and how we conceptualize it.

Unique to our relationship as co-editors and colleagues, it is important to share how much we appreciate each other and genuinely thank each other for challenging the other person – and our own selves – to grow as culturally responsive scholars as we went on a collective journey to edit this volume.

The cover of this volume centers the intergenerational. We honor e's mother, whose favorite color is purple, hence our choice for a purple book cover. We also honor Penny's mother, Suzanne Margaret (Agnello) Haberstroh (– 2021) whose original artwork adorns the cover and complements the purple. This book cover symbolically pays tribute to the generations that have come before us and the generations after us.

We would also like to thank the College of Education and Human Ecology at The Ohio State University for its support of the Advanced Methods Institute (AMI) and QualLab. Specifically, we acknowledge the culturally responsive efforts of Dean Donald Pope-Davis, Senior Associate Dean Noelle W. Arnold, Associate Dean Natasha Slesnick, and Director Kimberly Lightle.

Importantly, thank you to all the scholars, postdoctoral researchers, and graduate students who supported the international success of the Advanced Methods Institute in 2021. This includes all the participants who attended AMI and encouraged us to think more deeply – in the Institute workshops and in the writing of this volume – about transforming concepts of culturally responsive research into research practice. Further, we appreciate the boundless energy of Chelsea Gilbert, AMI and QualLab Graduate Research Associate (GRA), for all your leadership, thoughtfulness, and support with AMI 2021 and beyond. We appreciate the efforts of Bakari Lumumba (QualLab GRA) in helping one of our chapter authors. We also offer a special thanks to Ruth Lu and Tess Smith (QualLab GRAs) for your assistance in indexing this volume.

Finally, we would like to thank our editor, Hannah Shakespeare, and the entire Routledge team, for championing this important contribution about culturally responsive research and researchers toward a post-paradigm war era. We appreciate your dedication to the concepts in this book and your role in advancing the next iteration of research methods poised to make concerted change.

1

INTRODUCTION

The Importance of Culturally Responsive Research and Culturally Responsive Researchers

Penny A. Pasque, e alexander

As scholars, we play an instrumental role in researching and addressing myriad complex issues facing the world today in education and human sciences (Ladson-Billings, 2015; McMahon, 2009; Pasque, 2010/2014). Research informs policies, laws, programs, and practices in order to address inequities and transform lives. For example, our research impacts early childhood professional development, youth homelessness, racial and socioeconomic educational disparities in rural and urban environments, access to college, undergraduate and graduate student success, physical wellness, counseling in schools, federal and state court cases, our land, and beyond.

Yet, there is a problem. Despite the influence that our work has on society, approaches to academic research have not evolved at a pace that keeps up with societal changes. The past decade has brought us tremendous shifts in discussions about race, ethnicity, gender, class, coloniality, nationality, systems of oppression, and personal, organizational, and systemic power. It has also given us advancements in ontoepistemic technologies and the dissolution of civil public discourse in the face of difference among groups. Across the globe, we have witnessed scores of cataclysmic events: state violence against Black peoples and Peoples of Color, desecrations of Indigenous peoples and their lands, climate events at unprecedented magnitudes, global pandemics that have claimed millions of lives, colonization through war, and many others. Meanwhile, we have often continued using academia's traditional methodologies and methods as though these events are not occurring daily and impacting every aspect of our lives. To be sure, "approaches to research often follow similar patterns, admittedly from a place of academic privilege, with violence, systemic policy, and white supremacy infused throughout dominant research practices, programs, and policies" (Pasque et al., 2022, p. 3). Consequently, as we default to our familiar approaches

DOI: 10.4324/9781003126621-1

to, and methods of, research – we perpetuate the trope of us being disconnected from the world through our Ivory Towers.

If we as researchers continue to reify decades-old methodologies and methods and perpetuate the qualitative vs. quantitative paradigm wars, we cannot position our scholarship to adequately address contemporary issues *and/or* pervasive social inequities that have evaded us for centuries (Pasque & Carducci, 2015, in press). Said differently: *our approaches to research must evolve to keep up with the times.*

As Denzin and Giardina (2015) reflect,

> We are, to put it bluntly, at a pivotal crossroads: We live in a historical present that cries out for emancipatory visions, for visions that inspire transformative inquiries, and for inquiries that can provide the moral authority to move people to struggle and resist oppression.
>
> *(p. 12)*

As such, it is imperative that we, as researchers, are well-versed in the latest cutting-edge methodological approaches and their congruent methods – whether (post)qualitative,[1] quantitative, mixed, or transcendent of these labels – for research to make practical change in communities of which we are a part. *It is our responsibility, and yours, to make decisions reflective of culturally responsive research.* This book helps scholars to answer that call.

The authors intentionally created this volume to encourage you – scholars, community activist researchers, practitioner-scholars, and all readers – to design and engage in methodologies and methods that place cultural relevancy, including the voices and needs of people who have been historically minoritized and the environments that we inhabit, at the center of your inquiry. As such, every decision of the research process (i.e., conceptualization of orienting research questions with local stakeholders or co-conspirators, embodied methods, dissemination of research and implementation of inquiry-informed action plans) should reflect axio-onto-epistemologically[2] culturally relevant approaches. This includes topics *and* designs that are attentive to issues of power and inequities (Hurtado, 2015; Pasque & Pérez, 2015; Pasque & Carducci, in press). We hope this book helps you to engage in thoughtful, culturally relevant decisions in and with your research.

Culturally Responsive Research

Culturally responsive research is derived from the pedagogical change that Gloria Ladson-Billings (2014) fostered as she "dared to ask what was right with these [African American] students and what happens in classrooms of teachers who seemed to experience pedagogical success with them" (p. 74; also see Ladson-Billings, 1990). This approach includes cultural competence (e.g., the ability to appreciate and celebrate cultures of origin while gaining knowledge of and fluency in cultures oneself) and sociopolitical consciousness (e.g., using knowledge and skills to identify, analyze, and solve problems) in a sustainable way (Ladson-Billings, 2014, p. 75).

Culturally responsive research takes up Ladson-Billings' concept and enacts it throughout research processes from beginning to end, in an iterative manner. As such, culturally responsive research centers relational discourses as it challenges traditional research notions of distance and neutrality (Berryman, SooHoo, & Nevin, 2013).

To be sure, culturally responsive scholars take up research from different paradigmatic, ontological, epistemological, axiological, and methodological approaches – yet, with the adherence to centering cultural responsiveness in each research decision. For example, one could approach research from a postpositivist (Creswell & Plano Clark, 2011; Guba & Lincoln, 2005), constructivist (Charmaz, 2014), transformative (see Hurtado's chapter in this volume), critical (Denzin, Lincoln, & Smith, 2008), critical advocacy (Pasque & Carducci, 2015, in press), or poststructural paradigm (Belsey, 2002), among many others. Further, scholars may take up culturally responsive research from quantitative, qualitative, mixed methods, philosophical, historical, and/or approaches that extend beyond these labels. In this way, culturally responsive research pushes us past the paradigm wars that stunt innovation as it requires numbers *and* stories that, taken together, have the potential to move us toward sustained equity and justice.

Similarly, the authors in this book take up various philosophies, methodologies, and methods – *each with cultural responsiveness centered in their research design*. We hope you learn about various approaches to culturally responsive research from each author and *your* research extends the concepts presented in this volume.

This Book's Story

As an introduction to this volume, we want to share with you how its group of authors came together from different universities across the United States. Under the leadership of Dean Donald Pope-Davis, the College of Education and Human Ecology at The Ohio State University has been investing in strengthening knowledge and innovative research designs of faculty, post-doctoral researchers, graduate students, and scholars as we work collectively toward equity and social justice in social and behavior sciences. Penny was invited to lead the efforts of the biennial Advanced Methods Institute (AMI) within two months of her arrival at Ohio State as a director of qualitative methods for the college. There were numerous cutting-edge scholars that could have been invited; invitations went to some (but nowhere near all) of the most esteemed methodologists in the country, a true gathering of visionary and engaged scholars.

The contributors to this volume presented at the first biennial AMI in 2021. The Institute was hosted by Ohio State's QualLab (https://u.osu.edu/quallab/) in the Office of Research, Innovation and Collaboration, which was established in 2020 by both of us (Penny as director and professor; e as a graduate research associate, then post-doctoral researcher, and now assistant professor) with support from Dean Donald Pope-Davis, Associate Dean Natasha Slesnick, Director Kim Lightle, Sandy Reed, and Graduate Student Research Associate Chelsea Gilbert.[3]

AMI 2021 focused on *Advancing Culturally Responsive Research and Researchers*. The Institute title signifies the importance of researcher reflexivity and positionality in culturally responsive research processes. AMI provides an opportunity to engage participants in the latest research approaches that impact the cultural relevance and sustainability of scholarship in the social-behavioral sciences. This book makes said approaches more accessible to researchers. Please see AMI information and companion exercises to this volume's chapters at https://u.osu. edu/quallab/advanced-methods-institute/. Also see the numerous efforts of the QualLab, including the webinar series, video, and publication *Unapologetic Educational Research: Addressing Anti-Blackness, Racism and White Supremacy* (Pasque et al., 2022) (co-sponsored with the Department of Educational Studies), monthly QualLab Lunches, the Dashboard of Resources, and links to resources across the country (https://u.osu.edu/quallab/).

More specifically, the book includes four sections about (1) Contexts and Concerns for Quantitative, (Post)Qualitative, and Mixed Methods Research, (2) Qualitative Approaches (e.g., autoethnography, hip-hop research, intersectionality), (3) Quantitative and Mixed Methods approaches (e.g., sampling, GIS mapping, measurement, coding), and (4) The Future of Culturally Responsive Research. Each chapter in the second, third, and fourth sections offers *activities* that you can workshop in a class or with your research teams. The activities are focused on methodological issues in support of advancing scholarship to help you (and us) better understand frameworks, approaches, and considerations for undertaking more innovative social science research. We thank the contributors for their assistance in introducing the chapters to you here – for your ease in navigating the volume.

Of note is that the contributors do not seek to provide readers with concepts that simplify processes of (post)qualitative, quantitative, or and mixed-methods inquiry: others have already done so in previous works. Instead, our aim is to advance scholarly discussions on how research methodologies and methods might benefit from *innovative and cutting-edge strategies* that simultaneously contribute to equity and social change. The volume contributors illustrate the potential for advancing culturally responsive research – and the importance of your/our choices as researchers in supporting said movement and moment in time. In other words, each chapter seeks to extend understandings of social inequities, methodologies, and/or methods – and to contribute to meaningful and evolving social change. We implore you to explore how you will advance these efforts through your own scholarship.

Section I – Contexts and Concerns for Quantitative, (Post)Qualitative, and Mixed Methods Research

The three contributors to Section I, "Contexts and Concerns for Quantitative, (Post)Qualitative, and Mixed Methods Research," address concepts of transformative, social justice, and ethical research important for setting the context for the remainder of the book. Each provides important considerations that transcend quantitative, qualitative, mixed methods, philosophical, and/or historical approaches to culturally responsive research.

In the first chapter, Sylvia Hurtado reflects on her own journey as a scholar as she discusses "*The Transformative Paradigm: An Evolving Journey in Methods and Social Justice Aims.*" She addresses the distinctive approach of the transformative paradigm, rooted in a critique of power relationships with emancipatory goals for individuals and transformative goals for institutions and systems of oppression. This paradigm embraces multiple theories, methods, participants' realities, and variations in the stance of the researcher in relation to participants. Dr. Hurtado examines her journey through paradigms using examples in mixed methods research and case studies of the campus climate for racial/ ethnic diversity and organizational change in higher education. Key challenges are important to consider as methods evolve to fully embrace a transformative approach.

In "*Culturally Responsive Post-Qualitative Research,*" Patti Lather narrates the methodology of two books on race and schooling in order to address two questions: (1) What light do they shed on shifting imaginaries in the human sciences, and (2) What are their implications for fieldwork? Engaging post-critical, post-human, and post-qualitative ideas, she explores theories of anti–Blackness, especially a strand of work in Black studies termed Afro-pessimism, in relation to social justice methodology. Her engaging central argument is that the methodological elaboration of such contemporary currents in social theorizing offers rich resources for qualitative research.

Also important to researchers across methodology or approach, Winston C. Thompson asks us to consider the question "*Must an Education in Research Ethics Engage Issues of Culture, Context, and Community?*" Specifically, Thompson interrogates how the research community might benefit from identifying social justice-based ethical and moral concerns as essential elements, rather than incidental obstacles, to the work of research. That is to ask: by what research practices might culturally responsive research be advanced – and by extension, how might scholars be prepared for doing that work in meaningful ways? Thompson identifies this charge as an explicitly educational question, in that it focuses on a few normative (i.e., concerning what should be done) dimensions of a particular curriculum for researchers.

Section II – Qualitative Innovations

In Section II, five authors explore qualitative innovations to culturally responsive research. The authors comprise primarily Scholars of Color (e.g., all except one), who stand firm that research should not cause violence – in historical or contemporary contexts. To be sure, this does not mean that the authors hold the same definitions of nonviolent research – but each is committed to methods that center cultural responsiveness.

In the first chapter of this section, *"Teaching and Engaging Autoethnogaphy as Qualitative Engagement"* Bryant Keith Alexander demonstrates a use of autoethnography as a mode of teaching, examining, and illuminating aspects of everyday lived experience. Innovatively, he outlines strategies of engagement and theoretical perspectives of doing autoethnography as public, performative, and border pedagogies in a performance of possibilities. He contextualizes the methodology in an autoethnography on a Black father/son relationship in an epistolary form, a letter to his father. Next, Alexander uses the procedural considerations of the method – through questions he asks of his students – and applies them to his own offered autoethnography as a template of analysis. The chapter ends with Alexander asking you/the reader questions about their orientation to doing autoethnography as critical and creative endeavor.

Next, Kakali Bhattacharya explores *"Critical, De/colonial and Contemplative Approaches to Qualitative Inquiry."* She addresses how qualitative research, historically and currently, has been primarily produced in predominantly white countries. Under such circumstances, it is difficult to ignore the embedded oppressive, dominant sensibilities that have been rendered ubiquitous, ahistorical, acultural, and value neutral. Within such a context, critical and de/colonial qualitative researchers interrogate the entangled oppressive effects of multiple power structures and colonialism. Drawing on embodied experiences from her travels and contemplative practices, Bhattacharya demonstrates the discursive and materialistic difference between geographically privileged and marginalized locations. She juxtaposes insights gained from an acute awareness of existing in two locations to inform an interconnected, discursive understanding of qualitative research. Bhattacharya offers provocations throughout the chapter to encourage you/readers to create their own pathways of inquiry, informed by ethics, reciprocity, and relationality across differences. By engaging in generative and expansive methodological possibilities, options and justifications for non-traditional methods of inquiry emerge. Thus, this chapter is interactive, dialogical, and invitational, inviting readers to journey beyond stuck places in qualitative inquiry into places of possibilities previously unimagined and unthought.

In the next chapter, Antonio Duran and Susan R. Jones focus on *"Intersectionality as a Lens in Qualitative Research: Possibilities, Problems, and Practices."* As an analytical framework, intersectionality continues to gain traction across academic disciplines due to its potential to illuminate the influence of overlapping systems of marginalization and oppression. However, with this increase in popularity has come misuse and misappropriation of the term and a turn away from the historical origins of intersectionality that insist upon a focus on structures and power-based analyses. As such, Duran and Jones provide an overview of core constructs of intersectionality with an emphasis on the possibilities, problems, and practices the framework offers qualitative researchers. The chapter examines the practical implications of applying intersectionality in research by examining different elements of a study design, and how an intersectional approach might shape these elements. Consider reading this chapter with the Blake et al., chapter in Section III, which also takes up the concept of intersectionality.

Casey Philip Wong's chapter, "*good kid, m.A.A.d research: Culturally Sustaining Research and Calling Out the White Gaze in Our Epistemologies*," interrogates the current regime of knowledge production and investigates what it means to engage in education research outside of the politics of knowing that has been naturalized, within prominent guides like the AERA's "Standards for Reporting on Empirical Social Science Research" and "Standards for Reporting on Humanities-Oriented Research." Wong enters into conversation with education researchers and theorists of collective freedom from Black, Indigenous, Latinx, Asian, Pacific Islander, and intersecting and overlapping Communities of Color who have developed ways of gathering, interpreting, sharing, and valuing knowledge outside of the "White gaze." These education scholars and theorists confront the assumption that ideal education research should contribute to knowledge that focuses on improving nation-state schools, as conduits for producing workers who contribute to racial capitalism and ongoing processes of colonialism. Signifying on how Hip-Hop artist Kendrick Lamar accomplishes this epistemic labor in his classic album *good kid, m.A.A.d city*, this chapter explores how our epistemologies are bound to systemic processes of injustice and offer culturally sustaining strategies for engaging Hip Hop to conduct research "otherwise."

Section III – Quantitative and Mixed Methods Innovations

Section III includes five chapters focused on culturally responsive quantitative and mixed methods innovations in social science research. The authors comprise primarily Scholars of Color who offer different innovations to quantitative and mixed methods research.

Odis Johnson, Jr. and Jason Jabbari explore "*Using Counterfactual Modeling and Machine Learning Generated Propensity Scores to Examine Black Social Control and Mathematics.*" Specifically, work from the Race, Gender, and Social Control in STEM (RGSC-STEM) Lab[4] has established important and long overdue connections among state violence, schooling, and racial inequities in mathematics. In this way, the chapter offers an important exploration of social control, policy, and critical quantitative research. The RGSC-STEM work has been guided by the question of whether our national priority to fill the STEM pipeline in schools requires administrators to first drain the school-to-prison pipeline, since minoritized students tend to be underrepresented in the former and overrepresented in the latter. Using data from the Educational Longitudinal Study 2002 and the High School Longitudinal Study 2009, this chapter highlights how the Lab has sought to examine these concerns through methodologies that offer stronger inferences of association, if not causal inferences. Notably, Johnson and Jabbari find that Black students are at greatest risk for surveillance and exclusionary discipline, and that both lower the mathematics performances and the likelihood of college attendance. The discussion concludes with a summary of what RGSC-STEM Lab has learned related to policymaking, research, and justice.

Particularly important for school researchers and practitioners, in "*Examining Discipline from an Intersectional Lens,*" authors Jamilia J. Blake, Siqi (Lucy) Chen, Naomi Ruffin, and Lyric Jackson provide steps to analyze and interpret school discipline data from an intersectional lens considering both race and gender. The authors share this quantitative application of intersectional analyses as it relates to educational disparities and how to conceptualize research questions, based on intersectional theory within education, to drive questions related to discipline disparities. Consider reading this chapter along with the Duran and Jones chapter on intersectionality, listed in Section II.

Minjung Kim and Junyeong Yang focus on "*Detecting Differential Effects Using Regression Mixture Models: Applications Using Mplus.*" They argue that culturally responsive methods have been mostly developed under the qualitative research methodology framework, because quantitative methods tend to totalize and homogenize different population groups based on the majority group. When quantitative methods are used, regression analysis with interaction (or moderation) effects is one way to better understand the heterogeneity in the effects of predictors on an outcome. In this chapter, Kim and Yang describe the regression interaction approach with an example context of perceived discrimination and antisocial behavior. Next, they introduce another quantitative method, the regression mixture modeling, to explore the potential heterogeneity in the effects of predictors on an outcome in regression analysis. For interested readers, the authors provide the step-by-step tutorial for analyzing the regression mixture models with an example data using statistical software, Mplus 8; its answers are available on the website at https://u.osu.edu/quallab/advanced-methods-institute/

In "*The Utility of Critical Race Mixed Methodology: An Explanatory Sequential Example,*" Jessica T. DeCuir-Gunby, Whitney N. McCoy, and Stephen M. Gibson explore combining mixed methodology and Critical Race Theory (CRT) through Critical Race Mixed Methodology (CRMM). To do so, the authors discuss how CRT is used to help frame an explanatory sequential mixed methods design (quant → QUAL). Within such a design, quantitative data are initially collected followed by the collection of qualitative data. The qualitative data are used to confirm (or not confirm) quantitative data. Specifically, DeCuir-Gunby et al. illustrate how to engage in CRMM by focusing on a research study examining African American college students' experiences with racial identity, racial microaggressions, and belonging. Implications are provided for engaging in CRMM research.

In the final chapter of this section, Verónica N. Vélez offers "*Advancing Critical Race Spatial Analysis: Implications for the use of GIS in Educational Research.*" Vélez guides readers through how critical race spatial analysis (CRSA) can extend geographic information systems (GIS) from its traditional use in geography and urban planning into new avenues and possibilities; this is specifically useful in examining educational inquiry concerned with the social, cultural, political, and historic role of space and place as it relates to schools and educational (in)opportunity. By (re)imagining how socio-spatial relationships are explored, analyzed, and displayed, CRSA positions GIS as a critical research tool for furthering racial justice efforts within education. Vélez's chapter shares the methodological journey to CRSA, which was shaped by a case study of migrant mothers who led a GIS project to reveal uneven geographies of opportunity in and across the schools attended by their children. By rooting the analytical capabilities of GIS in their own lived experience, the mothers drove an iterative inquiry that built a counter-cartographic narrative – which spoke back to post-racial narratives taking hold of educational reform in their local context. Based on this work and conversations at the AMI, Vélez offers new developments in CRSA that wrestle more explicitly with the computational methods upon which much of GIS mapping relies. She concludes with implications for the continued use of GIS in educational research, particularly inquiry that seeks to build spatial models of the world from the lived experiences of Black, Indigenous, and People of Color.

Section VI – The Future of Culturally Sustaining Research

The volume closes with our contemplation of *The Future: Advancing Innovations of Culturally Sustaining Research and Researchers*. In reviewing the methodologies and methods that the volume's contributors have offered, we summarize common themes, practices, and considerations in each of its three sections. First, we elaborate on the necessity of transformation, expansion, and specificity as part of setting the context for doing and sustaining culturally responsive work. We then identify common qualitative themes of researcher liminality, community work, and resistance of white supremacy as part of innovating scholarship. Next, we summarize quantitative and mixed methods themes of problematizing traditional modeling and computational methods, using unique modeling and adjusting computations, and operationalizing literature and theory through analyses in promoting culturally responsive research. We end by offering readers a vision for the future of culturally responsive research, including recommendations and reflexive questions in support of you developing and sustaining your own culturally responsive research practices.

Tips for Reading This Book

What should be evident to readers throughout this volume is our urgency for you to actively engage contexts, cultures, and communities as integral to conducting culturally responsive research – rather than to avoid or erase these constructs of the environments in which your scholarship takes place. For example, readers may want to reflect on the differences between Patti Lather's use of the word "spooky" and Bryant Alexander's use of the word "spook." Lather takes up "spooky at a distance" with a quantum physics approach using Einstein's definition of the word which, importantly, challenges the Newtonian perspectives of ontology and epistemology. This use of the word opens up questions of how to "do" or conduct science. Alexander takes up a sociohistorical use of the word "spook." Herein, he refers to a white man using the word to call a Black man a phantom, or absent presence – denying the full humanity of the Black man. Notably, Alexander encourages readers to understand the use of the word by sharing, "I am not a phantom as something apparent to sense but with no substantial existence: or an object of continual dread or abhorrence."

Reflective of our need to evolve our (post)methodologies and methods: acknowledging and engaging with historical *and* contemporary meanings of constructs are important, including in how we move the field into future iterations of understanding culturally responsive research that is fully human, embodied, environmental, economically equitable, and beyond. Taken together, both uses of "spook/y" encourage researchers to (1) be cognizant of sociohistorical contexts while working in contemporary ones, (2) see entire persons as integral to research processes, and (3) simultaneously be sensitive to the realities of persons and communities that are involved in research. The same may be said about various uses of "intersectionality" throughout this volume. There are numerous nuances like these – to be explored and extended by you.

We encourage you to reflect on the numerous concepts offered in this book, consider how they are used, and *put yourself in conversation with the authors as you read their perspectives and advance your own perspectives*. We address this, and more, in the final chapter as we explore tensions in doing culturally responsive research, including in ways that scholars make decisions about conceptualizing, collecting, analyzing, sharing, disseminating, and enacting the knowledge that their projects bring to bear.

In Closing

We hope that you take up these advances in culturally responsive research – including approaches that are critical quantitative, critical/decolonizing qualitative, mixed methods, the "posts," and beyond. As scholars who make intentional choices with (or without) communities toward educational equity and social change, *how you choose to engage in culturally responsive research (and the degree to which you do so) is up to you*. Your decisions – the axio-onto-epistemological, paradigmatic, and methodological; your approaches to collection, analysis, and dissemination; as well as the future of culturally responsive research – are up to you and us.

We hope this book and the corresponding AMI information (see https://u.osu.edu/quallab/advanced-methods-institute/) inspire you to advance culturally sustaining research, as culturally sensitive scholars who go beyond traditional approaches in important ways to engage with the world as it evolves. We thank you for answering this call, and for joining us on this journey to advance the work of the academy.

Notes

1 Our reference to "(post)" is meant to include qualitative and post-qualitative approaches.
2 To quickly define the term axio-onto-epistemology – axiology is to ethically do, ontology is to be or embody, and epistemology is to know or come to know (Pasque et al., 2012). Praxiology is to practice and, while some critical scholars importantly separate praxiology from axiology – for the purposes of this chapter, we evoke both simultaneously.
3 Presenters (also book chapter contributors) represented universities across the United States and the approximately 1,000 attendees represented nine different countries.
4 For more information, see https://education.jhu.edu/event/hopkins-at-home-odis-johnson-on-stem-inequities/.

References

Berryman, M., SooHoo, S., & Nevin, A. (Eds.) (2013). *Culturally responsive methodologies.* San Francisco, CA: Emerald Group Publishing.

Belsey, C. (2002). *Poststructuralism: A very short introduction.* Oxford, UK: Oxford Press.

Charmaz, K. (2014). *Constructing grounded theory* (2nd ed.). Thousand Oaks, CA: SAGE.

Creswell, J., & Plano Clark, V. (2011). *Designing and conducting mixed methods research.* Los Angeles, CA: SAGE.

Denzin, N. K., & Giardina, M. D. (2015). Introduction. In N. K. Denzin, & M. D. Giardina (Eds.), *Qualitative inquiry – past, present, and future: A critical reader* (pp. 9–38). Walnut Creek, CA: Left Coast Press.

Denzin, N. K., Lincoln, Y. S., & Smith, L. T. (2008). *Handbook of critical and indigenous methodologies.* Thousand Oaks, CA: SAGE.

Guba, E. G., & Lincoln, Y. S. (2005). Paradigmatic controversies, contradictions, and emerging confluence. In N. K. Denzin & Y. S. Lincoln (Eds.), *The SAGE handbook of qualitative research* (3rd ed., 191–215). Thousand Oaks, CA: SAGE.

Hurtado, S. (2015). The transformative paradigm: Principles and challenges. In A. M. Martinez-Aleman, B. Pusser, & E. M. Bensimon (Eds.), *Critical approaches to the study of higher education: A practical introduction* (pp. 285–307). Baltimore, MD: Johns Hopkins University Press.

Ladson-Billings, G. (2015). Education research in the public interest. In N. K. Denzin, & M. D. Giardina (Eds.), *Qualitative inquiry – past, present, and future: A critical reader* (pp. 171–185). Walnut Creek, CA: Left Coast Press.

Ladson-Billings, G. (2014). Culturally relevant pedagogy 2.0: A.k.a. The remix. *Harvard Educational Review, 84*(1), 74–84. doi: 10.17763/haer.84.1.p2rj131485484751.

Ladson-Billings, G. (1990). Like lightning in a bottle: Attempting to capture the pedagogical excellence of successful teachers of Black students. *International Journal of Qualitative Studies in Education, 3*(4), 335–344.

McMahon, W. W. (2009). *Higher learning, greater good: The private and social benefits of higher education.* Baltimore, MD: Johns Hopkins University Press.

Pasque, P. A. (2010/2014). *American higher education, leadership, and policy: Critical issues and the public good.* New York, NY: Palgrave Macmillan.

Pasque, P. A., & Carducci, R. (2015). Critical advocacy perspectives on organization in higher education. In M. B. Paulsen (Ed.). *Higher education: Handbook of theory and research, 29*(30). (pp. 275–333). New York, NY: Springer.

Pasque, P. A., & Carducci, R. (in press). Critical advocacy inquiry. In J. Salvo & J. Ulmer (Eds.), *Routledge encyclopedia of qualitative methods*. Routledge.

Pasque, P., Carducci, R., Kuntz, A. K., & Gildersleeve, R. E. (2012). Qualitative inquiry for equity in higher education: Methodological innovations, implications, and interventions. *ASHE Higher Education Report*, *37*(6), 1–121.

Pasque, P. A., Patton, L. D., Gayles, J. G., Gooden, M. A., Henfield, M. S., Milner, I. V. … Stewart, A. (2022). Unapologetic educational research: Addressing anti-blackness, racism and white supremacy. *Cultural Studies – Critical Methodologies*, *21*(1), 3–17. doi: 10.1177/15327086211060451.

Pasque, P. A., & Pérez, M. S. (2015). Centering critical inquiry: Methodologies that facilitate critical qualitative research. In G. S. Cannella, M. Salazar Pérez, & P. A. Pasque (Eds.), *Critical qualitative inquiry: Foundations and futures* (pp. 139–170). Walnut Creek, CA: Left Coast Press.

SECTION I

Contexts and Considerations for Quantitative, (Post)Qualitative, and Mixed Methods Research

A critical dimension of investigating phenomena … is cultivating the research capacity to develop methodologies that harmonize with much older knowledge systems that have been genealogically passed on through eons of time. In practice, Indigenous research methodologies give greater salience to premodern sensitivities (i.e., praying, singing, dancing, beading, weaving, and other culture-centered faculties) that have been layered over with de-natured practices and approaches. Every research methodology has an umbilical origin. What cannot be overlooked is that Indigenous research methodologies include an ancestry that is embodied within the researcher (p. 15).

> ~ *Charlotte Davidson (Diné/Three Affiliated Tribes:*
> *Mandan/Hidatsa/Arikara)*
> *Heather J. Shotton (Wichita/Kiowa/Cheyenne)*
> *Robin Starr Zape-tah-hol-ah Minthorn (Kiowa/*
> *Apache/Umatilla/Nez Perce/Assiniboine)*
> *Stephanie Waterman (Onondaga, Turtle Clan) ~*

Davidson, C., Shotton, H. J., Minthorn, R. S. Z., & Waterman, S. (2018). The need for Indigenizing research in higher education scholarship. In R. Minthorn & H. J. Shotton (Eds.) *Reclaiming Indigenous research in higher education* (pp. 7–17). New Brunswick, NJ: Rutgers University Press.

DOI: 10.4324/9781003126621-2

Contexts and Considerations for Quantitative, (Post)Qualitative, and Mixed Methods Research

2

THE TRANSFORMATIVE PARADIGM

An Evolving Journey in Methods and Social Justice Aims[1]

Sylvia Hurtado

We often describe rules and methodological practices as a set, customary way of doing research when teaching methods and methodology within a specific worldview or paradigm (Creswell & Plano Clark, 2011). How often have we used the word "convention" to describe to a graduate student learning the rules governing the conduct and presentation of research? These "conventions" are actively constructed by communities of scholars that define research processes and principles for judging the quality of data collection, analysis, and presentation of findings.

In addressing research conducted under the umbrella of the transformative paradigm and the quest for social justice, it is evident that there is an evolution in practices surrounding methods, the role of the researcher in relation to those that are the focus of research, and the use of findings (Hesse–Biber, 2007; Mertens, 2009). Yet, in our roles, we face the tension between establishing and becoming guardians of convention on the one hand and advancing work in our fields by encouraging novel practices in method, methodology, and epistemology. The tension became clear as I transitioned from having been taught research in a post-positivist paradigm, using primarily survey methods, to conducting scholarship using mostly case studies and mixed methods to study institutional change related to equity and inclusion. I found ways to educate myself and educate others – graduate students, peer reviewers, and colleagues in promotion reviews – to use research and methods that advance a deeper understanding of the populations and campus contexts that hold promise in achieving social justice aims.

In this chapter, I will use examples of campus climate research and reflections on my own praxis journey to illustrate how research methods are not static when driven by a guiding paradigm that centers the desire to achieve more equitable outcomes for marginalized communities and educational institutions. Innovation and collective ways of defining new standards for research are especially needed

DOI: 10.4324/9781003126621-3

to answer questions about persistent inequity, to counter bias, and reverse erasure of marginalized communities, reclaiming their voices in society and its institutions. I conclude with suggestions for creating spaces to foster innovation and continued development of methods to achieve transformative institutional goals and emancipatory aims for participants in our studies.

> Innovation and collective ways of defining new standards for research are especially needed to answer questions about persistent inequity, to counter bias, and reverse erasure of marginalized communities, reclaiming their voices in society and its institutions.

Personal and Collective Evolution in Methods

We are on our own evolving journeys in practicing research, which include methods or various techniques for gathering evidence; methodology, "a theory of and analysis of how research is done or should proceed"; and epistemology described as what can be known, who can be a "knower," and what tests must be passed to be legitimated as knowledge (Harding, 1987, p. 3). Epistemology also involves understanding the relationship between the researcher and those being researched, reflecting "insider" or "outsider knowledge" of participants' communities, or a combination insider-outsider or outsider/within roles (Brayboy & Deyhle, 2010; Collins, 1999; Creswell & Plano Clark, 2011). All of these aspects are also shaped and reinforced by the collective research and disciplinary communities, the types of methods training we offer in coursework and professional development opportunities, and peer reviewers whose roles are to ensure the quality of published research.

At the same time that we adhere to professional standards in our fields, we are driven by our need to answer questions that are important to us and the communities that we desire to help. When I first began my own journey as an education scholar, there were no words to describe the type of work I was doing that focused on Latinx and other groups marginalized in higher education. At one point, I remember hearing it categorized as "diversity work," in reference to its use in affirmative action court cases, but that description was not satisfying because it failed to capture the complexity of basic beliefs and aims that underlie the research. Like many others, I was trained in postpositivism as an example of quality research and began to focus on advanced quantitative methods that would recognize differences in perspectives gathered in surveys. I expected different models to emerge for racial groups and, for example, sought advanced methods such as invariance testing to compare populations (Hurtado, Cuellar, & Guillermo-Wann, 2011). In other words, I paid attention to advances in quantitative methods that would help me document the multiple realities that co-exist on college campuses, and the multilevel contexts that have distinct effects.

That is, I was the "outsider/within" (Collins, 1999) that believed that different racial groups experience the world and campus racial climates differently, educational contexts matter, and these have implications for interactions with others and outcomes. I sought methods that addressed this set of beliefs because of my own undergraduate experiences in a predominantly white college environment. I knew deep down that this was not just my unique story as a woman of color, but a common one for those coming from similarly raced and classed communities that entered college and were struck by how unequal the pathway had been and would shape the journey ahead.

Although survey methods were helpful in showing distinct experiences and perspectives, it is clear that different methods and paradigms are needed to better capture institutional structures and practices in the quest to address key equity issues. There was an evolution in many fields about how to do research and judge it, as well as compare the different assumptions that underlie distinct paradigms that guide research (Creswell & Plano Clark, 2011; Mertens, 2009).

Research in the transformative paradigm is "rooted in a critique of power relationships, with emancipatory goals for individuals and transformative goals for institutions and systems of oppression" (Hurtado, 2015, p. 286). Revisiting aspects of transformative research is timely after the summer of racial reckoning that was sparked by traumatic racial violence in the news (i.e., the murders of George Floyd, Breonna Taylor, and Ahmaud Arbery among others), a rise in social identity and racially motivated hate crimes (McCarthy, 2020), and the national and international protests for social justice in 2020. The pandemic also revealed stark inequalities in access to education and health, with Black, Latinx, and Indigenous communities severely impacted by COVID-19 (Kendi, 2020; National Center for Health Statistics, CDC). These events also sparked national and wide-spread academic conversations about identifying and eliminating systemic racism in institutions and dismantling harmful policies or practices surrounding funding of research or programs (see, e.g., National Institutions of Health nih.gov/ending-structural-racism). Several of the most prestigious journals have devoted special issues to systemic racism and committed to diversifying editorial boards as a result (e.g., *The Lancet, American Educational Research Journal, Cell*). How much of this recommitment to racial equity and dismantling of structural racism will result in more transformative research and methods in these journals? We do not know yet, but it signals a need for more work that is committed to address the uplift and empowerment of marginalized communities and a reexamination of institutional practices to achieve institutional transformation.

I would have benefitted greatly from learning about the distinctions in research paradigms that help shape the role of the researcher in relation to marginalized communities, and more specifically about the beliefs and assumptions underlying the transformative paradigm as a graduate student. I would have more easily understood why my white, male advisor and I argued about theory, method, and interpretation during my dissertation research. Overhearing us one day his wife, who was a feminist scholar, immediately identified our debates as epistemological differences – we both did not see it at the time. We were not just disagreeing about the use of quantitative methods, it was actually about our differences in assumptions underlying our paradigmatic approaches. I realize now that it was more specifically about how a postpositivist frame did not align with the concept that multiple realities co-exist in predominantly white racialized campus environments that I was trying to highlight, and the disproportionate effect of the climate on Chicanx, Black, and white Students. To obtain the doctoral degree and accept the postdoctoral position that awaited me, I knew I needed to compromise and complete this study. Subsequently, I could follow my passion and interest in advanced methods that highlighted the experiences of students of color in different college contexts. Each day since that dissertation, I evolve in developing my scholarship and research path (and those of student research partners) within the transformative paradigm.

Defining the Transformative Paradigm

Inspired by social movements, the transformative paradigm originated from the dissatisfaction of researchers and members of marginalized communities with dominant research paradigms and practices (Mertens, Bledoe, Sullivan, & Wilson, 2010). It is described by Donna Mertens (2003) as an umbrella for scholarship (including feminist, critical race, queer, praxis-oriented, and Freirean participatory research) that may employ different research methods (techniques) where researchers not only identify and critique power relationships, but also seek active engagement in social change and reform. This represents an epistemological shift from the notion of the distanced, presumably unbiased, and all-knowing researcher prevalent in mostly postpositivist but also other paradigms that guide research. Researchers that employ the transformative paradigm for their research begin with an intentional plan to challenge inequality and focus on social justice that "permeates the entire research process, from problem formulation to the drawing of conclusions and use of results" (Mertens, 2003. p. 159). Mertens' (2005, 2009) conceptual work built on Guba and Lincoln (1989, 2005) and Lather (1992) to help distinguish the emancipatory elements of this paradigm from the dominant paradigms of postpositivism, constructivism, and pragmatism. Mertens later changed the terms from calling this approach the emancipatory paradigm to calling it the transformative paradigm to emphasize not only liberation from oppression but also to recognize participant agency and demonstrate respect for marginalized groups, and how researchers work alongside communities to achieve personal and institutional transformation.

Table 2.1 is a summary of the four beliefs or basic tenets that characterize research under the transformative paradigm. Other literature has contrasted all other paradigms along these dimensions (Creswell & Plano Clark, 2011; Guba & Lincoln, 2005; Hurtado, 2015; Mertens, 2009), so the focus here is on the key characteristics and transformative researchers' guiding assumptions in the areas of axiology, ontology, epistemology, and methods/methodology.

TABLE 2.1 Key Characteristics and Beliefs in the Transformative Paradigm

	The Transformative Researcher and Research Team:
Axiology – Values and nature of ethics	Emphasizes the values of human rights and social justice; recognizes ethical considerations in interactions with and respect for marginalized populations.
Ontology – The nature of reality and truth	Acknowledges multiple realities and lived experiences co-exist in a research context that are subject to the influence and consequences of power and privilege; rejects cultural relativism.
Epistemology – The nature of knowledge and relationship among knowers	Advocates culturally competent relations with participant communities; recognizes different ways of knowing situated within cultural/social identity groups; values participant knowledge; and explicitly addresses power and privilege.
Methods – Appropriate approaches and systematic inquiry	Employs culturally appropriate methods tied to social action, acknowledging contextual and historical factors; uses dialogic qualitative methods and any method of systematic inquiry so long as it accommodates cultural and contextual complexity.

Source: Adapted summary from Mertens (2009, p. 49) with my own additions.

> Researchers that employ the transformative paradigm for their research begin with an intentional plan to challenge inequality and focus on social justice that "permeates the entire research process, from problem formulation to the drawing of conclusions and use of results" (Mertens, 2003. p. 159).

We begin our studies with a set of values (axiology), even though we may not be explicit about them, and typically we are trained in ethical research behavior (and certified) before our campuses allow us to use human subjects. However, not every researcher has a key concern for social justice or even respect for marginalized communities that experience adversity and are socially and economically oppressed. Transformative researchers understand these vulnerabilities and identify the resilience/resistance among the populations they are studying. They respect the forms of agency that participants show in spite of social and economic constraints and demonstrate a strong intent on inclusion of voices that have not been heard or are divergent. For example, in a study centering women of color's experiences with campus sexual assault (CSA), the authors use a racially conscious and healing lens approach, with a specific focus on resilient forms of support (Harris, Karnaratne, & Gutzwa, 2021). Findings identify women of colors' community-based healing strategies that were often intertwined with culture and race, whereas previous work disregarded the significance of race in CSA healing.

With respect to ontology, it is clear that there is not one reality or truth, as some researchers seek to find. Multiple realities must be captured within a context where some are valued and others are either devalued or made invisible. I found this especially true in researching campus climates, requiring us to not only gather the same data on all groups to assess differences (quantitatively), but also allow for each social identity community to tell their stories and share their perspectives on the campus climate (qualitatively). For example, we worked at every site to match the researcher's identity with the social identity community represented in focus groups, establishing facilitators as outsiders/within (Collins, 1999) so that there was a better probing of race and gender issues, and to create comfort among student participants willing to share their views. It was an attempt at a more culturally responsive research approach to gathering data.

The concept of multiple worldviews is also related to epistemology, which addresses how knowledge is produced and negotiated, the relationship between the researcher and study participants, who can be a knower, and what can be known. Invariably, in many other research paradigms, the researcher is the knowledge constructor and also is in the position to validate or devalue participant knowledge. In reality, cultural responsiveness enhances validity of findings with culturally distinct communities (Mertens, 2009; also see other chapters in this volume). If the researcher is culturally incompetent, it is highly unlikely that they would be able to generate new knowledge or valid insights into participant ways of knowing and consequent behaviors. Some even question if a neutral observer can even get the facts right for culturally distinct communities (Christians, 2005; Mertens et al., 2010). Thus, this tenet involves relationships between the researcher and participants, negotiated knowledge development, with transformative researchers seeking reciprocity while being mindful of power differentials and adopting an epistemology of liberation (Zuberi & Bonilla-Silva, 2008). All of this requires a greater awareness of self and other epistemologies in the research context that can be enhanced with reflexive activities for "strong objectivity" (Harding, 1991, p. 151), where researchers reflect on their own cultural particularities and biases in order to maximize objectivity.

It is important to note that although no single method of data collection is considered to be uniquely tied to the transformative paradigm, "the inclusion of qualitative methods is seen as critical" (Mertens, 2009, p. 49). The method of data collection should aim to capture the contextual and cultural complexity that surround and emerge from participants in the study. In fact, mixed methods is well-suited for this work because the approach can best capture cultural elements and multiple levels of contextual complexity, acknowledge the historical legacy of inclusion or exclusion (using documents), and broader structural factors that shape the environment (e.g. unequal distribution of resources, compositional diversity of the student body or faculty). In a subsequent section, I will provide a mixed methods example of how the cultural complexity and historical legacy was integrated in a campus climate study that began with a focus on racial group differences.

Collective Innovation: The Mixed Methods Comunity

How do we learn together to collectively devise new methods and standards for research excellence? I have a specific experience to share that shows this can occur at any stage of one's evolving methods journey. In presenting my second mixed methods research paper at a national higher education conference, I ran into a colleague who invited me to the International Mixed Methods conference. This was an opportunity to learn and gain insight into how we were actually mixing methods and understand developing standards on method. It was here that I was first exposed to Donna Mertens' work on the transformative paradigm where she was on a panel along with others that represented four paradigms of research (i.e., postpositivist, social constructionist, pragmatic, transformative). I experienced the excitement among a group of scholars who were shaping the contours of mixed methods research. It was lively, engaging, and interesting to hear a variety of perspectives about what constitutes mixed methods. I felt like I was in a cauldron of creative work, listening to researchers from different disciplines engaged in trying out and asking for feedback on their methods – encountering novices and experienced/well-known researchers in methods from a variety of fields from education to science. It was life-changing because it was the first time that I did not experience methods as static but evolving and collectively determined. John Creswell and Vicki Plano Clark had just released their second edition of *Designing and Conducting Mixed Methods Research* and we attended a workshop on design and presenting mixed methods in a paper. I realized that almost my entire career I have been conducting multiple methods – collecting Quant and Qual data, using the new language of the mixed methods – in the same projects but had not been "mixing" data sources, results, and findings. I treated them as entirely separate methods in terms of data collection and analyses to address different research questions.

To guide ourselves and others, one of the most important strategies or developing conventions that we were taught was to map how both forms of Quant and Qual data would be collected, and how they would be mixed (or talk to each other) in a graphic form to aid readers in understanding steps in mixed method. After attending that conference, we were well-armed when confronting journal reviewers of our paper. We pushed back on reviewers' suggestions to present Quant and Qual findings separately and defended our mixed method approach, educating reviewers. It was only the second mixed methods paper to ever be published in that journal, which speaks volumes about the editorial team focus and reviewers that are unaccustomed to innovations in method. We were fortunate to have one reviewer versed in mixed methods and called our paper "an innovative and good example of presentation of mixed results." In short, I felt I had become a member of a community of scholars innovating in mixed methods, determining what would later become ways to judge the quality of mixed methods (Papadimitriou, Ivankova, & Hurtado, 2013).

> We pushed back on reviewers' suggestions to present Quant and Qual findings separately and defended our mixed method approach, educating reviewers.

The Transformative Paradigm and Campus Climate Studies

While many may claim climate studies are developed to help identify discrimination and transform the campus environment, and although an informative indicator of potential areas of exclusion and inequality, not many climate studies are used directly for institutional transformation or action. This may be because there is a disconnect between researchers collecting the data and use of the climate study to critically assess normative elements of the institution. The transformative paradigm serves as a useful guide for methodology toward achieving the goals of individual empowerment and institutional transformation for improving the climate for racial and other minoritized social identity groups.

We intentionally implemented the transformative paradigm in a qualitative study of a campus climate (Hurtado, Gasiewski, & Alvarez, 2014). We began with several tenets of the transformative paradigm, compared with other campus racial climate studies conducted in the past that lacked this approach. First, there was no assumption of a single campus climate reality and our methods were designed to acknowledge multiple coexisting realities that are differentially valued and appreciated. We used focus groups to include students from different racial, class, and gender-identity group perspectives. Second, we paid attention to observed power differentials on campus and identified themes of privilege that prevailed on the campus from access to physical spaces to assumptions about wealth in college classrooms. We sought to make visible the experiences of students that were subject to erasure in other research methods that heightened their feelings of invisibility. This was particularly important to do with Indigenous communities on campus whose data were obscured in survey methods due to a uniform policy that prevents reporting of results with small sample sizes. Third, in order to encourage social action, we assembled students' stories regarding different types of microaggressions so that they could name their experiences and others could identify bias incidents.

> We sought to make visible the experiences of students that were subject to erasure in other research methods that heightened their feelings of invisibility.

We used examples with student quotes connected with a research basis so that these could be used in teaching, and their experiences could become part of common knowledge about specific ways marginalized groups experience the campus. To increase inclusion, we used a web-based set of focus group questions for any student who wished to offer comments. Every member of the community could offer recommendations for improving the climate that we assembled into a chapter, which concerned administrators because they felt they would be obligated to implement all of the recommendations. No matter, the important point was that members of the campus community could be heard and included. The report gave voice to students who felt invisible on campus; it was creative, informative, and empowering. In reviewing preliminary results, the campus-wide task force was involved to help determine how the report could best be used to inform their planning for diversity, equity, and inclusion initiatives. The report was posted on the campus website for all to learn how different student communities experience campus climate based on race, class, and gender-identity.

After learning more about the transformative paradigm and mixed method techniques, I was able to reanalyze an earlier study of a campus climate, using Quant and Qual methods to achieve crystallization with the data, or identify multiple dimensions presented in results from different forms of data coming together to gain a better understanding of African-American students' racial climate experiences. Instead of triangulation using different forms of methods and data to validate findings, crystallization allows for exploring multiple dimensions of context and experience. The "metaphor of the prism (crystal) in the transformative paradigm conveys the central point of knowledge is multifaceted, and therefore a triangle is not adequate to the task (Mertens, 2009, p. 62). Crystallization includes an "infinite variety of shapes, substances, transmutations, multidimensionalities, and angles of approach" (Richardson & St. Pierre, 2005, p. 963). More specifically, crystallization brings the many facets together to better understand events and experiences to achieve a more complete portrait of experience in context.

I offer an example from a mixed method climate study to illustrate how the concept captures the cultural and contextual complexity essential in transformative research. Further, this example reveals how a more comprehensive portrait of student experiences on campuses can be achieved, using multiple sources of data and methods. The campus climate survey we administered as part of the study captured many of the key elements of the unique culture at the campus, but understandably, the survey could not answer why particular racial groups differed on behaviors and forms of engagement. Specifically, we asked students how frequently they participated in campus rituals, many of which were annual traditions. One of the main traditions was the annual building and lighting of a bonfire before the big football game of the season. The survey revealed that virtually 93% of white students frequently or occasionally participated in bonfire activities, and numbers for other groups were also approaching 80–90%. However, only about 70% of African-American students said they frequently or occasionally participated in activities. It is hard to know from the survey data alone why these differed, or if lower participations rates are simply based on student preferences. From our site visit, we learned that participation is very high because the campus offered classes (Bonfire 101) that helped students learn the science of building a bonfire structure and safety measures. The campus not only sanctioned the event, alumni had participated as students and some continued to take part in the ritual over nearly 90 years.

Moreover, preparation for the event included engagement that went above and beyond some students' comfort zone. The expectation was that the evening, or whatever free time students had, would be devoted to building the bonfire structure. Groups of students would go out, chop wood from trees in designated areas, and begin constructing a tall pile of wood that became the structure that was to be lit later on the night of the event. We learned from focus groups that organizers went knocking, door to door, in the dorms look-ing for volunteers in the middle of the night to build the bonfire structure. Moreover, we learned why African-Americans had lower participation rates, as one student explained:

> … being an African American, I'm not about to go out to the woods with a bunch of drunken white boys with axes … all it takes is a little spark and they'll be looking for the one who's different … I don't want to put myself in that kind of predicament." African American male

The qualitative data revealed that reservations held by African-American students with lower engagement rates in this campus ritual were based on safety concerns that were due to race and context. Other items in the survey also revealed that African-Americans were less likely to binge drink than white classmates, further illustrating a major difference in experience and substantiating concerns about "drunken white boys" voiced in focus groups.

The context of the institution was also important, located in the South with a predominantly Black college down the road, the campus was part of a segregated system of higher education. This was further evidenced by the presence of white, male confederate statues that stood as a tribute and reminder of a racially exclu-sive past on the predominantly white campus. We observed these and received comments in open-ended questions on the internet that mentioned that none of the statues represented women or students of color. Perhaps the most chill-ing evidence collected came from local newspapers, as one had recently run a story on the history of the nearest town that documented how the lynching of Black males was celebrated by the light of a bonfire. Although it is unclear if all African-American students were aware of the local history of racial oppression, these documents added the historical legacy that can shape the lower partici-pation rates in campus rituals that are based on white supremacy and helped to clarify why students of color stated in focus groups that they felt these were not "our traditions." Two years after the climate study, the event was no longer offi-cially sanctioned by the University after 12 students were killed and 27 injured when the bonfire structure collapsed in the middle of the night. However, some students and alumni continue the bonfire tradition without University sanction or involvement.

The story of students' racialized experiences comes together (crystallizes) in a way that is deeply cultural and contextual after reviewing the evidence using different forms of data, each of which add a new layer of understanding and complexity. Note that any single source of data is somewhat incomplete, and the mixing of results in the previous paragraph provides a more complete account. Student behaviors are not just determined by individual preferences but have a rationale based in social and historical contexts, and systemic issues of oppression over which they have had little or no control. Triangulation would use one source of data to verify another (as in the example of the abuse of alcohol on campus documented on the survey and student accounts about white peers), whereas crystallization uses the different sources of evidence like a "prism, that grows, changes, and alters" (Mertens, 2009, p. 62) how we see the phenomenon in greater complexity. In short, the mixed method analysis allows for capturing oppression that exists culturally and historically, while also respecting students' choice to resist dominant and potentially physically unsafe campus rituals. Prior to the study, the campus was unlikely to see it from the perspective of African-American students or the systemic connections that showed how the campus holds onto racist legacies. Further, even if the majority of students participated in some aspect of the event, the African-American students' concerns about safety documented in the report should have received validation and attention before the fatal accident.

The transformative paradigm has also fostered new forms of data collection with vulnerable groups and serves as an impetus to facilitate empowerment. For example, in a racial climate study example in Canada, researchers captured Indigenous youths' understandings of resilience that are strongly connected to space and place. In Liebenberg, Wall, Wood, and Hutt-MacLeod (2019), students were given equipment to engage in filming spaces and places and subsequently participated in interviews about locations where they felt a sense of belonging and connections that help them become resilient. This approach respected and validated students' ways of knowing, engaging them in the research process. Student participants were subsequently involved in developing a thematic analysis of photos they selected that guided the research team in their analysis, and the youth were also involved in creating ways to disseminate findings to their communities This study offers many details on how researchers engaged student participants in different phases of the research process from data collection, initial analysis, and dissemination of results. We need more examples of participant-empowering research activities for solutions to longstanding inequities, and studies that also make participant knowledge primary (see also Bensimon, 2007 for a discussion about integrating practitioner knowledge in the scholarship of student success).

In another example, Harris (2016) shows how researchers can honor the ways of knowing among participants and engage them in empowerment aims. Harris (2016) writes about using the method of the "walking interview" in campus climate research with students of color and multiracial students. The technique elicits "participants' perceptions, spatial practices, biographies, social architecture, and the social realms within the campus environment" (p. 365). In other words, participants' ways of knowing are prioritized. Each participant can guide the researcher toward seeing the campus from their perspective, including how they navigate the physical and social environment. The technique provides a more deeply contextualized understanding of how marginalized students experience college campuses.

Other transformative paradigm principles are embedded in the approach. For example, the method can build rapport between the researcher and participant. Specifically, Harris advocates for an unstructured approach for the walking interview, so that students and the researcher can co-construct knowledge. A more structured interview approach depends on the researcher's epistemic assumptions and is subject to the same the limitations of "sit down" interviews and field observations that are often much more dependent on researcher's ways of knowing. The spaces, places, and people encountered during the walking interview can elicit memories that bring about reflection on racial barriers to engagement and self-esteem. Participants can find that "sharing these narratives may be cathartic and empowering," especially if they are able to point out everyday experiences to someone they believe is interested in improving the campus racial climate. Harris sees the method as an opportunity for campus administrators and staff, who are willing to listen and learn, to gain a better understanding and build relationships with marginalized students. However, researchers and practitioners must work together to develop more responsive practices when entrusted with insights. Validating students' perceptions and experiences is a pathway for individual empowerment and institutional transformation.

Conclusion

> The transformative paradigm is inclusive of multiple methods, social movements, and interdisciplinary critical studies on diverse communities. It is muticontextual and relies on crystallization of multiple perspectives and data sources. It requires different forms of researcher engagement and commitment to work alongside marginalized communities.

In its entirety, the transformative paradigm is inclusive of multiple methods, social movements, and interdisciplinary critical studies on diverse communities. It is also muticontextual and relies on crystallization of multiple perspectives and data sources. It often requires different forms of researcher engagement and commitment to work alongside marginalized communities. These are all promising new directions, however, to create sustained social change and empower communities sets a very high bar for scholars who aspire to achieve transformative aims. In fact, when I introduce the frame to doctoral students, only a few embrace it because they do not feel that they are capable or have the time to engage with communities. However, it is a requirement of some communities that researchers establish a relationship, such as Indigenous communities that are wary of "drive by research," or worse have been robbed of their histories and artifacts, and now impose stricter access and require relationships before researchers can gain entry into their communities (Zape-tah-hol-ah Minthorn & Shotton, 2018). Other students are concerned that it would not meet the approval of their dissertation advisors. I empathize with their concern about power dynamics associated with choice of paradigm and methods at the dissertation stage. At minimum, however, if we are truly interested in linking research with improvements in practice and institutional change, we should begin to ask doctoral students for an action plan to engage communities in understanding and use of their findings. Similarly, as peer reviewers of others work, we can begin to ask for more culturally responsive approaches as well as empowering uses of research results in studies.

Before beginning a new racial climate study, I now ask campus representatives specific questions about how the study will be used for institutional transformation and how we can tailor our approach to achieve progress on diversity, equity, and inclusion goals. That is, such evaluative work requires inclusion with communities about research questions, challenges, and voices that need to be heard. I once surprised a college president with a large report that addressed students, faculty, and staff racial and gender-identity climate issues, and he remarked, "I didn't ask you to do all that!" I replied, "no sir, you asked me to work with a 17-person task force and this reflects the myriad issues and concerns they had." He had a narrow sense of the problems and solutions, whereas a grassroots task force composed of staff and faculty had many long-standing issues that they wanted to be addressed in the report. I made sure that every community had a voice that was documented and could use the report as evidence for future institutional change, even if the President was not ready to grasp the range of issues on campus.

As for our own responsibilities as gatekeepers, no matter the paradigm, we have to begin to encourage innovation in method, methodology, and the changing role of researchers in relation to communities. At one conference, I was identified as an example of a critical quantitative researcher and the convenor, Fran Stage, encouraged us to help define the work we were doing for social justice aims. According the Stage (2007), critical quantitative researchers have two tasks: 1) to use data to "reveal inequities and to identify social and institutional perpetuation of systematic inequities" in educational processes and outcomes (p. 11); 2) question and offer competing models, measures, and analytical practices that better describe the experiences of those who have not been adequately represented.

Researchers must continue to come together to innovate and help to establish new standards shaped by social aims. In short, scholars have identified how both quantitative and qualitative methods are essential to understanding inequity and "questioning the status quo on approaches to problems, actively seeking to improve the state of the art, including models, measures, and application of analytic methods" (p. 11). I found the transformative paradigm immediately appealing because it embraces multiple methods. The traditional divides between quantitative and qualitative methods are set aside to determine how both can address social justice aims, adjusting for the limitations of single method approaches. It also begins to tie different critical perspectives, research inspired by social movements, and encourages linking research with social action. At last, I found a paradigm and feel a strong connection with a community of scholars that sets social justice goals as primary and provides flexibility for researchers, encouraging innovation of methodological techniques to achieve equity for individuals and social identity groups while also addressing long-standing, systemic issues of inequity and oppression.

Note

1 Originally presented as keynote address at virtual conference, Advanced Methods Institute, Columbus OH, June 2–4, 2021, sponsored by the QualLab in the College of Education and Human Ecology, The Ohio State University.

References

Bensimon, E. M. (2007). The underestimated significance of practitioner knowledge in the scholarship of student success. *Review of Higher Education, 30*(4), 441–69.

Brayboy, B., & Deyhle, D. (2010). Insider-outsider: Researchers in American Indian communities. *Theory into Practice, 39*(3), 163–69.

Christians (2005). Ethics and politics in qualitative research. In N. K. Denzin & Y. S. Lincoln (Eds.), *The Sage handbook of qualitative research* (3rd ed.). Thousand Oaks, CA: Sage.

Collins, P. H. (1999). Reflections on the outsider within. *Journal of Career Development, 26*(1), 85–88.

Creswell, J., & Plano Clark, V. (2011). *Designing and conducting mixed methods research*. Los Angeles, CA: Sage.

Guba, E., & Lincoln, Y. S. (1989). *Fourth generation evaluation*. Newbury Park, CA: Sage.

Guba, E. G., & Lincoln, Y. (2005). Paradigmatic controversies, contradictions, and emerging confluence. In N. K. Denzin, & Y. S. Lincoln (Eds.), *The Sage handbook of qualitative research* (3rd ed., pp. 191–215). Thousand Oaks, CA: Sage.

Harding, S. (Ed.) (1987). *Feminism and methodology*. Bloomington, IN: Indiana University Press.

Harding, S. (1991). *Whose science? Whose knowledge? Thinking from women's lives*. Ithaca, NY: Cornell University Press.

Harris, J. C. (2016). Utilizing the walking interview to explore campus climate for students of color. *Journal of Student Affairs Research and Practice, 53*(4), 365–377.

Harris, J. C., Karunaratne, N., & Gutzwa, J. A. Effective modalities for healing from campus sexual assault: Centering women of color undergraduate student survivors. *Harvard Educational Review, 91*(2), 248–272.

Hesse-Biber, S. N. (2007). *The handbook of feminist research: Theory and practice*. Thousand Oaks, CA: Sage.

Hurtado, S. (2015). The transformative paradigm: Principles and challenges. In A. M. Martinez-Aleman, B. Pusser, & E. M. Bensimon (Eds.), *Critical approaches to the study of higher education: A practical introduction* (pp. 285–307). Baltimore, MD: Johns Hopkins University Press.

Hurtado, S., Cuellar, M., & Guillermo-Wann, C. (2011). Quantitative measures of students' sense of validation: Advancing the study of diverse learning environments. *Enrollment Management Journal, 5*(2), 53–71.

Hurtado, S., Gasiewski, J., & Alvarez, L. C. (2014). The climate for diversity at Cornell University: Student Experiences. Retrieved from https://www.diversity.cornell.edu/sites/default/files/Qualitative-Study-of-Student-Climate-Full-Report.pdf.

Kendi, I. (2020). Stop blaming Black people for dying of the Coronavirus. The Atlantic, April 14th. Retrieved July 1, 2021, from heatlantic.com/ideas/archive/2020/04/race-and-blame/609946/

Lather, P. (1992). Critical frames in educational research: Feminist and poststructural perspectives. *Theory and Practice, 31*(2), 1–13.

Liebenberg, Wall, Wood, & Hutt-MacLeod, (2019). Spaces & places: Understanding sense of belonging and cultural engagement among indigenous youth. *International Journal of Qualitative Methods, 18*, 1–10. https://doi.org/10.1177/1609406919840547

McCarthy, N. (2020, November 17). U.S. hate crimes at highest level in over a decade. *Statista*. Retrieved July 1, 2021 from https://www.statista.com/chart/16100/total-number-of-hate-crime-incidents-recorded-by-the-fbi/

Mertens, D. M. (2003). Mixed methods and the politics of human research: The transformative-emancipatory perspective. In A. Tashakkori, & C. Teddlie (Eds.), *SAGE handbook of mixed methods in social and behavioral research* (pp. 134–164). Thousand Oaks, CA: Sage.

Mertens, D. M. (2005). *Research and evaluation in education and psychology: Integrating diversity with quantitative, qualitative and mixed methods* (2nd ed.). Thousand Oaks, CA: Sage.

Mertens, D. M. (2009). *Transformative research and evaluation.* New York, NY: Guilford Press.

Mertens, D. M., Bledoe, K. L., Sullivan, M., & Wilson, A. (2010). *Utilization of mixed methods for transformative purposes.* In A. A. Tashakkori, & C. C. Teddlie (Eds.), *SAGE handbook of mixed methods in social & behavioral research* (2nd ed., pp. 193–214). Los Angeles, CA: Sage.

National Center for Health Statistics, CDC. Health disparities data reviewed and downloaded from https://www.cdc.gov/nchs/nvss/vsrr/covid19/health_disparities.htm

Papadimitriou, A., Ivankova, N., & Hurtado, S. (2013). Addressing challenges of conducting quality mixed methods studies in higher education. In J. Husiman, & M. Tight (Eds.), *Theory and method in higher education research, international perspectives on higher education research* (Vol. 9, pp. 133–153). Bingley: Emerald Group Publishing Limited.

Richardson, L., & St. Pierre, E. A. (2005). Writing: A method of inquiry. In N. K. Denzin, & Y. S. Lincoln (Eds.), *The sage handbook of qualitative research* (3rd ed.). Thousand Oaks, CA: Sage.

Stage, F. K. (Ed.). (2007). *New directions for institutional research: Using quantitative data to answer critical questions,* No. 133. San Francisco, CA: Jossey-Bass.

Zape-tah-hol-ah Minthorn, R., & Shotton, H. (Eds.) (2018). *Reclaiming indigenous research in higher education.* New Brunswick, NJ: Rutgers University Press.

Zuberi, T., & Bonilla-Silva, E. (Eds.). (2008). *White logic, white methods: Racism and methodology.* Lanham, MD: Rowan & Littlefield Publishers, Inc.

3
CULTURALLY RESPONSIVE POST-QUALITATIVE RESEARCH[1]

Patti Lather

Introduction

In what follows, I narrate the methodology of two books on race and schooling in order to address two questions: 1) what light do they shed on shifting imaginaries in the human sciences and 2) what are their implications for field-work? The shifting imaginary to which I refer is captured in the title of a recent collection of my works, *(Post)Critical Methodologies: The Science Possible After the Critiques* (2017). Here terms and phrases like "post-qualitative," "post-critical," "post-human ontologies of entanglement and intra-action" and "subjugated knowledge" circulate across a career of writing about the shifts in feminist methodology and qualitative research in education.

If one can encapsulate the history of qualitative research from an early qualitative/quantitative binary through the multiple paradigms of the late 1980s to the qualitative/quantitative re-alignment of a post-paradigm era, what does today's qualitative research look like? While I have an interest in the implications for **quantitative** research (post-quantitative?),[2] in this paper, I look at the "positivist qualitative" dominant as a disciplining reduction of interpretive approaches and turn to the post-qualitative or post-critical as an undoing that moves deeper into complication and accountability to complexity.

If critical theory is the focus on structures of power and post-critical is that which takes post-structural and post-colonial theories into account, then post-qualitative is that which re-engages with the beyond of the linguistic turn.[3] This is NOT old school Marxist materialism with its identity politics and economics in the last instance, but, rather, an engagement with questions of objectivity AFTER deconstruction (Melville, 1996) and the post-human and agentic realism of Karen Barad (2007) and quantum physics (Wendt, 2015). Its move is toward the political value of not being so sure toward a research imaginary

DOI: 10.4324/9781003126621-4

that finds shape and standards in what we are making in its name. This includes practices that no longer have such a hold on us where we struggle with ghosts as terms collapse.

After a short foray into post-qualitative research in a post-human context, I turn to what all of this might mean for fieldwork. With a focus on what different designs, methods and theories enact and an ethics of critical engagement, I call upon two exemplars to argue that the field is our best friend in developing practices toward a different kind of science. My two exemplars are Bettina Love's, 2012 qualitative study of Black teenage girls and their experiences of hip hop music and Savannah Shange's, 2019 ethnography of abolition and anti-Blackness in a San Francisco progressive school.

What Kind of Science for What Kind of Politics?

In 1986 Arthur Fine, a philosopher of science, published *The Shaky Game: Einstein, Realism and The Quantum Theory*. What I remember most about this book was Fine's statement that "We have to grow up in our attitudes toward science." While I came to this area through feminist critiques of science as a deeply cultural practice (Fonow & Cook, 2005), what Fine's book helped me see was that the science most of us were taught, the science of certainty about a world of stable, inanimate objects knowable through stable, objective methods is neither the science of laboratory practice nor a science adequate to a view of the world that even Einstein had trouble accepting.

This shift from Newtonian to quantum ontologies of entanglement, complicity, and co-constitutive intra-actions is evident in daily life, for example, understandings of ecology, technology, and medicine. Here the lack of an outside vantage point, the meltdown of categorical separations, measurement interactions, indeterminacy, and the limits of knowing, even what Einstein called "spooky action at a distance": all of these quantum concepts help us make sense of our world even while attachments continue to the classic view of science with its God's eye view of objectivity.

This heroic science, this patriarchal science, has been eroded for a long time both epistemologically and ontologically. Claims of procedural objectivity have been questioned for some 50 years by feminists, AIDS activists, people of color, animal rights, and the citizen knowledge movement. This sort of **epistemological** questioning of the authority granted via scientific method has gained heft in the popular imaginary in the wake of meltdowns in claims from women's health (see Boston Women's Health Collective, 1971) to COVID vaccines. Habermas (1975) called this a legitimation crisis across social institutions, a crisis accelerated by everything from Watergate to surveillance shocks to the intrusions of media into the corners of our lives.

The questioning of the **ontological** base of science has been around since at least Einstein who, somewhat in spite of himself, unleashed an alternative story about how the world works under the sign of quantum physics. Here intra-actions, fuzzy objects, and "spooky action at a distance," movement across time and place that challenge Newtonian views, open up profound questions of how to do science in a world of intra-relationalities, becomings, and entanglements (e.g., Barad, 2007; St Pierre, 2013; Wendt, 2015).[4] In the social sciences, in educational research, some of this work goes on under the banner of post-qualitative.

Since Bettie St. Pierre first coined the term in 2011, "post-qualitative" has particularly become a site for developing methodologies in keeping with the philosophical turn away from language and toward the ontological and its re-engagement with questions of "the real." Here "things talk back" (DeLanda, 2010, p. 47) in excess of the signifier's free play. Attempting to recover footing in a mind-independent world (Coole & Frost, 2010), focus shifts from isolated objects to intra-related assemblages and from proliferating and competing paradigms to meta-method across disciplines. Moving toward experimental exemplars that advance the edges of critical practice, the effort is not to debunk science but to recast and reimagine it as community based, community sustaining, and community serving in ways that might help alter the structures of institutions in more expansive, democratizing ways.

Embedded in an immanence where our knowing is in our doing, practice is the motor of such change. Here the ontological turn provides fruitful ground for registering the "making indeterminate" out of the "call of the other" that was, perhaps, the insistence that mattered most in the post-modern turn (Spivak, 1999, p. 426). "Unfolding into a future that must always be folded back into its past" (Rajan, 2002, p. 32): This is a very different temporality than that of successor regimes, endisms, and apocalyptic breaks. Complicating any linearity and untroubled claims to truth, objectivity, and reference, what the ontological turn might offer, finally, is the opportunity to make a science out of indeterminacy. Such a science is not only less imperialistic but, in meeting the world "half-way" (Barad, 2007), also more in touch with contingencies, relationalities, instabilities, and history. This calls for a science more attuned to innovation and a critique more attuned to the weight of the material in our knowing. What becomes thinkable is a science that grows out of practical engagement with the world within a different ontology of knowing: This might be the beginnings of not only (post) qualitative research but also a science worthy of the world.

Post-humanism, Subjugated Knowledge, and Theories of Anti-Blackness

In this next section, I bring post-human ontologies of entanglement and intra-action in relation to anti-Blackness as a social justice methodology. For our purposes today, post-humanism is simply the move away from what has been called "human exceptionalism": the idea that we are the center of everything and can, hence, command and control.[5] If you read at all in ecology, you know this idea has gotten us in a lot of trouble, trouble so deep we may not be able to get out of it. If you are from a marginalized group that has experienced subjugation, you know that inclusion in the category of the fully human has not necessarily been your history.

Many social theories have arisen to help explain and change this situation. Post-colonialism, critical race theories, feminist/womanist theories, all are essentially humanist in the ways they read the world and the sort of changes they urge. In contrast is a range of feminist materialist and post-critical theories that have explored post-humanism in developing a body of exploratory research, but it is the ways that post-humanism is at work in theories of anti-Blackness that is my interest here. Foregrounding its estrangement from the humanist theories that undergird most social justice work, I explore anti-Blackness as an enabling counter-narrative for grasping "the specificity of anti-Black racism" at work in schools and elsewhere (Dumas, 2016, p. 12). I return to what all of this might mean for research methods in the final part of the chapter.

A Post-Social Justice?

"Decolonizing is the new Black" said a dancer at a 2020 panel I attended based on the question, "Does Abstraction Belong to White People?[6] I took this to signal a sort of "basic" insistence that work that acknowledges the end of empire and the contest of margins and centers is *de rigueur* in order to have purchase in our historical moment of diasporas of people, ideas, and movements. Additionally, culturally responsive, social-justice themed work has occupied the space of the "new-new" (Spivak, 1999, p. 67)[7] long enough that the panel evidenced an emergent internal critique regarding the frustrating confines and predeterminations of resistance and identity at play in discourses of social justice. While the idea of critical discourses running out of steam, hollowed out with repetitions and stuck places, is not new (Latour, 2004), what was striking about this panel was the way that insight came not from theory but from the inside of practice, in these cases, dance, painting, and teaching. Here the "new new" is student resistance to the limits and cliches that can arise, resulting in a "post social justice" move.

It is here that the post-human comes into play in terms of offering a post-critical move beyond such stuck places. Getting our feet on the ground in a period of neoliberal structural readjustments (Lather, 2020) requires a sense of how, whatever theory is in play, all is in transit, including gender,[8] race, and social justice methodology. In this place and time that might be termed a post-Trump era where the secret of racist malice is a secret no more across a wide demographic, theories of anti-Blackness offer a critique of the limits of the humanism of what has come before. Rising out of frustration with the aporias of both civil rights as a multicultural social movement and critical race theory, and perhaps Black feminism too, including intersectionality theories,[9] my argument is that anti-Blackness is a theory whose "threshold moment" has come.[10]

Afro-Pessimism

Frank Wilderson and Jared Sexton launched Afro-pessimism at a University of California Irvine symposium some years back based on the work of Franz Fanon, Sylvia Wynter, and Hortense Spillers. Wilderson's recent (2020) *Afro-pessimism*[11] collects philosophy of Blackness, lyrical memoir, political history, and cultural critique in order to lay bare the roots of our social and historical time as fed by anti-Black violence. An uncompromising argument for how the prison has replaced the plantation, anything short of a disintegration of American civil and political society is held to be accommodationist. Blackness is viewed through the lens of perpetual slavery and anti-Black hatred and modernist Black subjectivity are displaced by ontological death (Hartman, 1997).[12]

"The end of redemption" is a hard place to be (Wilderson, 2015). An intensi-fication of the wound of racism, Afro-pessimism is based on a refusal of catharsis via resolution, redress, and hopefulness. In what Wilderson calls a "meta-aporia for Humanist thought and action," Blacks are not political subjects; they are "coterminous with Slaveness... social death" (Ibid.). For the socially dead, there is no humanity, the very humanity posited on the *necessity* for violence against Black people (emphasis in the original). This "abject inhumanity" is totalizing and analogy with other oppressed groups is a denial of the truth of the excep-tionalism and foundationalism of Black suffering.[13] Here Afro-Pessimism refuses humanist assumptions of the self-possessing, rights-bearing human beings of modernity. Neither therapy nor politics nor coalition has purchase in this place of gratuitous violence that is beyond narrative. This is the unbearable nature of Blackness (Sexton, 2015).

Anti-Blackness

Sometimes meshed with Afro-pessimism, theories of anti-Blackness are per-haps less totalizing although nonetheless demanding both recognition and accountability in terms of overturning dominant systems. Reparations,[14] truth-and-reconciliation processes,[15] practices well beyond the sort of "anti-racism training" the Trumpian government tried to forbid:[16] perhaps this is the "wake work" (Sharpe, 2016) that is being called for. Built on entanglements of refusal, exhaustion, and betrayal, more interesting than its definition is the question of why it is now finding its moment of theoretical articulation (Sexton, 2016).

Invested more in how to think Blackness in an anti-Black world than in the analysis of white supremacy, anti-Blackness is about cultivating a new Black subjectivity. Coalition with its inclusive, democratic, and multiracial "solutions" results in "fraught political formations" on the part of non-Blacks who do not recognize "the underlying anti-Black historical logic that produces Black oppression and suffering" (Costa Vargas, 2018, p. 6, 11). An imposed abjection through terror has produced a libidinal economy in a way not commensurable with any framework that stresses common denominators. Anything less than "unapologetic Black perspectives and collective practices" (p. 15) dilutes and crowds out, negating the specificity of Black experience. "Imagined familiarity" with Black oppression and suffering denies "anti-Blackness as foundational" (p. 17). Hence, "nothing short of detecting and destroying our structuring codes of what is means to be human in society will get rid of it" (p. 18).

The Field as Our Best Friend

> It was "the doing" of research, experiencing the ontological practices of methodology, that helped me to think through and move through… Fieldwork is an affective event where the materiality of the field rises up to meet us, rubs against us, pushes back on our interpretations.
>
> *(Childers, 2013, p. 602)*

We turn then, finally, to my big task: to lay down a methodological blueprint for post-critical qualitative research in such a space. To do this, I will compare two ethnographic studies, one firmly in the critical paradigm and the other in a post-critical space that draws strongly on anti-Blackness theory. After an overview of each book, I will do a comparative narration of their methodologies. I think what this means is that my "data" will be the fieldwork, textwork, and headwork (Van Mannen, 1995, p. 4) as evidenced through a "methodological story" of what each researcher has done in the name of design and analysis.

Exemplar 1: Hip Hop's Li'l Sistas Speak

Love's, 2012 first book grew out of her dissertation.[17] It combines autoethnography, hip hop as critical pedagogy and the "muddled, impulsive, and discernible bond" that young Black women have to rap music (p. 2). Methodologically exploring her queer Northern-born researcher self in relation to a two-year ethnography of Southern straight girls in Atlanta, this is as much a study of place and time as of people.

Love takes the reader through her journey as a teacher delineating how her "romanticized views" of hip hop and attachments to her "hood story" led her to view her own students through "a deficit cultural lens" (p. 4) before she comes into a critique of Black popular culture in her doctoral work. Drawing on her fieldwork journals to illustrate how this played out in the research, she says "I thought I knew who I was until I met these six young women" (p. 64). Hence, what we have here is an interpretive, critical, reflexive study that pays close attention to the girls' stories as well as to Love's own experiences and multiple identities as a researcher.

Two aspects are particularly noteworthy. One is the rich cultural mix Love offers that never forgets the socio-political in a portrayal of some very urgent and evocative "voices." The second is how she presents a very complicated story in an accessible manner. Situating the girls as "informal cultural critics" (p. 24), her research provides the foundation for them to learn critical thinking skills to negotiate the contradictory culture of Black girlhood. In this, Love is scrupulous about studying them "where they are" instead of where she wishes they were. Her study is, she says, "a snapshot... without intervention" (p. 31) that "unpacks" how the girls make sense of their time and place.

Perhaps the most gripping part of the book is the words of these girls in relation to watching rap videos. Here the theory that Love has in her bones is put to work in making sense of what the girls say, but never in an impositional way. This is particularly strong in the chapter on how "the beat" can paralyze critical thinking as Love brings to empirical life the concept of ideological splitting, the lived experience of hegemony, and how we consent to our own oppression. What comes across is the girls' "intellectual prowess" (p. 99) as they engage "in the complicated and contradictory work of negotiating the space of hip hop music and culture" (p. 103). Her lamentation is not their "false consciousness" but, rather, that they have to do this work alone. In "the intellectual fight of their lives" (p. 107), Black youth are neither "dumb nor dopes" in "the corporate-manipulated space of Black popular culture" (p. 108), but their shift from consumers to critical citizens needs to be aided by others, especially schools.

I'm usually pretty crabby about dissertations turned into books in what Deborah Britzman calls the "too soon," but this book made me think twice about that. By my reading, what Love has accomplished grew very much out of her esteem for these girls and her own struggles, including her imperfect self as a researcher. Love loves the girls; she loves hip hop as a paradoxical site of freedom; she loves Black culture; she loves Black feminist work in education. She loves ethnography and draws heavily from the qualitative methodological literature in education.

While Love regrets not situating her work as a "social justice" project that would have "empowered" the girls "to challenge misogyny and heterosexist male fantasies instead of just narrating them" (p. 113), I wish she had not been so hard on herself. Calling her work "inefficient and ineffectual," (p. 113), she wishes she had been less an observer so that her work could have been "more impactful" (p. 113) and urges readers to not be as fearful as she was of creating change.

While I strongly believe that no one gets out of the difficulties of researching the lives of others innocently, it seems to me that what Love has accomplished is a gift to these girls and to once and future qualitative researchers. This is so exactly because she has managed to eschew both romantic illusions of resistance and researchers as what Foucault terms "the Great Liberator, the master of truth and justice." While situating herself as a cultural theorist with great delicacy in making sense of the girls' understandings, she demonstrates both the limits and the possibilities of voice and theorizing and poking around in other people's lives. This is good stuff and I urge her to appreciate what she has made here and not only not sell it short for what it is not but to recognize the strengths of what it is.

Exemplar 2: Progressive Dystopia: Abolition, Anti-Blackness + Schooling in San Francisco

My second exemplar is Shange's, 2019 book that is also based on dissertation work[18] in what she calls "the Austin school of Black diasporic anthropology" (p. 162).[19] Shange's site is a small public San Francisco high school that offers culturally responsive, social justice-themed education in a working-class neighborhood for low-income youth of color. The product of a hard-fought campaign led by a multiracial coalition of parents, students, and teachers, the school thinks of itself as progressive, whereas Shange finds it dystopic, a place where "slavery never stopped" (p. 2) and efforts toward racial solidarity "cannibalize Black suffering" (p. 3), resulting in a perpetually colonial place.

Theories of anti-Blackness guide Shange toward an understanding of social justice practice as essentially a reconstruction project within liberal logics (p. 14). Abolition is a "messy breakup" with the antiracist, distributive state (p. 4), and anti-Blackness the weather in which we live. The book is, in short, a refusal of "the terms of the progressive promise" premised on the exclusion of Blackness from the social body (p. 140).

In this "dystopian narrative" that "attunes us to death, dispossession, and disposability" (pp. 13-14), what Shange terms "willful defiance" as a "practice of Black refusal" (pp. 15-16) becomes the agency the dispossessed use to think outside of the systems of their betrayal. Her interest is in an "abolitionist anthropology" that brings anti-Blackness theory and critical anthropology of the state together. Her movement is toward what she calls "a reparative caring" accountable to the more than we can know in the ruins of our world and discipline, an engaged anthropology, a practice of Black refusal that offers "a grammar to speak beyond the state" (p. 16).

Topics that she debunks include the messianic notion of teachers and the tensions of coalition, particularly the fragility of white liberal allyship that centers white emotional experiences at the denial of Black subjectivity, what she calls "#WhiteFeels" and "#WhiteTears" hashtags (p. 79). Endorsing what she calls "Black sass in the face of affective norms," she urges embodied abolitionist practices that challenge the "painful naivete of respectability as a strategy for Black citizenship" (p. 91). From loving discontent to uncivil disobedience, she develops "a North Star logic" (p. 101) that grows out of chattel slavery in its refusal of both a "libidinal economy that is repulsed by unruly Blackness" (p. 102) and the disappearance and disposability of Black girls.

In her methodological section, she expands on this through what she calls a "Black girl methodology" (p. 94) that flummoxes the multiracial progressive project and puts a kink in efforts to manage dissent. Placing Black girls' experience at the center of freedom's landscape (p. 114), she tries not to demand access to Black girl interiority, letting girls be absent, respecting the lines they draw. She calls this ethnographic refusal. Through the prism of an "Afrarealist imperative,"[20] her argument is that the reclamation of black girl sovereignty requires "thin description," a "nonknowing that disentangles" the ethnographic desire to know everything from the willed opacity of a participant, a refusal to concede to the terms in which we wish to know her (p. 121).

Daring to interrupt anti-Black authority and the alibi of democracy, Shange's refusal of confinement logics addresses the many burned bridges between social movements and social reforms to conclude on the impossibility of Black liberation in late liberalism. Like Love (2012), Shange faces her own complicity, "betrayed by my own research" (p. 154) in the context of a member check gone amuck. Facing squarely her romantic attachments to both the school "as a site of liberatory social transformation" (p. 155), and her intervention, she laments her "collaborative treachery" (p. 154) as she falls out of love with the school.

Starting out to do "'wake work'" (p. 156) in the aftermath of a slavery never meant to be survived, she concludes by claiming space for an ethic of "caring, seeing, and being *in the wake* of Black dispossession" (paraphrasing Sharpe, original emphasis, p. 156). This is work that won't "write light into dark" but, rather, insists on a non-knowing ethic of care, a "reparative care" (Shange, 2019, p. 121)[21] toward a political imaginary that disavows the nation-state as "any place we could call home" (p. 159). Enacting a "willful defiance of the afterlife of slavery" (Ibid) toward the possibility of Black lives lived otherwise, she terms this "departing dystopia" (p. 157), an evocative but under-theorized move. As the daughter of poet Ntozake Shange, of *For Colored Girls who Have Considered Suicide When the Rainbow is Enuf* (1975), Shange insists on abolition before utopia, indicating, perhaps, her desire for something beyond the seeming finality of the very theories that fed the study.

Fieldwork Lessons

What can be learned about fieldwork from these two exemplars? Both meet the sort of minimal standards for activist fieldwork for transformative practice: reflexive, dialogic, and participatory. These are the core of activist research for the Austin School of Anthropology (Gordon, 2007, p. 95) as well as any contemporary delineations of critical methodology.

Reflexivity is evident in their self-critiques. Love writes of not being interventionist enough; Shange unpacks a member check that feeds the very disappearing of Black girls she is trying to disrupt. Both undercut their own romantic attachments, Love to hip hop and her own "hood story," Shange to the school in which she taught for six years prior to two years of fieldwork. Dialogic elements include drawing on their fieldwork journals to provide vivid enactments to ground their analytic points. As is typical in ethnography, many voices are woven together to tell data-based stories. And while participatory elements are minimal, both use member checks, Love in a reciprocally educative manner where she sets herself up to think *with* the girls in trying to make sense of hip hop in their lives. Shange's extensive member check makes clear that she listened to those of whom she was critical, but she is unapologetic in her analysis of teachers and schools as complicit in an anti-Black system (Dumas, 2016).

In terms of theory as a prism through which data are read, while Love surely makes sense of what the girls say through the lens of critical theory, she tends much less than Shange to use the strictures of theory to set herself apart from her participants. While some of the teachers in Shange's study are presented as ambivalent in negotiating progressivism, she is much harder on them than Love is on the girls who are rigorously not taken to task for being exactly where and how they are.

This is the difference in the theories they use. While critical fieldwork in education started out positioning teachers as the "bad cops" of capitalism and the researcher as the good cop of one or another liberatory theory, as critical ethnography developed, it became much more aware of the ambivalence and contingency of complex subjectivities on the part of both researcher and researched. You can see this in how Love's effort was very much a visibility and recovery project of reclaiming Black women's subjugated knowledge as they negotiate Black cultural production.

Anti-Blackness shapes a different perspective altogether. While Shange ends up somewhat unexpectedly endorsing a reparative caring, this is little in evidence in how she tells the tale of the ruins of a multiracial progressive school where Black punition and disposability are much in evidence. Shange's surety in saying unpopular things and calling out complicity rubs against post-critical calls to foreground the insecurity of knowing and to displace the rescuing researcher. Her task is more a deconstruction of the claims of progressive multiculturalism where all but a handful of Black students, especially girls, are taken to task for reproducing Black suffering. Shattering myths of civil rights progress, like Barry Jenkins' *The Underground Railroad* in presenting a direct hit to the nervous system, she is invested in creating a foundational "grammar" of refusal as a necessary corrective, a refusal built on the sense that the old "Afro-pessimism" was "pessimistic" about Black capacities, while the new "Afro-pessimism" is "pessimistic" about non-Black capacities for change (Woods, 2018).

While both are love letters to Black culture and resilience from, interestingly, Black queer women, they have very different messages for those committed to improving schools for Black lives. Love's narrative comes across as much more hopeful while Shange channels the willful defiance of abolitionist theorizing that calls into question progressive pathways. "Plantation futures" and multiracial solidarity are dangers in her dedication to Black movement beyond survivance where complicity is everywhere in a world "'structured by anti-Black solidarity'" (Sexton, 2016).

Comparing the very recent *The Underground Railroad* with *Roots* from 1977, searing awareness of that complicity is unavoidable. Here, after endless police shootings, street protests met with wildly different responses, and the branding opportunism evident in the corporate commodification of Blackness,[22] Jenkins' no apologies depiction of slavery takes its sense. Perhaps it is as simple as *Roots* was formed out of a white gaze, well leavened with family drama and heartwarming moments, perhaps what the traffic could bear at the time. Jenkins enacts a Black gaze (Costa Vargas, 2018, p. 35) that offers "a praxis for imagining," to use Sharpe's words (2016, p. 113), a vehicle for engaging the "more" that exceeds "all of the violence directed at Black life" (p. 134) via the use of magical realism to tell a difficult tale.[23]

Perhaps this is what I mean by anti-Blackness as a theory whose time of field forming elaboration has come. Perhaps thinking with, through or against it can be of use in "reframing racism as a relation grounded in anti-Blackness rather than white supremacy" (Sexton, 2016). Here the insistence on a Black/non-Black binary that is unapologetically totalizing and anti-dialectical, creates a kind of anti-Black base and global racial superstructure that decenters both whiteness and the "liberal political narrative of emancipation and enfranchisement" (Day, 2015, p. 110) to, instead, focus on the "precarity and irrationality of Blackness" (Ibid., p. 115).

In terms of trustworthiness, both display the work of the labor involved in a way that intensifies the reaching, making visible the time put in. This propels the reader into an intimate relation with particular aspects that are put into service for that something "more" – be it critical edge or transcendence or "life" and its questions. This is a sort of "methodology section" that makes visible "the skin in the game," the diligence involved, so that the work is EARNED for the reader by presenting the agency and intentionality of the researcher in rechoosing the rituals of fieldwork.

Love's ethnographic tale is the more familiar as she uses critical theory to wrestle with the implications of research as praxis that can be evaluated according to long-established criteria (Lather, 1986), whereas Shange presents a non-apologetically "anti–anti-Blackness" via "a world not structured by a type of sociability that demands Black abjection" (Costa Vargas, 2018, p. 48). In this, she demonstrates that "true" is a deep question that we mean – really a prayer. This is less the kind of work that takes away the ability to judge by the usual criteria than that which demands/evokes a different value, research that functions more like a wound.

Neither of these exemplars is post-qualitative. Neither troubles voice, agency, and emancipatory goals although the liberatory researcher is undercut and complicity is wrestled with (Childers, 2013, p. 606). Neither breaks new ground in terms of how both practice and the objects of a field are redefined and reconfigured.[24] While both enact common elements of critical ethnography, they are neither particularly experimental in form nor interested in the kind of reflexivity that enacts doubled(d) practices of representation that both represent the researched and trouble representation simultaneously (Lather, 2007). And neither explores what it might mean to endorse anti-identitarian critical thought. While Shange gives some attention to "non-knowing" in her ethic of reparative caring, this gets displaced by a more typical portrayal of the researcher as "the one who knows" in not departing from a position of certainty,[25] and the "identitarian force" that drives social justice work is largely untroubled (Wiegman, 2004).

What we have, then, is the instantiation of critical ethnography in two modes, one a story of a researcher falling in love with her participants but sad about the limits of her intervention, the other a story of falling out of love with a school in which the researcher was much invested in order to intervene in an exhausted narrative of anti-racist schooling. Both find themselves in a "bruising" affect sphere of "what is already not working" (Berlant, 2011, p. 263), performing the impasse where critical ethnography has arrived: the loss of innocence regarding the possibilities of the progressive narrative.

Conclusion: Toward a "Woke" Methodology?

What we need must be acknowledged as conceptually beyond our conceptual grasp and yet, anachronistically, potentially here in our very present. This potentiality is ...what I take to be the methodological significance of our confrontation with unknowability... it is not something we say so that we can settle again for what we've already thought. It is the recognition that unknowability is the activity of our own limits: to think *here* is to inhabit a politics generous enough not to punish us for our failure to arrive now at the future imaginary we seek.

(Wiegman, 2004, p. 116, emphasis in the original)

As educators in the service of fostering capacities in those we serve, we reside uncomfortably betwixt and between Enlightenment beliefs and some recognition and even welcoming of a post-humanism that might save the world from us. Maybe this entails a new brain, rewired out of ecological necessity to what Claire Colebrook (2014) terms, after Deleuze and Guattari (1987), "'becoming imperceptible'" (p. 38): a self beyond what we are, a counter ethics beyond self-furtherance given our seeming inability to adequately witness planetary crisis.

"And so, here we are, everywhere *in* it and *of* it – the world's mess'" (Spillers, 2003, p. 40, quoted in Sexton, 2016, emphasis in the original), trying to figure out how to do "wake work" that takes into account both planetary and on-the-ground everyday lived crises. While "woke" is derided as the new "politically correct" by the Right,[26] the "wake work" that Sharpe (2016) aspires toward feeds off the paradox of both the persistence of the "racial calculus" that skews Black life in the afterlife of slavery AND what survives under conditions of "this insistent Black exclusion, this ontological negation" (p. 14). Perhaps best evident in Black expressive culture, this is both a refusal of blackness-as-victimization and an acknowledgement of anti-Black violence as a "constitutive aspect of this democracy" (p. 7).

This is Black work, this work of forging Black political imaginaries on their own terms and we can see what might be possible for "wake work" in qualitative research in the ethnographies I have featured in this paper. But who is this "we," white girl?[27] This was a question I asked in an earlier paper regarding a trip I took to South Africa where I lost my voice after many seminars about doing empowering research in schools (Lather, 2004).

As a white woman living in a perpetually strange time where whatever authority I have is grounded in the prejudices of the historical context, hope for solidarity is, perhaps, best thought along the lines of what Fred Moten (2018) terms "reciprocal nonexistence of the white man and the black man, dwelling in and on the im/possibility of proper self-possession" (quoted in Row, 2018, para 11). This is a sort of Buddhist place where the dualisms of identity "'consent not to be a single being'" via practices always incomplete, always in-the-making, keeping communication open, listening hard in the midst of self-doubt, questioning redemption, and damnation alike. Here becoming imperceptible means occupying many "scrupulously differentiated" positionalities (Spivak, 1999, p. 193) where we all have work to do out of our particular combinations of privilege and struggle.

For non-Blacks, the "woke methodology" that might be possible in qualitative research, hence, might mean using fieldwork as a site of unlearning privilege as loss (Spivak, 1990), alert to the workings of uneven power, compelled to address ourselves as *other* on the way to becoming *something other* as we learn how to live in de-authorized space.

In sum, in terms of a blueprint for post-critical qualitative research, out of mutated dominant practices, we move forward through a convergence of intensity and emergence. Here, in a very Foucauldian vein, practice itself is the motor and mode of change (Nealon, 2008, p. 43). Infiltrating, embedding, infusing, intensifying, multiplying, and extending its realms of application, such change is wholly immanent. This is a kind of "hacking" of a series of conflicting points and issues: this is our (post)critical project that is not about individual but collective procedure, a very social enterprise where we start where we are.

Notes

1 Originally presented as keynote address at virtual conference, Advanced Methods Institute, Columbus OH, June 2–4, 2021, sponsored by the QualLab in the College of Education and Human Ecology, The Ohio State University.

2 I am particularly interested in what I have termed "smart mixed methods" and what Harry Torrance has called "less stupid assessment" (Lather, 2016). See, also, special issue of *Cultural Studies<->Critical Methodologies* on "Alternative Ontologies of Number: Rethinking the Quantitative in Computational Culture," 16(5), 2016. As but one example of the blurring of qual/quant distinctions, see Advances in Quantitative Ethnography: Second International Conference, Andres Ruis and Seung Lee, eds. NY: Springer Nature, 2021.

3 Post-critical has a newish meaning in feminist theory that has to do with a move from a critical hegemony to reparative engagement that is affirmative. Building on Eve Sedgewick's (1997) distinctions between "paranoid" and "reparative" readings, thinking "with" rather than "opposed" to one's object of study is key. Here what Robyn Wiegman calls "the critic's performance of interpretative mastery" is situated in "the twilight of the hermeneutics of suspicion" (2014, p. 18) when "faith

in the equation between knowledge and political transformation" (p. 7) is shaken. The Ur-text appears to be Rita Felski, *The Limits of Critique* (University of Chicago, 2015).

4 Alexander Wendt has organized a virtual format "Quantum Social Science Bootcamp" for July 12-16, 2021, funded by Carnegie Corporation and sponsored by the OSU Mershon Center. Follow-up in-person bootcamps are expected in 2022 and 2023. See https://u.osu.edu/quantumbootcamp/program-schedule/

5 See Braidotti, 2013a, 2013b, for an introduction to the constellation of ideas that come together in post-anthropocentric thought, from digital/technology to animal studies, post-colonial, race and gender studies, and environmentalism.

6 Ohio State University Wexner Center discussion, January 20, 2020, based on work of Miguel Gutierrez. See Gutierrez, 2018. Comment by Nadine George-Graves, OSU Department of Dance and Theater.

7 Spivak is referring to "the indigenous dominant" (1999, 67-68). See Walter and Anderson, 2013, on Indigenous quantitative methodologies.

8 "Trans in Transit Conference," Turku Finland, November 2018.

9 Tyron P. Woods (2018) situates both Black feminism and intersectionality as post-civil rights phenomena but considers them "dead-end" in conceptual limits, coopted into "institutionalized decadence," symptoms of the sorry state of Black power today. Woods provides a concise history of Black pessimism through anti-slavery, Black nationalism, and civil rights up through the critical race theory movement. From Derek Bell's "racial realism" to Wilderson's "Afro-pessimism," this is a long-standing response on the part of black intellectuals to crisis, with largely unacknowledged roots in the tradition of pessimism regarding the African continent's capacity to rise up. "The original 'Afro-pessimism', then, is merely the post-colonial extension of the 19th-century racist tracts on civilization and history created to justify Western empire." For a genealogy, of the "old" Afro-pessimism, see Noah, 2011. For a critique of intersectionality marked by its nostalgia for Black Power, see Bruce A. Dixon's three-part essay in *Black Agenda Report*, January 27, February 1–16, 2018. For a more loving insider critique, see Jennifer Nash (2014, 2019).

10 Hortense Spillers (2003) identifies the threshold moment as when a concept moves into theoretical elaboration in the academy, as cited in Wiegman, 2004, note 5.

11 The book was long-listed for a National Book Award in nonfiction.

12 See *Afro-Pessimism: An Introduction*. Minneapolis: racked and dispatched (publisher), 2017. Free download: rackedanddispatched.noblogs.org. It includes chapters by Wilderson, Spillers, Sexton, and Hartman.

13 In earlier work (2010), Wilderson makes an exception for Native Americans.

14 A now classic essay on reparations is Coates, 2014. For a critique of reparations as part of the liberal project of inclusion, see Jamilah Martin, http://jamilmartin.wordpress.com/2014/05/26/on-reparations-resisting-inclusion-and-co-optation. See, also, Wilderson's critical documentary, *Reparations... Now*, available on Vimeo.

15 For a history of such commissions, see Zvobgo and Crawford, 2020.

16 Trumpian efforts to forbid training that endorses "structural racism" has more recently segued into the hysteria around critical race theory. Several state legislatures are trying to prevent the "indoctrination" of students by prohibiting teachers and curriculum from any mention of what former Vice President Mike Pence refers to as "systemic racism as a leftist myth."

17 Love's 2019 book, *We Want to do More than Survive*, combines recent information on race and schooling with memoir. More a polemic than research study, it is not an ethnography. While it uses the term anti-Blackness, it is a clarion call for intersectional social justice and solidarity across oppressed groups that stand in stark contrast to Afro-pessimism.

18 At the University of Pennsylvania.

19 See Gordon, 2007, "The Austin School Manifesto: An Approach to the Black or African Diaspora."

20 Afrarealism uses Black radical, feminist-womanist, and queer theories to theorize democracy's aggressions and terrors in the production of Black suffering. "In conversation with 'Afro-pessimism,'" (Joy James, 2013, p. 129), it both uses Wilderson's work and offers a more inclusive analysis that is less insistent on refusing analogies with the experience of other oppressed groups, especially anti-indigenous genocide.

21 Eve Sedgewick, 1997, argued for reparative as opposed to "paranoid" critique.

22 One could add: that only 160 of the 2000 remaining confederate monuments have been removed or renamed, and those few often at great contest.

23 Jenkins filmed a preamble to *The Underground Railroad* called "The Gaze" where the Black "extras" look silently into the camera for extended times. He said he decided to do this when he looked around the set and realized these folks could have been his ancestors. Available on Hulu.

24 For a post-qualitative exemplar, see Lather and Smithies (1997), *Troubling the Angels: Women Living with HIV/AIDS*.

25 Sexton (2016) argues that such certainty may be more doubled than it first appears. Citing Lyotard at the front of his paper "Afro-pessimism: The Unclear Word," he argues for a certainty that is both absolute and "'at the same instant, completely deprived of all security.'" In Shange's case, I would argue that this might be a place where waiting to publish after the rush of dissertation might have benefited her, allowing her to develop this more doubled vantage point, what Moton (2018) calls "the terribly redoubled double edge" of freedom.

26 The Republican "war on woke" is everywhere in the news media (e.g., Edsall, 2021). But one example is an Ohio Senate candidate and former chair of the Ohio Republican Party who published an editorial on "the socialist agenda" of critical race theory and the 1619 Project before launching a "listening tour" of concerned parents across Ohio (Timken, 2021).

27 Sexton (2016) cites Wilderson's suspicion of the "we" of coalition as too much the coherent modern individual and too much "'a Humanizing inspiration.'" See Sexton, note 3.

References

Barad, K. (2007). *Meeting the universe half-way: Quantum physics and the entanglement of matter and meaning*. Durham, NC: Duke University Press.

Bassil, N. R. (2011). The roots of afropessimism: The British invention of the 'dark continent'. *Critical Arts, 25*(3), 377–396. doi: 10.1080/02560046.2011.615141.

Berlant, L. (2011). *Cruel optimism*. Durham, NC: Duke University Press.

Boston Women's Health Collective. (1971). *Our bodies, ourselves*. Boston, MA: Women's Health Collective.

Braidotti, R. (2013a). *The posthuman*. Cambridge: Polity.

Braidotti, R. (2013b). Posthuman humanities. *European Educational Research Journal, 12*(1), 1–19.

Childers, S. (2013). The materiality of fieldwork: An ontology of feminist becoming. *International Journal of Qualitative Studies in Education, 26*(5), 599–609.

Coates, T. (2014, June). The case for reparations. *The Atlantic*. Retrieved from https://www.theatlantic.com/magazine/archive/2014

Colebrook, C. (2014). *Death of the posthuman: Essays on extinction, Vol. 1*. Ann Arbor, MI: Open Humanities Press. Retrieved from http://dx.doi.org/10.3998/ohp.12329362.0001.001

Coole, D., & Frost, S. (2010). *New materialisms: Ontology, agency, and politics*. Durham, NC: Duke University Press.

Costa Vargas, J. (2018). *The denial of antiblackness: Multiracial redemption and black suffering.* Minneapolis, MN: University of Minnesota Press.

Day, I. (2015). Being or nothingness: Indigeneity, antiblackness, and settler colonial critique. *Critical Ethnic Studies, 1*(2), 102–121.

DeLanda, M. (2010). *Deleuze: History and science.* New York, NY: Atropos Press.

Deleuze, G., & Guattari, F. (1987). *A thousand plateaus: Capitalism and schizophrenia.* Minneapolis, MN: University of Minnesota Press.

Dixon, B. A. (2018, January 25). Intersectionality is a hole. Afro-pessimism is a shovel. We need to stop digging. Part 1 of 3. *Black Agenda Report.* Retrieved May 15, 2021, from http://www.blackagendareport.com

Dixon, B. A. (2018, February 1). Looking down that deep hole: Parasitic intersectionality and toxic afro-pessimism. Part 2 of 3. *Black Agenda Report.* Retrieved May 15, 2021, from http://www.blackagendareport.com

Dixon, B. A. (2018, February 16). Are intersectionality or afro-pessimism paths to power? Probably not. Part 3 of 3. *Black Agenda Report.* Retrieved May 15, 2021, from http://www.blackagendareport.com

Dumas, M. J. (2016). Against the dark: Antiblackness in education policy and discourse. *Theory Into Practice, 55*(1), 11–19.

Edsall, T. (2021, May 26). Is wokeness "kryptonite for democrats"? *New York Times.*

Felski, R. (2015). *The limits of critique.* Chicago, IL: University of Chicago Press.

Fine, A. (1986). *The shaky game: Einstein, realism and the quantum theory.* Chicago, IL: University of Chicago Press.

Fonow, M. M., & Cook, J. (2005). Feminist methodology: New applications in the academy and public policy. *Signs, 30*(4), 2211–2236.

Gordon, E. T. (2007). "The Austin school manifesto: An approach to the Black or African diaspora. *Cultural Dynamics, 19*(1), 93–97.

Gutierrez, M. (2018). *Does abstraction belong to white people? Thinking the politics of race in contemporary dance.* Theory and Practice series, supported by the Andy Warhol Foundation for the Visual Arts. Retrieved from Bombmagazine.org/articles/Miguel-gutierrez-1/

Habermas, J. (1975). *Legitimation crises.* Boston, MA: Beacon Press.

Hartman, S. V. (1997). *Scenes of subjection: Terror, slavery, and self-making in nineteenth-century America.* Oxford: Oxford University Press.

James, J. (2013, November 10). Afrarealism and the Black matrix: Maroon philosophy at democracy's border. *The Black Scholar, 43*(4), 124–131.

Lather, P. (1986). Research as praxis. *Harvard Educational Review, 56*(3), 257–277.

Lather, P. (2004, April). Ethics now: White woman goes to Africa and loses her voice. Paper presented at the annual conference of the American Educational Research Association. San Diego, CA.

Lather, P. (2007). *Getting lost: Feminist efforts toward a double(d) science.* Albany, NY: SUNY Press.

Lather, P. (2016). Post-face: Cultural studies of numeracy. *Cultural Studies/Critical Methodologies, 16*(5), 502–505.

Lather, P. (2020). Updata: Post-neoliberalism. *Qualitative Inquiry, 26*(7), 768–770.

Lather, P., & Smithies, C. (1997). *Troubling the angels: Women living with HIV/AIDS.* New York City, NY: Westview/HarperCollins

Lather, P., & St. Pierre, E. (2013). Post-qualitative research. *Qualitative Studies in Education, 26*(6), 629–633.

Latour, B. (2004). Why has critique run out of steam? From matters of fact to matters of concern. *Critical Inquiry, 30*(Winter), 225–248.

Love, B. L. (2012). *Hip Hop's li'l sistas speak: Negotiating hip hop identities and politics in the new south*. New York City, NY: Peter Lang.

Love, B. L. (2019). *We want to do more than survive: Abolitionist teaching and the pursuit of educational freedom*. Boston, MA: Beacon Press.

Melville, S. (1996). Color has not yet been named: Objectivity in deconstruction. In J. Gilbert-Rolfe (Ed.), *Seams: Art as philosophical content* (pp. 129–146). Wilton, CT: G&B Arts.

Moton, F. (2018). *Black and blur (consent not to be a single being)*. Durham, NC: Duke University Press.

Nash, J. (2014). *The black body in ecstasy: Reading race, reading pornography*. Durham, NC: Duke University Press.

Nash, J. (2019). *Black feminism reimagined: After intersectionality*. Durham, NC: Duke University Press.

Nealon, J. (2008). *Foucault beyond Foucault: Power and its intensification since 1984*. Stanford, CA: Stanford University Press.

Rajan, T. (2002). *Deconstruction and the remainders of phenomenology: Sartre, Derrida, Foucault, Baudrillard*. Stanford, CA: Stanford University Press.

Row, J. (2018, April/May). Declarations of independence: Fred Moten's improvisational critique of power. *Bookforum Magazine*. Retrieved from https://www.bookforum.com/print/2501/fred-moten-s-improvisational-critique-of-power-19407

Sedgwick, E. (1997). Paranoid reading and reparative reading; or you're so paranoid you probably think this introduction is about you. In E. Sedgwick (Ed.), *Novel gazing: Queer readings in fiction* (pp. 1–37). Durham, NC: Duke University Press.

Sexton, J. (2015). Unbearable blackness. *Cultural Critique, 90*, 159–78.

Sexton, J. (2016). Afro-pessimism: The unclear word. *Rhizomes: Cultural Studies in Emerging Knowledge, 29*. Doi.org/10.20415/rhiz/029.e02

Shange, N. (1975). *For colored girls who have considered suicide/when the rainbow is enuf*. San Francisco, CA: Shameless Hussy Press.

Shange, S. (2019). *Progressive dystopia: Abolition, antiblackness + schooling in San Francisco*. Durham, NC: Duke University Press.

Sharpe, C. (2016). *In the wake: On blackness and being*. Durham, NC: Duke University Press.

Slaby, J. (2020). The weight of history: From Heidegger to Afro-pessimism. In L. Guidi, & T. Rentsch (Eds.), *Phenomenology as performative exercise* (pp. 173–195). Leiden: Brill.

Spillers, H. (2003, January 16). *Women in/of the Academy*, Address at the First Annual UNC-Duke Lecture in Women's Studies.

Spillers, H. (2003). *Black, white and in color: Essays on American literature and culture*. Chicago, IL: University of Chicago Press.

Spivak, G. (1990). *The post-colonial critic: Interviews, strategies, dialogues*, Sarah Harasym (Ed.). London: Routledge.

Spivak, G. (1999). *A critique of postcolonialism: Toward a history of the vanishing past*. Cambridge, MA: Harvard University Press.

St. Pierre, E. (2011). Post qualitative research: The critique and the coming after. In N. K. Denzin & Y. S. Lincoln, (Eds.), *Handbook of qualitative inquiry* (4th ed., pp. 611–635). Thousand Oaks, CA: Sage.

Timken, J. (2021, May 25). Radical left using race theory to advance agenda in schools. *Columbus Dispatch*.

Van Mannen, J. (1995). An end to innocence: The ethnography of ethnography. In J. Van Maanen, (Ed.) *Representation in ethnography* (pp. 1–35). Thousand Oaks, CA: Sage.

Walter, M., & Anderson, C. (2013). *Indigenous statistics: A quantitative research methodology.* Walnut Creek, CA: Left Coast Press.

Wendt, A. (2015). *Quantum mind and social science.* Cambridge: Cambridge University Press.

Wiegman, R. (2004). Dear Ian. *Duke Journal of Gender Law and Policy, 11*(93), 93–115.

Wiegman, R. (2014). The times we're in: Queer feminist criticism and the reparative 'turn.'. *Feminist Theory, 15*(1), 4–25.

Wilderson, F. (2010). *Red, white & black: Cinema and the structure of U.S. antagonisms.* Durham, NC: Duke University Press.

Wilderson, F. (2015, October 20). *Afro-pessimism and the end of Redemption.* Durham, NC: Duke University: Humanities Futures: Franklin Humanities Institute. Retrieved from https://humanitiesfutures.org/papers/afro-pessemism-end-redemption/

Wilderson, F. (2020). *Afropessimism.* New York: Liveright Publications.

Woods, T. P. (2018, August 8). Putting afro-pessimism, intersectionality, and solidarity to work. *Black Agenda Report.* Retrieved May 8, 2021, from: http://www.blackagendareport.com

Zvobgo, K., & Crawford, C. (2020, October. 21). Some people want a U.S. truth commission. But truth commissions have limits. *The Washington Post.*

4

MUST AN EDUCATION IN RESEARCH ETHICS ENGAGE ISSUES OF CONTEXT, CULTURE, AND COMMUNITY?

Winston C. Thompson

Introduction

For some persons, it may be tempting to look at the call for culturally responsive research as something of a niche concern. "Surely," such persons might assert, "even though culturally responsive research is a fine goal for institutions to state, placing their articulations on promotional brochures and public-facing websites, much serious and 'good' research can be pursued without meeting or, indeed, even being evaluated against that standard." When tasked with the preparation of the next generation of researchers, such persons might view cultural responsiveness as an incidental rather than essential element of their education. From such a perspective, research ethics and the education that initiates researchers in their practice, then, should be squarely about ensuring that aberrant ethical errors do not disrupt the objective pursuit of knowledge. To some extent, it is precisely this view that will be explored within this chapter.

The following pages interrogate how the research community, and individual researchers and scholars, might benefit from identifying social justice-based ethical and moral concerns as essential elements – rather than incidental obstacles – to the work of research. That is to ask: *by what research practices might culturally responsive research be advanced and, by extension, how might scholars be prepared for doing that work in meaningful ways?* This charge will be identified as an explicitly educational question in that it focuses on a few normative (i.e., concerning what should be done) dimensions of a particular curriculum for researchers, specifically framed as: Must an Education in Research Ethics Engage Issues of Context, Culture, and Community?

Before continuing in engaging that work, this introduction will frame much of the course of the exploration to follow. As the chapter is written by

DOI: 10.4324/9781003126621-5

a philosopher of education with the expectation that it will largely be read by those who do not similarly identify, a few notes about that field might be appropriate.

Firstly, philosophers of education often engage in a form of scholarship that, for many scholars, might challenge clear classifications of research methods. The usual discussion of quantitative, qualitative, empirical, or theoretical may or may not serve useful for all (or even most) philosophers of education. As such, it is worth acknowledging that this chapter is written from within a tradition of scholarship that places primary value on the justification of arguments. Essentially, this asks for reasons to endorse a particular claim or conclusion.

Secondly, though philosophy of education is a field that, as readers might presume, has much to say about what happens in traditional public-school classrooms, it also stands to study and analyze other environments and domains of education. This is a field that is also concerned with, among other subjects, epistemological issues emergent in the process of knowledge creation and distribution by essentially asking: how do/should we come to know what we know and how do/should we share that knowledge with others? Of course, these processes are central to what most readers of this chapter will recognize as research. Given this, the chapter will argue for a social justice-based understanding of research ethics education.[1]

The chapter aims to lead readers through a response to its core question in the following stages. First, it suggests that a subset of the concerns of research ethics is moral in nature. This insight contributes to reconsideration of research ethics education programs as a type of moral education. This moral educational work is operationalized to provide broad attention to matters related to developing an appropriate relationship to standards of conduct in relation to research activities.

Second, the chapter explores what such an educational program might offer as methodological foundation for increasing the moral quality of research activities. These examples serve as evidence of the ways in which a reconsideration of research as a moral practice might work toward responding to often underaddressed aspects of social justice.

Third, the chapter provides a limited, working definition of social justice. This definition embraces special consideration of "context," "culture," and "community" within these invocations of social justice in research ethics. Against the backdrop of these definitions, the chapter returns to its central question, namely, whether a coherent and defensible account of a reconsidered version of research ethics education (as a domain-specific type of moral education) can be pursued without reference to social justice concerns of context, culture, and community.

Finally, in direct response to this question, the chapter outlines responses to a few likely forms of resistance opposing the creation and execution of these new educational programs. In this, the chapter pursues the view that the moral educational work of research ethics education has an unambiguous duty to engage issues of social justice, arguing that these social justice concerns are an important expression of moral concerns contextualized in the world in which one lives, the cultures through which one makes epistemic claims, and the communities that result from both.

Having described what the chapter will do, a brief statement follows about what it will not do. Though written by a philosopher, this chapter is not written *for* philosophers. Essentially, this means that many of the choices made in regard to the presentation and manner in which ideas are articulated and expressed have been made less with concern for philosophically nuanced minutiae. Rather, the chapter favors a speculative approach that welcomes readers to a generalist account of ideas that have emerged from the field, pointing to their potential (rather than conclusive) use in defining and promoting appropriately responsive research. With regrets, this means that some justifications will not be fully presented – though these omissions will often be noted, should a reader wish to pursue them through other texts.

Additionally, and relatedly, this chapter aims to be accessible for scholars of all ranks across fields and disciplines. This includes students, full professors, and all those in between. It is expected that the examples and explorations will allow this range of academically engaged persons to find some elements of value in the arguments and values – which might also compromise an approach to methods – on offer via this chapter. These dual decisions have been made in the interest of offering a rigorously supported invitation to further explore the arguments that are sketched as possibilities for use. The chapter operates on the assumption that the questions that follow from this invitation to imagine and explore the limits of research ethics education might be of direct use to those outside of the discipline of philosophy (of education) yet interested in the insights that intersect with the usual work of research in education or other similar fields of study.

Exploring the Question

To begin in earnest, this chapter will focus its attention on a way in which "research ethics" might be understood as a category containing far more than is typically assumed. Stated differently, the chapter asks whether a nuanced understanding of research ethics might make clearer the answer to the question located in its title. Toward establishing that understanding of research ethics, a few points of definition and interpretation are useful.

Firstly, many plausible accounts of ethics situate that field of concern in various competing relations to the category of morality. On some accounts, one might regard ethics (i.e., right or proper action) as a subcategory of morality. On another account, morality (i.e., related to right action for the right reasons or values) could appear to be a specific type of ethical conduct. On some accounts, morality and ethics are largely interchangeable.[2] Despite these divergent views, however, it seems appropriate to identify a close relationship between these two normative categories.

In this chapter, the reader is asked to consider a form or extension of research ethics, namely, *research morality*. That is, rather than only the usual question of proper actions (i.e., avoiding plagiarism, securing research subject consent, etc.) that populate a typical research ethics outlook, questions of values and motivation might be invoked. Why do we study the subjects we do? Given the background circumstances within which we operate, what obligations might we have to produce knowledge? Further, what types of obligations might we have in relation to the types of knowledge we produce, or the ways in which that knowledge is disbursed? The questions potentially engaged here are as profound as they are numerous.

Secondly, as alluded to above, a view of research ethics with a mind to matters of research morality might allow for a thoughtful engagement with epistemological questions that are not easily sidestepped in the pursuit of "good" research. Indeed, these questions can be considered central to the very picture of what it means to engage with the thoughts and evidence of others responsibly and responsively.

In his captivating work on reasoning, philosopher Anthony Laden (2012) provides an account of reasoning that defends it as a reciprocal and responsive social practice. Following Laden, reasoning could be described as an activity that invites others to join together in the mutually endorsed conclusions justified by evidence and consideration. On this view, one might regard the research community itself as a large and continuous mechanism for facilitating the reasoning of our shared society.

If research is a social practice with moral dimensions, the preparation for that practice ought to be a form of *moral education,* focused upon the moral dimensions of knowledge creation.

Viewed in this way, research ethics ought to be concerned with, among other things, how well the research produced can stand as an invitation for others to take up the evidence and perspectives on offer. "Good" research, then, is intelligible and responsive to the justified perspectives of those it wishes to engage. Research ethics programs ought to be aimed at increasing the likelihood that this moral standard for a social practice will be met.

From this it follows, then, that research ethics (here understood as research morality) programs ought to consist of more than mere behavioral training schemes aimed at ensuring specific and predetermined actions by rote repetition or rehearsal of formal accounts of infractions. Rather, these programs must be richly educational in that they aim at preparing researchers to act, by way of curating within them the appropriate values, under the often unpredictable and morally weighty circumstances of social life. Stated differently: if research is a social practice with moral dimensions, the preparation for that practice (i.e., what is now typically considered research ethics education) ought to be a form of *moral education*, focused upon the moral dimensions of knowledge creation. This is a task that requires careful consideration of the epistemic stakes and consequences of research as a social (and political) activity.

Rethinking Research Ethics (Education)

A view of research morality might ground mandates for a number of compelling obligations and standards for scholarship. Toward providing a generative example of this area of consideration, this chapter will now explore some of the epistemological matters that might be located within the moral educational project usually understood as research ethics education.

Of course, on the existing model of research ethics, one could be forgiven for concluding that that the main elements of concern are the falsification of data, matters of plagiarism, and the like.[3] But, with the enlarged perspective afforded by the concept of research morality, one might also engage concerns of ethics and morality, deeper questions of value, in the domain of the epistemic and conceptual. Two examples of this follow.

Firstly, philosopher Miranda Fricker (2007) has done foundational work in what she (and now others) has called epistemic injustice. As articulated via her groundbreaking work, epistemic injustices are forms of injustice that are related to one's status as a knower. In her early work, Fricker explores two sub-categories of epistemic injustice: testimonial injustice and hermeneutical injustices.

A testimonial injustice is an injustice visited upon a person when they are not deemed sufficiently credible (often for some reason attributable to aspects of their identity) in regard to their claims to knowledge. Here, one might consider the increasingly popular call to "believe women" when they communicate their knowledge of sexual harassment, assault, or violence. This prompt acknowledges the unjust background conditions of our society in which women's voices are often ignored; they are perceived as less than sufficiently credible in their claim to knowledge. In this and other examples, research morality might then recognize the need for care and attention regarding whose perspectives and voices are deemed credible in the creation of knowledge (or, written differently, it might further interrogate what gets recognized as knowledge, in addition to who gets recognized as knowledgeable[4]).

A hermeneutical injustice is an injustice that is visited upon a person when the very concepts available to make sense of their experiences, to distill these into more legible knowledge, are unjustly insufficient. In a stirring example (linked to the one above), Fricker describes the historical case of women navigating similar, but in some sense illegible, experiences within their workplaces. Their identification of the (newly named at the time) concept of "sexual harassment" allowed for their communicating with one another about the nuances and details of their individual and collective experience, empowering their action in response to these unwelcome and predatory experiences. Research morality might recognize the ways in which having insufficient concepts masks the lived experiences of persons and renders attempts at analyzing (and addressing) their experiences difficult.

Following these analyses, it would seem that "good" research ought to be appropriately attuned to the epistemic issues of research/participant credibility and the concepts available in the construction of knowledge. Indeed, these insights suggest that scientific study is far less objective than is sometimes suggested. Scientific studies necessarily reflect the society and culture in which they operate. Structural and individual biases related to gender, race, or ethnicity operate in scientific inquiry just as they manifest in the broader culture. While some philosophers of science have defended ideal versions of the objectivity of the academic experience, these commentators rely on a rational model of the scientific process in which deductive reasoning and observational refutation provide the basis for "objective" results.[7] By contrast, other scholars have argued that science does reflect the culture in which it evolves, including its biases. In the literature on the sociology of knowledge and the history and philosophy of science, for example, Mannheim (1936) and Kuhn (1970), and those who follow them, posit that we can only relate to any experience on the basis of our social and historical understanding.[5] In other words, some subjectivity is unavoidable. Research morality (as informed by, e.g., analyses of epistemic injustice) must contend with this degree of contingency in science.

Secondly, engagement with the contingency of concepts and credibility might incline action in what philosopher Sally Haslanger (2000) has called ameliorative projects; this work, aimed at resolving injustices stemming from concepts as they replicate oppressive structures, is also known as conceptual ethics. In a groundbreaking work, Haslanger sought to analyze the concepts of gender and race, asking not only what they are, but (perhaps even more importantly for a forward-looking project), what we might want them to be. Here one might ask: is the concept of race a useful and morally justifiable way of interpreting or analyzing a set of, say, social phenomena? Might that answer shift depending on the definition of race that is operationalized in the study? If so, it would seem that ethical questions about the very concepts of a study themselves – questions of their construction, their usage, what they clarify and/or obscure – are necessary.

Seeking moral research might require the researcher (and the research community) to consciously and explicitly attend to the concepts in use, designing and engineering them to explain and explore elements of phenomena that might previously have been unjustly obscured. In one example of compelling work in this area, philosopher Robin Dembroff (2016) analyzes the concept of sexual orientation. They note that the existing dominant concepts used in the West are premised on the value and salience of reproduction. That is, the categories of sexual orientation are demarcated by whether the pairings typically allow for procreation: heterosexual couplings are presumed to do so and homosexual couplings are presumed not to do so. Dembroff observes that this creates rather diverse groupings of sexual attraction within these categories. That is, within the category "heterosexual" are persons attracted to, for instance, women. But the category "homosexual" also contains persons attracted to women. The examples could continue as it becomes clear that the categories are essentially about reproduction rather than sexual attraction and/or the tendency to be in a relevant relationship with a person of a particular sex, gender, and/or gender expression. Consider how these categories of sexual orientation, biased and flawed as they might be, reify particular configurations as "natural" or "normal." What injustices follow from these categories and their uncritical invocation as default categories of human orientations and attractions? One might here imagine that research morality could endorse researchers thoughtfully engineering the concept of, say, sexual orientation in the very ways that Dembroff's work suggests, creating new and improved conceptualizations of an existing concept. Further, perhaps "good" research ought to reflect this example and similar others as research morality prompts researchers to consider engineering relevant and meaningful concepts in the process of creating new knowledge that resists existing forms of bias which might have historically been presented as "natural" or "objective."

The examples above serve as theoretical orientations to the very methods that researchers employ in their practices. A program of research morality education might embrace these insights, preparing researchers to (1) pose the questions that an awareness of epistemic injustice invites and/or (2) engineer concepts that respond to enduring forms of immorality, in the ways the research community both knows the world and creates knowledge about it. Such an educational program for researchers forwards a mission of social justice, here understood as morality in social contexts.

Engaging Social Justice

Though the label of social justice might seem to be a matter of some personal preference and reasonable disagreement (more on this later in the chapter), this chapter endorses the view that while the content of social justice might be contentious, the subject itself, properly framed, is rather generally endorsed. As the chapter interrogates a view of research ethics (morality) education that aims at encouraging researchers to engage questions of a social justice orientation (some examples of such efforts were provided in the previous section), a very brief definition and defense of that category (i.e., social justice) follows.

Social justice might be broadly understood as an account of what is owed to persons within social circumstances.[6] As such, though social justice can be understood as a political category, it is necessarily moral in that it articulates the values that ought to guide interactions with others. With this view of social justice in mind, for this chapter's purposes, an exploration of research morality education might meaningfully intersect with three categories within which salient matters of social justice can be engaged in the service of pursuing good research.

Firstly, the *context* within which one researches must be engaged. That is, in order to operate with an appropriate consideration of research morality, one must be able to comprehend the moral context within which choices might be selected. For example, a researcher would be hard-pressed to navigate the moral minefield of race in the US reliably and accurately without a due sense of the conceptual, historical, and social context in which race is constructed and reified.[7] Stated differently, ethical or moral principles are not enough to guide research. These principles must be appropriately indexed to the contexts within which a research acts as they attempt moral practice in their activities constructing knowledge (i.e., research).

Secondly, a specific aspect of context to which the researcher ought to be sensitive is that of *culture*. If, as described in the previous section, scientific knowledge is beholden to cultural norms, default concepts, and the accompanying expectations, a researcher would do well to be mindful of the conclusions that are based within a particular cultural context (especially if that context is marked by structural injustices). How universal (if at all) might they be? How might cultural framings of a research question reveal or obscure elements of the phenomena it aims to analyze? These matters ought to be concerning not only to the social scientist; they are essential matters of "good" research that cannot merely be brushed aside by the "objective" scientist.

Finally, a social justice minded researcher ought to be attentive to matters of the *community* (or communities) discovered, cultivated, or dissolved by the knowledge they create. That is, if, as earlier referenced in relation to Laden's (2012) work on the social practice of reasoning, research is well understood as an activity that invites others to share in recognizing the legibility of one's evidence, a researcher would do well to consider how knowledge might be created (and communicated) in ways that welcome others as social and moral equals in the practices of knowing and coming to know.

These three pillars, briefly described, constitute a provisional image of some of the sensitivities needed for the moral researcher to conduct their work. This chapter now turns to a few considerations regarding how one might be prepared for the practices described.

Pressing Beyond Desirability to Duties

As the preparation for these and other potential practices of research morality will require a considered and intentional educational program (similar in some, and dissimilar in many, ways to the motivations for research ethics training/education), some attention to the justifications for such education should be given.

Indeed, the research community might fully agree that research morality (pursued in some of the ways articulated in previous sections) is *desirable*, but that need not imply any *duty* to teach/educate researchers for this work. This chapter grants that distinction and, given its aforementioned speculative and exploratory nature, invites thoughtfulness on these topics rather than conclusive arguments; it does not provide detailed arguments for this duty, though it will seek to strengthen the intuition that the existence of such a duty can be defended. Those arguments require a more complex treatment than the one upon which this chapter is focused. Therefore, it may suffice to state that insofar as persons have duties to do what is ethical (which includes research ethics, which itself includes epistemological aspects of research ethics), and they have duties to do what is moral (which includes social justice issues linked to values in a social context), this chapter has provided some foundation for accepting the claim that these sorts of duties may exist.

For most readers, a full account of these duties may do little to forward the type of work described herein. That is, *principled* arguments in favor of or against the existence of these duties are not likely to motivate readers' peers and associates (one major exception here are other academic philosophers but, as mentioned earlier, they are not the audience for this chapter). More likely, instead, to spur action or respond to disquiet are arguments of a *practical* nature. Colleagues and administrators, with busy schedules, may be little inclined to the abstract moral reasons for this work, but may respond to more directly prudential concerns.

Toward embracing a more practical orientation, then, the chapter offers its readers a defense of these possible duties against some of the prudential arguments which may be asserted to curb the development and practice of a social-justice-based research morality educational program. In what follows, the chapter briefly argues against two concerns that could be invoked in limiting these elements of focus in research morality educational projects: indoctrination and generalizability.

Addressing the Worry of Indoctrination

In attempting to establish an educational program that might prepare researchers for the type of work earlier described, one might encounter objections based in what this chapter calls the "worry of indoctrination." In essence, the worry of indoctrination suggests that if research ethics education engages substantive social justice concerns, it runs afoul of a general prohibition against indoctrination in a (moral) educational project that ought to be impartial or neutral.[8] Stated simply: this view claims that, in the responsible and unbiased preparation of similarly responsible and unbiased researchers, one ought not direct scholars into particular worldviews if there exists reasonable disagreement about the value of these and other outlooks. Such a directive-based education on an open or uncertain matter constitutes indoctrination.

As such, issues of social justice (as earlier defined) are matters about which there exists reasonable disagreement such that they have no justified place within unbiased and objective research ethics/morality educational efforts. Examples of this type of argument are plentiful. Claims that a social justice education is a form of undue ideological coercion undergird much of the (recent at the time of this writing) outcry for limitations on critical race theory and other perspectives that engage with analyses of structural power in a social context.[9]

The worry of indoctrination can be addressed in a number of ways. Perhaps, most directly of use for the readers of this chapter would be to note that the worry (as a criticism of establishing the educational programs under discussion) operates on a misunderstanding of what might be called *knowledge ends* and *inquiry motivations*. That is, the worry about indoctrination here proceeds as if the exposure to the educational content deterministically results in persons endorsing a specific conclusion or knowledge end. The implication is that if such an educational program existed, it would produce "brainwashed" indoctrinated researchers rather than thoughtful persons with diverse views and disagreements on the matters at hand. The confusion here rests in an underappreciation of a research morality educational project that encourages engagement with various topics of social salience in research practices. That such a project provides attention to the value of asking questions of fairness, inclusion, and our obligations to one another as knowers and creators of new knowledge does not imply that persons will reach identical (or even similar) conclusions. Reasonable disagreement is still possible despite the fact that such disagreement rests on a foundation of generally held values. Identifying a set of considerations as worthy of researcher attention has long been a non-indoctrinatory practice in researcher education. As a matter of form, this need not be different.

Addressing Claims of Generalizability or Redundancy

Moving along to another worry, likely to emerge in practice as a further objection to a social justice-based program of research morality education, this chapter considers the worry of generalizability.

> Research morality education cannot rely on general moral education or the general application of existing moral standards to specific situations of knowledge creation.

Generalizability accounts of moral education as applied to research ethics education claim that such moral educational projects consist of those practices which bring people into moral conduct, in a broad and transferable sense. That is, a program of moral education for researchers ought to develop in these persons dispositions, habits, virtues, etc. that can be invoked across a wide range of circumstances – including those that reflect social justice concerns of, *inter alia*, culture, context, and community. As such, these issues of social justice need make no special claim of inclusion within the moral educational activities of research education; researchers can instead be educated for an awareness of general moral matters related to their work, such that social justice issues will "automatically" be addressed as a by-product of their actions. We can do this by hyper focus on existing research standards. For example, this worry (offered as a critique of efforts toward establishing these educational programs) could suggest that simply ensuring a representative sample in one's research makes sufficiently good headway to realizing justice of the sort implied by social justice. That is, achieving what we already identify as good practices in research will necessarily result in morally good research.

Depending on one's interpretation, this claim might be understood in two separate ways. Either (1) existing general standards for research ethics education are sufficient for achieving moral research or (2) existing general standards for moral education are sufficient (once applied to the specific activities of research) for achieving moral research. Both are unsatisfying.

Firstly, it should be acknowledged that specifics matter for morality. To invoke an earlier example, one might think of the subject of race. Though a general moral education, without specific references to the circumstances within which moral action might be conducted, might communicate values about the equal worth of human lives, it would fail to make a distinction between the expression of that general concern as manifest in (the most charitable interpretations of) the slogan "Black Lives Matter" and the slogan "All Lives Matter." In the specific contexts of historical and contemporary undervaluation of Black lives, the former is a call for achieving the moral ideal of recognition of the equal worth of all lives. The latter, though it seems to express the underlying moral value, evades the specific immorality to which the other slogan responds. This contemporary example is evidence that morality in social circumstances requires specificity and nuance of a sort that a general moral education may well overlook. So it is with the claim of generalizability in moral research education. The researcher may well be as likely as not to exacerbate the immoral structures of knowledge and knowledge creation at the very heart of this educational project.

Secondly, it should be acknowledged that the standards of research are unlikely to recognize their own limitations in these matters of specificity so long as they operate within enclosed systems of validation. To invoke an earlier example, one might think of the specific concept and standard of immoral action that is sexual harassment. It seems unlikely (and indeed there is a long history of empirical evidence to support the claim) that a workplace analyzed only by those persons who had been explicitly or implicitly complicit in the destructive behavior of sexual harassment would have recognized the impacts of the practices and the degree to which existing standards of functionality and desirability of workplaces were inadequate. As Fricker's (2007) work shows, the very nature of hermeneutical injustice represents a major obstacle to an awareness of these issues. Again, so it is with the claim of generalizability in moral research education. The existing definitions and practices of "good" research (understood via interpretation 1 or 2, above) are unlikely to recognize their own shortcomings absent the input and perspectives of persons from unjustly marginalized positions that challenge the status quo.

For these reasons, research morality education cannot rely on general moral education or the general application of existing moral standards to specific situations of knowledge creation.

Returning to Context, Culture, and Community

Having responded to some of the practical critiques of the form of research morality education earlier explored, the chapter acknowledges that some readers might still feel uncertain that the ideas presented are feasible or achievable in a research context. Toward calming these fears, the chapter now makes explicit the ways in which its own structure and content serve as an example of the very aims it has offered. That is, reading this chapter as a lesson in research morality might demonstrate the accessibility and proximity of some of the work to be done, more broadly.

First, a reader might note that this chapter's claims are provisionally offered. As a speculative work, it invites others to interpret and disagree. Instead of closing a discussion by settling "matters of fact," it offers a set of ideas that might be fodder for further ideas and improvement. The invitation might be expanded as readers share this work with others, inviting a broader community to participate in shaping the contours of mutually pursued work. Of course, it should be noted, many matters of fact do exist about which there ought to be very little reasonable disagreement; research should not claim ambiguity where certainty is present. However, "good" research can be conducted that reduces uncertainty about a matter without offering definitive statement of the same. Almost all researchers are aware of this truth, yet much research is written so as to obscure it. This chapter has attempted to model a form of epistemic humility, the understanding that one's knowledge is incomplete, in its pages.

Secondly, this chapter has attempted to identify forms of epistemic injustice in the practices of research itself – and the very research ethics programs that define the boundaries of "good"-ness in these practices. This focus has largely been aimed at matters of hermeneutical injustice. Indeed, testimonial matters appear to be more broadly discussed in other explorations of the potential shortcomings of the academy and its practices. As a matter of modeling an awareness of hermeneutical injustice, this chapter has asked its readers to consider whether the existing standards of research ethics (and the educational programs that pass these standards on to new members of the research community) capture all that a social justice-sensitive research community might desire.

Thirdly, finding some possibility for improvement, the chapter has begun to engineer the concept of research ethics, offering an account of research morality that might serve to support the type of expanded concerns, as essential to "good" research, which the chapter recommends. In line with the above considerations, research morality is provisionally offered. The chapter has intentionally created space for that concept to be reworked and re-tuned as necessary for the evolving social practices of knowledge creation at the center of this book's focus.

Finally, in all of this, the chapter has attempted to point to the ways in which appreciation for context, culture, and community might serve as guiding values for that moral work. The ideas forwarded in this chapter are placed within a social and historical context. Attention has been given to the contextual ways in which, for example, gender and race are often inadequately engaged as tangential to research practices. Further, the chapter has grounded itself in a specific disciplinary tradition (philosophy of education), acknowledging the norms and practices that constitute the culture of that approach to knowledge creation. In this, the chapter has sought openness to the ways in which these practices, seemingly justified when philosophers are in discussion with themselves, might be engaged by those outside of the culture that dominates that field. Attempting to welcome a diverse range of knowers, this chapter has intended to create space for community around the topics it discusses. As earlier described, this attention to the social aspect of research endorses scholarship as a dynamic and dialogical activity. The more persons who can find themselves within this discussion, the more perspectives and experiences it can incorporate, the closer the research inches toward being truly good in regard to both its epistemic quality and morality.

Notes

1 According to the Department of Health and Human Services, research misconduct involves "fabrication, falsification, or plagiarism in proposing, performing, or reviewing research, or in reporting research results." Arguably, most research ethics educational programs define themselves in aiming at avoiding these outcomes. Interestingly, "honest error" is explicitly excluded from this list. See, Office of Research Integrity, Department of Health and Human Services (2021).
2 See, for example, MacIntyre (1957), Hare (1981), Rawls (1971), Klenk (2019), Scanlon (2011), and Turiel (1983).
3 See, Office of Research Integrity, Department of Health and Human Services (2021).
4 For general orientation to these concerns, see Gilligan (2012) and Belenky et al. (1986).
5 See, Nagel (1961), Popper (1972).
6 This definition is, perhaps, too broad to be useful in most contexts, but the level of resolution is sufficient for the claims of this chapter, as described in the introduction.
7 See, Thompson (2017).
8 See, Erickson and Thompson (2019).
9 See, Iati (2021, May 29).

References

Belenky, M., Clinchy, B., Goldberger, N., & Tarule, J. (1986). *Women's ways of knowing: The development of self, voice, and mind.* New York, NY: Basic Books.

Dembroff, R. (2016). What is sexual orientation? *Philosopher's Imprint, 16*(3), 1–27.

Erickson, J. D., & Thompson, W. C. (2019). Preschool as a wellspring for democracy: Endorsing traits of reasonableness in early childhood education. *Democracy and Education, 27*(1), 1–22.

Fricker, M. (2007). *Epistemic injustice: Power and the ethics of knowing.* Oxford: Oxford University Press.

Gilligan, C. (2012). *In a different voice: Psychological theory and women's development.* Cambridge, MA: Harvard University Press.

Hare, R. M. (1981). *Moral thinking.* Oxford: Oxford University Press.

Haslanger, S. (2000). Gender and race: (What) are they? (What) do we want them to be? *Nous, 34*(1), 31–55.

Iati, M. (2021, May 29) What is critical race theory and why do republicans want to ban it in schools? *Washington Post*. Retrieved from https://www.washingtonpost.com/education/2021/05/29/critical-race-theory-bans-schools/

Klenk, M. (2019). Moral philosophy and the "ethical turn" in anthropology. *Zeitschrift Für Ethik Und Moralphilosophie*, *2*(2), 331–353.

Laden, A. (2012). *Reasoning: A social picture*. Oxford: Oxford University Press.

MacIntyre, A. (1957). What morality is not. *Philosophy*, *32*(123), 325–335.

Office of Research Integrity, Department of Health and Human Services. (2021). Research Misconduct. Retrieved from https://ori.hhs.gov/definition-research-misconduct.

Nagel, E. (1961). *The structure of science: Problems in the logic of scientific explanation*. New York, NY: Harcourt.

Popper, K. (1972). *Objective knowledge: A realist view of logic, physics, and history*. Oxford, UK: Clarendon Press.

Rawls, J. (1971). *A theory of justice*. Cambridge, MA: Harvard University Press.

Scanlon, T. M. (2011). What is morality? In J. Shephard, S. Kosslyn, & E. Hammonds (Eds.), *The Harvard sampler: Liberal education for the twenty-first century* (pp. 243–66). Cambridge, MA: Harvard University Press.

Thompson, W. C. (2017). Educational practice in pursuit of justice requires historically informed and philosophically rigorous scholarship. In A. Errante, J. Blount, & B. Kimball (Eds.), *Philosophy and history of education: Diverse perspectives on their value and relationship* (pp. 87–98). London, UK: Rowman and Littlefield.

Turiel, E. (1983). *The development of social knowledge: Morality and convention*. Cambridge, UK: Cambridge University Press.

SECTION II

Qualitative Innovations

Counterstories can build community among those at the margins of society … challenge the perceived wisdom of those at society's center … nurture community cultural wealth, memory, and resistance … facilitate transformation in education (pp. 14–15) …

So please, take these counterstories and hope at the margins of society. Retell them, add new characters, speak your truth, and take action to transform the Chicana/o educational pipeline. Storytelling is a 'genre of action.' How the story continues is up to each of us (p. 171).

~ *Tara J. Yosso* ~

Yosso, T. J. (2006). *Critical race counterstories along the Chicana/ Chicano educational pipeline.* New York, NY: Routledge.

DOI: 10.4324/9781003126621-6

DOI: 10.4324/9780367648626-6

5

TEACHING AND ENGAGING AUTOETHNOGAPHY AS QUALITATIVE ENGAGEMENT[1]

Bryant Keith Alexander

I have always engaged autoethnography as a qualitative research method; a method that allows me and encourages others to look to, validate, and articulate lived experience as a means of critical sense making and building theories of self in/for/with/society. This is to address current challenges, by looking to the past to plan toward new future possibilities of being and becoming – for self and others. A focus on the structural features of the word *auto • ethno • graphy* is a helpful starting point in defining the epistemological goals of the practice. "Auto" references *personal experience, "Ethno"* is a definitional frame that references culture, cultural context, or cultural experience. *"Graphy"* is a term that refers to a descriptive science or a technique of producing images to systematically analyze place, space, or human psychology. In the formality of its construction, autoethnography can thus reference a method and product of researching, writing with a systematic analysis of personal experience in a cultural context.This approach to research locates the personal experience of the investigator as the starting point of the subject of engagement (Ellis, Adams, & Bochner, 2010).

It demands a triple stage of seeing as a thrice relational orientation that includes *the subject of experience, the moment of re-engagement,* and *the re-orientation to knowing of that experience through theory and memory.* The process for me has always been the tripartite of *reflection, refraction, and reflexivity.* The difference between reflecting on experience linked with memory and recall, then refractively bending and turning those memories to crack open meaning, followed by engaging in a reflexive turn of looking at the self-looking at the self in a twice removed level of self-objectivity. Such objectivity does not dismiss the personal but identifies the personal as always and already political within the cultural context of engagement; always looking at the varying features of time, place, and space as

DOI: 10.4324/9781003126621-7

constitutive and informing of the happening, relative to the nature of how the experience is thus narrated with what meaning?

Norman K. Denzin (1997) writes that autoethnography involves the "turning of the ethnographic gaze inward on the self (auto), while maintaining the outward gaze of ethnography" on broader cultural structures (p. 227). This process keeps in mind that there is always *intentionality to research*, the motivating impulse of discovery for what purpose (self-gratifying or politically edifying), and to what outcome of research seeks to contribute back to society as both socially conscious act and act social justice (Adams & Holman Jones, 2008). In another framed intention – autoethnography like any form of socially conscious research should engage in processes of information, formation, and transformation seeking insight, using that new-found knowledge as a means of deepening positive convictions for purposes of transforming self and society.

In this sense, autoethnography is not only a qualitative approach to research and writing that seeks to describe and systematically analyze personal experience in order to understand cultural experience. But autoethnography is a strategic tool of illuminating, in any given situation, how structures of power are imbricated in the social and psychological, impacting others both by inhibiting and inhabiting their social reality. Hence, autoethnography becomes a communicative endeavor to share an exacting account of lived experience in a public forum of engagement whether in print or performance as a template of sociality. Not to code on the experience of others, but as a generative device that affords the reader/listener/viewer an opportunity to witness how they might begin to reflect on human experience and to delve into or unpack their own lived experience, and thus to transform their ways of seeing and knowing themselves anew. While also helping to transform systems of oppression that intentionally, and sometimes without reflection, replicate patterns of oppression.

Performance and cultural scholar Judith Hamera (2007) describe *templates of sociality* – as mechanisms of examining human social engagement that help to render extraordinary and everyday aspects of living "readable and reorganizing the relationships in which these readings can occupy" to make the knowing and politics of being accessible to self and others (p. 23).

Autoethnography becomes a rhetoric of finding *all the available means of persuasion*, shaping notions of change for social good. My own integrated approach of writing and performing autoethnography reinforces the notion of "exploring self with and for others" as a social endeavor that goes beyond the sometime presumed self-serve naval gazing of an *ethnography of the self* – to engage autoethnography as *cultural studies* that investigates the ways in which culture creates and transforms individual experiences, everyday life, social relations, and power; seeking to both illuminate and contribute to practices of cultural change (Alexander, 2009; Alexander, 2022b). In autoethnography, the researcher/investigator operates both within and outside culture, as both subject and object, pivoting on the relationality of experience as critique with a tempered recognition of self-implication in what is described, discovered, directed, and dictated as presumed insights of both process and product.

Allow me to offer a very recent attempt at autoethnographic writing in an epistolary form, as a letter to my father who passed away nearly 20-years ago, yet whose memory and the palpable realities of his being is consistently present in my life today. Point of reference: I called my father Dádēē – a southwest Louisiana and French informed version of daddy.

****

To Dádēē (*from Keith*)

Dear Dádēē,

It has taken me a long time to write this letter to you. I have written a lot about you in my scholarly work; sometimes trying to remember or memorialize you; and sometimes about the trials and tribulation of being with you.[2] But all those efforts seem to fail to capture the fullness of you to me and in me. So maybe this time I just want to say thank you. Thank you for being a strong Black father.

Thank you for being a consistently present Black father in my home upbringing.

Thank you for being you, in my own processes of being and becoming, me.

I used to think that we were so different. But now that I am coming closer to the age of your passing. And now that the implicity and complicity of blood is making you more present in my body – the aches, the pains, and the challenges; not to mention that your face appears with more frequency in the mirror when I look, I realize that we were not so different. Not just in body but in mind. The Ph.D. that you encouraged me to complete in relation to your fourth-grade education has finally taught me enough to come back to you, again and again. Maybe you would have predicted that return. You always had that form of intelligence that letters behind names could not achieve.

I was listening.

I was listening, especially in those quiet moments together watching reruns of the same old Westerns and military shows in which you deconstructed the ethics of war, race, class, white privilege and the role of Indigenous people and Black people on the short-end of manifest destiny and Americanism, in the reel and real-life adventures of our experiences in this country – both found and transported.

I was listening.

I was listening when you pointed out military movies with shifting "others" as enemies of war, or skirmishes with Native Americans (in those pained Cowboy and Indian movies) when parties retreated; retreated as a strategy of war; not a complete withdrawal or throwing in the towel or declaration of defeat, but a type of military operation that signified a pulling back of forces and energies while maintaining an obvious contact with the opposing faction. While you liked the strictly military versions in overt wars, you celebrated and cheered when Indians (Indigenous or Native Americans) used the same strategy in covert wars of manifest destiny, annihilating people for their land (like stealing and raping Black bodies for their labor – Dádēē – that was also a part of your lesson.) The Native Americans were (also) presumed to be savages with no critical sense-making skills and thus had no rights. When they retreated it was a variation of biding time; a variation of suggesting defeat by running away, but a reconnoitering of possibilities that came back to occupy a different ground (as in space or argument or position of defense) that was easier or a better positioned for an ambush, for an insurrection – as a strategic and acceptable skill in combat in defending their territory and claiming their sovereignty. When it was obvious that the "Indians" were making a perceivable risky move with some sacrifice to get the greater gain in a perpetual fight for dignity and destiny. You outlined those strategies, asking me, "Do you see it? See what they are doing?" You taught me about the importance of retreat as a strategy of survival.

I was listening.

I was listening to the lessons on performative masculinity which for you was about being resilient and resistive for the common good. Sitting at your knee watching television, just you and me, when everybody else was gone, I listened. But when everyone else was home, Mámēē and the other six children, I remember that you always seem to be in the process of leaving. Retreating from the activities of the everyday hustle and bustle of a big family. You would stay long enough to touch each; you would stay long enough to claim a certain dominion, you would stay long enough to declare and discipline, then you would retreat. Retreating to your bedroom where you listened to music alone, sometimes I would follow you thinking it was just to be with you. And sometimes you would retreat into a puff of cigarette smoke or into a bottle. I did not follow there, neither then, nor now. I wasn't sure, but it appeared that you were running away from the obligations of a large family or maybe the noise, or maybe it was just your need to be alone, a different retreat.

At varying times, when she would see the same behavior in me, Mámēē would say, "You are just like your father." And I hated that phrase. I hated it because it seemed like a curse. But maybe she was trying to help me understand you better, especially in those times when I would not talk to you for days because you had said something harsh. Maybe you were trying to get me to fight back. Unlike my four brothers and two sisters, I never learned to fight back with you in the same ways. But maybe you would be happy to know that I have learned to fight – in my own ways, with words, but still with the ferocity of getting even, or standing my ground, or putting people in their place – which were the postures of self-defense that you wanted to instill. You always said, "That one's got a mouth on him." Maybe my talking back then was a rehearsal for my professional life where words matter in shaping new realities and possibilities for self and others; a different kind of fight – and maybe not so different. Thanks for the early lessons.

Then and now. Then, the fifth child of seven, the fourth boy of five, the sensitive one who ran away to the back room to hide in a book; avoiding being an audience to performances of bravado or shame; never wanting to fully witness because I did not want to later have to testify to what I heard, to what I saw, to what I felt; the anger, the resentment, the hurt; knowing that I was never given the same stage. I was not the oldest child, or the oldest boy; not the youngest child or the youngest boy; not the presumed talented one, or the middle child who demanded attention. I was not the squeaky wheel that demanded oil and attention. I was always a little off center, and different – the one who learned to be self-sufficient, but still yearned for the attention of respect. Maybe that is why I followed you when you retreated –thinking that it was just wanting to be with you – it was probably my own need, an impulse that I was rehearsing in my own survival of retreat. *And now*, in my adult/professional life, the only Black administrator at my level and above–at a university engaged in *trans-race-formation* as a reckoning of the current historical moment but still *predominately white*, which is a term that is as much about sensibilities, and positionalities as it is about demographics – I also stand a little off center.

Both there and then, and here and now – I stay/ed to witness and watch, to contribute what I can in a double load of work and representation, and then I retreat. I retreat from large gatherings of mandated sociality saturated with the politics of positionality in which people are still strategically working the room. I stay long enough to touch each; long enough to claim a certain authority of my position. I stay long enough to represent as needed in the politics of difference and diversity, then like you, Dádēē, I retreat. Retreating to my office, or my car, or my home– maybe to listen to music alone or to write. Sometimes at such gatherings, I would have one too many drinks to lessen my anxieties, then think of you and restrain myself – wondering if your drinking was linked with your anxieties; to calm the social noise, white or otherwise.

Because of this behavior I was once described by a high-ranking university official as being a phantom. He was describing the fact that I seemingly appeared and quickly disappeared at social events. And of course, he was right in his adjectival description of a certain phenomenon. Though he also showed a lack of racial awareness in him being a white man calling me a Black man, a phantom; like the historical reference to Black people being spooks or bugaboos. I understood his description of a certain presencing and absenting, but without the recognition that I was fully present. And that I made my presence known. Then I made the conscious decision not to linger. Thus, I am not a phantom as *something apparent to sense but with no substantial existence: or an object of continual dread or abhorrence.*

That is the unfortunate construction of the Black man in the white imagination to which this country is still reckoning with in the year 2021. And whether "just" a poor choice of words or not, he, like so many others need to dig deep, with the pressure of a root canal, to extract the roots of their own actions that give teeth to impressions of racism, or how racism is also linguistically rooted in our references to the presumed other. I am not that kind of a phantom, nor were you Dádēē. *I see you.* And while you retreated from time to time, you stayed with your family; and you were always in arms reach when needed. I too retreat as a form of personal survival; to sustain enough energy to do the work, to mindfully mine future possibilities and support the greater effort for the ones who need me to be fully present; for the ones who are also in the margins, standing on the borders of their being and becoming.

I always saw you in the process of retreating but your never fully left. You stayed.

I wonder.

I wonder how many Black boys did not understand their Black father's anger or struggles or pains and scars.

I wonder how many Black boys coded on the anger without a deep sense of their Black father's desire for them not to relive the same experiences, and maybe feeling helpless of that inevitability.

I wonder how many Black boys didn't value their Black fathers because they didn't look or act like the Beaver's father (on "Leave it to Beaver") or Richie Cunnington's father (on "Happy Days") or the father of the Tanner kids (on "Full House"), or even Heathcliff Huxtable on that pseudo-rendition of an upper-class Black family (on "The Cosby Show"). I suggest that even the actors who played those fictional television fathers failed to live up to the fictive paternal image that they perpetuated, along with the network propaganda of the ideal American family which was typically white or engaged in a performative whiteness. We know for a fact that Bill Cosby failed miserably in living up to the idealistic Black man-father he played on "The Cosby Show," or even as the moralizing ranting and demonizing public figure who critiqued other Black men about how they treated their women and children, and not standing up as Black male role models. This is the same actor playing the same role on television and in the public sphere – demonizing/demoralizing other Black men, only to be revealed as a philandering man who drugged dozens of women in service of a necrophiliac-type sexual desire to have sex with their comatose bodies.

All of which shattered the hypocrisy of his crafted public persona and his constructed social mobility. He is now in prison for three counts of aggravated indecent assault, with some of the presumed basic Black men that he critiqued. I always hated Heathcliff Huxtable anyway. There was something unreal about the character. There was something in the refractivity of the moralistic induced rhetoric that Cosby rehearsed on Thursday nights, and his celebration of selective parts of Black culture (through Heathcliff Huxtable) that did not bend to shine the light on aspects of everyday Black culture, of everyday Black people. Cosby seem to believe that his class-based moralistic ranting through his fictional character of Cliff authorized his grandstanding in the everyday life of Black people, never deflecting from the actuality of his private practices as a serial rapist.

We used to watch "The Cosby Show" as a family; aspirational in nature because of class and representational to see Black folks living well. But Dádēē, I remember that you didn't like Cliff Huxtable either – you said the character *didn't sit right with you.* But you reminded me that you first introduced Cosby to me years before through his comedy albums, where he was touted as a "clean comic." We would listen to the albums on your portable record player in the back room, on one of those days when we were both retreating. Then, when you were home on Saturday mornings, we would watch Cosby through another alter ego, *Fat Albert and the Cosby Kids.* The animated cartoon that featured poor Black kids who often circulated in and around a Philadelphia junkyard.[3] The show always had an educational lesson through the frame of Dr. Bill Cosby, Ed.D. You preferred that version of Cosby more, maybe because that rendition of his public efforts and education still cared about representing and uplifting everyday Black folks, or at least those who were make-in-it by the hardest.

And maybe there you were Dádēē, less Cliff Huxtable and more Fred G. Sanford (of "Sanford and Son"). Fred, that somewhat sarcastic Black male junk dealer who operated a junkyard with his son Lamont in another Black television series. Fred, who was always a little cantankerous and grumpy but with a heart of gold, and fully present for his family.[4] Fred G. Sanford's flaws were obvious as he continually worked, episode by episode, to address his biases without claiming high moral ground but continually grappling with his humanity in family and the Black community where he lived. In the year 2021, when the challenges of being a Black person in America are still real. When Black people are still being killed under the regimes of racism and white privilege, the lessons you taught me about being steadfast in your commitments and the honor of being a Black man and father, are clearer to me today than when I was a boy. Because I understand more fully your struggle and your scars, and what you did to protect me for as long as you could. I stand stronger for possible futures. I am happy to claim you as more Fred G. Sandford than Heathcliff Huxtable – and I do so with great pride.

I listened and I remember.

I remember how many Black boys flocked to the corner lot of our humble house. The fact that you had five biological boys of your own increased the metric odds of the number of friends we would attract. Maybe it was the basketball court, or the card games on the front porch, or the tournament style marble games of my childhood that attracted them. But I also think that they were attracted to you. I remember so many of them were from homes with an absent father, with a turn style of new uncles or play daddies or nasty old men entering and existing their lives. They saw you as a Black father who stayed. I remember you telling them to "Pull up their pants" or "Put on your shirt." Not like a Bill Cosby moralistic rant, but as a set of expectations for your yard, in front of your wife, and in front of your daughters.

I remember that you kidded and jived with them, and you knew their names – because you also knew their parents. They called you, "Mr. Joe." And when they saw you coming around the corner – they adjusted themselves. Sometimes you made them help clean the yard, or pick up pecans after a rainstorm, or pick mulberries and figs from the trees for preserves. You said, "if you are going to spend so much time here – you might as well earn your keep." And they did, with no complaint or talk back. It is no wonder there was always a few extra mouths around dinner time. You would grumble because that was your way, but they would stay because they knew they were welcomed. And even when one of them knocked at the door late at night, because something was happening at their house – you would grumble about the time, but would pull them into the house – sometimes to talk, other times just to say, "You alright? Go in the back room and sleep – we can talk tomorrow." They knew there was love in the house because amongst other things, this Black daddy stayed. And I knew that as well. And you provided them, like you provided your children, a template of the Black masculine that they/we could pivot off in finding our own sense of being and relating to Black men in the world. At your passing, these boys now men, cried, and they squabbled for positions to be your pallbearers as a final act of appreciation for "Mr. Joe."

Dádēē, I don't know how to end this letter, so I won't.

It is an ongoing dialogue between you and me, and maybe with myself, that I will continue to write and unravel as evidence of my being and becoming in both your presence and your absence. I will continue being or trying to be the man that you and Mámēē wanted me to be (pictured below in Figure 5.1). I keep this picture of you both on my desk at work and at home as a reminder.

FIGURE 5.1 Velma Ray Bell-Alexander and Joseph Junius Alexander, Sr.

Joseph Junius Alexander Sr, passed April 11, 2001

Velma Ray Bell-Alexander, passed October 3, 2003

I cry for you and Mámēē on the regular. I miss your physical presence in the world and my ability to retreat with you into quiet spaces of our own.

With deep love and respect,

Your boy,

Keith

****

I offer you this autoethnography in the form of a letter to reinforce the personal and dialogical nature of doing autoethnography, with communication to a real and absented other.

Teaching autoethnography and autoethnographic pedagogy foregrounds that a critical explication of human experience often results in building theories and theorems of knowing that are always cross applied in everyday living and can serve as evidence of academic knowing through the body. Such an approach leads to the development of a sophisticated vocabulary of terms and terminologies that give voice to experience as a means of realizing, personalizing, foregrounding, and sharing histories and happenings that matter in assisting us – teachers and students – in seeing ourselves in relation to the politics of culture and scholarship with the ability to use our shared experiences through autoethnography as templates of sociality and tools of critique.

Teaching autoethnography and autoethnographic pedagogy foregrounds that a critical explication of human experience often results in building theories and theorems of knowing that are always cross applied in everyday living and can serve as evidence of academic knowing through the body.

Developing a Philosophy of Teaching Autoethnography/Autoethnographic Pedagogy

I believe that "teaching autoethnography and autoethnographic pedagogy" establishes an integrative relationship between why one uses or engages autoethnography in the classroom or in research as a means of making the personal both political and pedagogical for self and other across a range of strategic intentions including an autoethnographic pedagogy as critical performative pedagogy, border pedagogy, public pedagogy, a performance of possibilities.

Autoethnographic Pedagogy Acknowledges Critical Performative Pedagogy

Critical performative pedagogy promotes an active embodiment of doing as a key component of a pedagogical practice used toward libratory ends. Specifically, such practices are geared to having students (and participants) and researchers perform the possibilities of progressive cultural politics by exploring counter-narratives to the master narratives of everyday and educational life (engaging students and scholars in active rehearsals of social justice by using their lived embodied experience as source material – avoiding the distanciated and objec-tified search for knowing elsewhere and promoting a dialogical performance. "The aim of dialogical performance," which becomes *sine qua non* for any approach to critical performative pedagogy, "is to bring self and other together so that they can question, debate, and challenge one another" on both the local and global level (Conquergood, 1985, p. 9). Hence the fact that autoethnography is centered within the critical articulation of lived experience as a pedagogical engagement means there must be a deep philosophical commitment to encour-aging students and researchers to explore how their experiences, in a wide range of social encounters and political happenings, matter; and matter as a form of activism (Alexander, 2010; Alexander, 2022a).

It is a teaching, researching, and doing philosophy that is grounded in bring-ing lived experiences into the classroom; into the research and having those experiences bear upon and infuse the critical content and processes of what we are studying. In some ways in my own presented autoethnographic piece, I am studying many things that could be reduced to just a son reflecting on his rela-tionship with his father. But if so – you would then miss:

- The particularity of a reflection on a Black father and son relationship that cannot be generalized – even with my four biological brothers.
- The public constructions of a father in relation to his family, separate from issues of patriarchy, heteronormativity, or control.
- The commentaries on absentee fathers or abusive fathers to which most Black men are measured and demonized.
- Issues of race, sexuality, and gender performance that are imbued in being a Black man and being a Black father that are both co-informing and reduc-tive as a set performativities.
- Issues of family dynamics that speak to the relationality of beings in a com-plicity of blood and biology
- Issues of the media in the social construction of family dynamics, issues of race, class, and gender performance that belie the range of possibilities in the privacy of domestic place and space.
- The representation and misrepresentation of Black men baring the historical tropes of slavery and the slave market that necessarily needed to eschew our humanity.

- Bill Cosby and Heathcliff Huxtable as problematic social templates of the ideal Black man/father and Black cultural representative – as it relates to the public and private aspects of living. A fictive construction that is not without critique in the depiction of the ideal and the stark reality of the actual man.
- And more – all emanating from the critical reflective moment on a particular relationship of a Black father and son, with dynamic qualities and endless possibilities of reading.

And hence, if you did reduce the story to just that – then you would have missed my early theorizing on *family autoethnography*. Family autoethnography is not exclusively about autoethnography in relation to a family context, as much as it recognizes the *always and already ways* in which autoethnography often pivots from the granular spaces of lived experiences, identity politics, biological/psychological, and sociological aspects of the self with antecedents that we track back to family units; how we come to see and know ourselves both in the celebratory aspects of our intersectional identity, and in the dreaded aspects in our sense of self. Family as both the caldron and crucible of our being and becoming, and how we begin to process our sense of purpose. Along with the implications and complications of theorizing absented others as "conscripted collaborators" (Tamas & Tamas, 2021).

Autoethnographic Pedagogy Acknowledges the Political Importance of a Border Pedagogy

Teaching autoethnography and using autoethnography as a research and performative methodology provides the opportunity for students and researchers to critically articulate conflicting cultural experiences, especially in the between spaces of culture, schooling, and the places that they call home. In *Postmodern Education: Politics, Culture, and Social Criticism*, Aronowitz and Giroux. (1991) discuss the construct of *border pedagogy*.

> Border pedagogy offers the opportunity for students [and researchers] to engage the multiple references that constitute different cultural codes, experiences, and languages. This means educating students [and retraining our research and scholarly practices] to read these codes critically, to learn the limits of such codes, including the ones they use to construct their own narratives and histories.
>
> *(pp. 118–119)*

It is a logic that promotes students and researchers to bleed the borders of the classroom and scholarly production with lived experience.

In more specific terms, Aronowitz and Giroux write that border pedagogy helps students to understand that "one's class, race, gender, or ethnicity may influence, but does not irrevocably predetermine, how one takes up a particular ideology, reads a particular text, or responds to particular forms of oppression" (p. 121). Hence, there is the potential of seeing the links that bind humanity and not the borders of difference that we presume divide us. In my open autoethnography – I seek to explore the relational dynamics of my relationship and orientation with my father in my family in other aspects of my personal and professional life:

- How my father is mapped onto so many aspects of my being, both private and public spaces, physical and psychic realities.
- How I read cultural and political contexts through the lens of watching television with my father
- How my Black male body is implicated and interpellated in spaces by virtue of being and the social construction of my being in relation to a Black father.
- And how my reflections and recognitions map back to experiences with my father and in family – as a quintessential source of cultural knowledge that is as valid academic and intellectual knowledge; a form of cultural capital that is very seldom validated in marginalized populations – or cultural knowledge broadly writ that we don't give credit but on which we all barter as we navigate our ways through life.

In these ways, autoethnographic engagement can move education, teaching, and research toward a pedagogy that strategizes purposeful learning with an awareness of the social, cultural, and political contexts in which learning and living take place. Autoethnography as a particular pedagogical and research strategy can then move even further to encompass a *critical pedagogy* by revealing, interrogating, and challenging normalizing social and cultural forms and opening spaces for additional voices in a meaningful human discourse. Such an act would always be moving toward becoming a *revolutionary pedagogy* or research for social change that helps to enact the possibilities of social transformation by bleeding the borders of subjectivity and opening spaces of care (McLaren, 1999).

Autoethnographic Pedagogy Acknowledges the Importance of Public Pedagogy

Henry Giroux (2001) constructs as *a public pedagogy*, a process in which the efforts and effects of such critical processes are not limited to the sterilizing confines of the classroom or traditional educational discourse and traditional notions of Research (but are presented to and enacted in the public sphere in ways that work to transform social life). Giroux writes,

> Defined through its performative functions, public pedagogy is marked by its attentiveness to the interconnections and struggles that take place over knowledge, language, spatial relations, and history. Public pedagogy

represents a moral and political practice rather than merely a technical procedure.

(p. 12)

Through the performed engagement of a cultural dialogue, autoethnography becomes a public pedagogy/a public research/scholarship with several characteristics:

- It is designed to make public the often privatized, if not secularized, experiences of others.
- It is designed to begin the painstaking process of deconstructing notions of difference that often regulate the equal distribution of humanistic concern.
- It makes present and visible the lived experiences of self and others – giving students, performers, audiences and other research access to new knowledge (knowledge that is often cloistered in private pains/sorrows and joys) that one hopes will open spaces of possibility.
- Which I hope you can read in my offering and in my recovered relationship with my father.

Autoethnographic Pedagogy Acknowledges the Importance of "A Performance of Possibilities"

D. Soyini Madison's (1998) construction of *the performance of possibilities* offers both validity and direction for performance ethnography in general, giving gravity to the particular practice of autoethnography.

- The *performance of possibilities* as applied to autoethnography invokes an investment in politics of "self, other, and self as the Other," always negotiating the tensions and tensiveness between *cynics and zealots.*
- The *performance of possibilities* as applied to autoethnography takes the stand that the articulation of lived experience matters because it does something in the world by illuminating personal experience and activating social consciousness.
- The *performance of possibilities* as applied to autoethnography moves away from prediction and control toward understanding and social criticism as both process and product.
- The *performance of possibilities* as applied to autoethnography does not accept being heard and included as its endpoint but only as a starting point to present and represent self and other as products and producers of meaning, symbols, and history in their fullest sensory and social dimensions.
- Therefore, the *performance of possibilities* as applied to autoethnography is a performance of voice wedded to experience, of critical thinking wedded to the emotionality of remembrance, and of the power of invoking presence that *moves away from facts (pure and simple) and toward meaning (ambiguous and complicated).*

In its fullness, Madison's (1998) construction of possibilities might also res-
onant with José Esteban Muñoz's (2006) delineation between possibility and
potential. Muñoz writes: "Possibilities exist, or more nearly, they exist within a
logical real ... Potentialities have a temporality that is not in the present but, more
nearly, in the horizon, which we can understand as futurity" (p. 11). Madison's
possibilities make salient Muñoz's potentialities, which I believe directs an essential value in autoethnographic work, in that the critical reflection and articulation of lived experience offers potential emancipatory ends to both performers
and others.

Methodological Considerations in Teaching Autoethnography

In this section, I offer a brief sketch of one approach to teaching autoethnography used for both undergraduate and graduate classes in performance studies and
with graduate students as a qualitative research methodology. In outlining these
practical stages, I then apply them back to the construction of the autoethnography that I previously shared just as a point of reference.

1. First I ask students to recall a kernel moment, a narrative fragment, *lexias* of
   a happening, an incident, or occurrence that left a palpable impulse in you;
   an experience *that changed your life*, a *transformative moment* an "epiphany"
   that had a significant impact that you seek to theorize, to make sense of in a
   broader socio-cultural-political context.

In the case of my own performance, it was a moment of taking the opportunity
to thank my father – knowing that each aspect of the thanking was a recognition linked with histories that are both celebratory and revelatory in speaking as
much about our relationship to each other – becoming somewhat of an apologia
for the delay of the thank – and why.

2. After identifying the kernel moment and outlining the details of the happening, I encourage working through the logics in telling of the experience.

How is the story specific and *contingent* upon particular variables and the actuality
of the happening?
   How might you relay the facts of the story but also occasion the story as an
analogy to offer the reader or listener multiple points of entry into the story, to
see the experience from differing perspectives? In this case autoethnography is
both particular to the teller and plural to diverse audiences.
   In my offering you saw that the story moved from very specific relational
observations and then broader observations in which both my father and I are
implicated and maybe complicit – and my knowledge of him is not exclusive to
just me and him

- My mother and siblings are implicated in the telling of a story that is both about father and family – each inexplicable to the other.
- Our family life is outlined via birth order and social relations.
- Boys from the neighborhood are summoned forth in the story not just as minor players but as evidence in the building of character – theirs and my father's character.
- Observations, testimonies, and witnesses of/to my father are made from differing perspectives.
- And then recognitions and parodies of him in me are recognized, acknowledge, and celebrated, and more.

3. I ask: Who or what is the socio-cultural-political context for this kernel moment?

To whom and what is the story being told in relation to (e.g., family, religion, government, particular cultural practices and expectations, cultural politics of race, gender, sexuality, and so forth)?

What are the assumed logics, expectations, power systems, norms, values, and beliefs within these locations?

In my own story, it becomes obvious that the story is within family but extends to my professional life. The lessons that I learned from my father and the parts of him that are always in me (e.g., biological, psychological, political, and social) impacts every aspect of my grown personal and professional self.

4. I ask students to then begin to build a story about the kernel moment by establishing context through critical self-reflection.

- The dramatisitic questions of when, where, why, how, what – are good guides in developing the specificity of both the past and present.
- What are the details of the happening that are key (for the audience) to understand the social, cultural, and political milieu/context of the happening?
- What are the power structures at play in these moments (e.g., time, place, relationships between players)? What is your relation/ship to/in those structures?
- What is your location, positionality in the story, to the story, to the happening? What is your sense of empowerment or entrapment, agency of oppression in this situation/context?
- Who are the players in the story, in the happening? What was your orientation to them and how did they impact the nature of the experience? What are the connections between the persons *at/in* play with socio-cultural-politics that you have defined?
- How do you intend to represent or characterize these particular others in the story? What is your ethical responsibility and commitment to representing these others relative to critical remembrance of how they existed and the impact of the happening (Conquergood, 1985)?

In my own autoethnography, I use an epistolary format to simulate me talking to my father outlining and fleshing out the factual and emotional components of my experience with him and what I come to now know about myself. Listing and detailing, shifting in time from my childhood to my adult current moment; bringing in a range of examples and situations that are both particular and plural, but always circulate around and bringing me back to him.

5. I ask students to establish the argument of the story, not as a form of persuasion but as structure of intent:

   - The descriptive details of the story from the preceding steps can begin to serve as the evidence.
   - The rationale of sense making as you tie the variables together in the story can serve as the reasoning.
   - The conclusion is the logical intention of telling the story, which may only fully emerge as the process unfolds.

And in my own autoethnography – while the beginning started with a desire to say thank you to my father, I did not know how I was going to do that. But then each reason offered its own justifications; each example took me to new places of knowing him and knowing him and me both together and apart. Some of which is celebratory and other parts are mere aspects of sense making – no critique, no complaints, but recognitions of knowing me better through theorizing and recognizing him. All of which leads to a conclusion that could only come after the critical reflective, reflexive, and refractive work was done. Only after I had truly travelled the distance from him, through him in me, and back to him and me again.

6. In the process, I ask students to invoke emotionality, contingency, and activism.

   a. How are you positioned within these factors?
   b. What is your emotional response to the original happening and how do you imagine or intend an audience to respond?
   c. Could your intention be a less exclusively empathic connection with the experience; a refashioning of the self in the other, and maybe a display of your own critical sense-making that produces an analytically rich and accessible text that reflects their personal change and found knowledge through the process, as an offering to an interested audience for purposes of potential change (Holman Jones, 2005, p. 764)?
   d. Is there a charge or further invitation to the audience in this performance?

There is no explicit charge to the audience at the end of my presentation; but I take the personal charge to continue to be the type of person, the type of man, the type of Black man that I believe my parents wanted me to be. In that utterance, I am covertly asking the audience to reflect on the same questions and answers, the same desire and distain relative to their own parents or fathers; and where they stand in relation to their being and becoming, and what they imagined their parents had in mind for them.

7. I ask students to explore the residual effects of the experience. How do you negotiate the "snaking temporality," the shift in time between when the experience occurred and the time of the current telling; "between tellers and audiences," between the person you were and the person you are approaching in the assignment and at the end of the assignment (Gingrich-Philbrook, 2005, p. 305)?

> The performance is also refractive, as I bended time between the there and then, and the here and now – to shift the directionality of effect and meaningfulness of my relationship with my father – with who I have become.

In my own autoethnographical offering, the piece is clearly *reflective*, as I revisit my relationship with my father and experiences with him. The presentation is *reflexive* as I try to critically make sense of my life with my father and how that has been implicated in my sense of self now. The performance is also *refractive*, as I bended time between the there and then, and the here and now – to shift the directionality of effect and meaningfulness of my relationship with my father – with who I have become. And in the end, I am renewed in my love and respect for him – with a deeper understanding of myself through and from the process.

8. I ask students: How can you draw upon memory to inform the current moment in a reflexive mode that provides you both connection to the story and critical distance to share experience without being consumed in the moment of reliving or replicating experience, but instead uses that sensed knowing to provide the audience with access to an experience worth sharing? What do you come to know differently through critical reflection on the particularity of experience?

Separate from the recounting of actual events in the process of critical reflection, are there any unforeseen elements (truths/realities/experiences) you wish to recall? Maybe the story you discovered, or the memory that you recovered is not the one you seek to tell, but a story that now demands telling. What other emergent possibilities of telling the story circulated around the same kernel moment? In other words, are there other versions of this story to be told?

9. Where and how is your body in this critical remembrance, and in the critical retelling of experience? How was your body situated and read in the happening (e.g., gender, race, skin color, body type, ableness)? Did the reading

or situatedness of your body play a unilateral or bilateral role in the happening? In other words, the body as *unilateral* references the one-sided physical
postures of being, and the body as *bilateral* represents the duality of the body
as a site of critical sense making.

In my own presentation that pivots between melancholy and joy, through recognition and renewal, through confusion and discovery – about him and myself,
I am renewed.

10. And finally – I then ask students to tie together these elements into a mean-
    ingful whole in a voice or mode that is uniquely theirs (e.g., narrative,
    poetry, song, choreographic movement and I just engaged an epistolary
    from in a letter to my father) – recognizing that any good story has a begin-
    ning, middle, and end; a crafted argument that is revealed in both intent
    and form, with language that is evocative of thought and imager, with a tug
    of emotionality that reveals the human investment in feeling, and knowing
    and sharing with an audience of readers or a lived audience reading for felt
    understanding.

In my own presentation, I offered you a story that is both simple and complex;
a short and I hope well-crafted narrative – that invites you into the story with
a simple intent – and then draws you into the complexity of a happening that is
both particular and plural. A story about a particular father son relationship in
the context of a particular Black family – but with insights of how *the particular*
becomes *the plural*, offering you a template of sociality; offering you a generative
modality of engagement that might apply to your own self-exploration in similar
(or different) family contexts. This knowing that our family situations are different – as they circulate around issues of race, sex, sexuality class, gender and cir-
cumstance but also how a deep critical reflexivity of the self; as a form or research
and scholarly inquiry; and theorizing the self in a public context can offer others
new ways of seeing and doing the work of knowing the self in a cultural context.
All of which is for purposes that are far from privatized naval gazing – but private processes made public; as public scholarship, as public pedagogies, as border
pedagogies; as critical performative pedagogies; and as performances of and for
diverse possibilities for self and others.

Critical Intention and Passion of Purpose in Autoethnography: A Conclusion

These are the things I see as the important practices, processes, and possibilities of
autoethnography as research (and pedagogy) within the pantheon of qualitative
methodologies – as an *interpretive and naturalistic* approach to human sense-making
(Denzin & Lincoln, 2000). And what autoethnography can achieve as a culturally responsiveness modality of engagement that values the articulated lived

experience of all – inviting the possibilities of diversity, equity, and inclusiveness in research and pedagogies of resistance.

Throughout this short explication of autoethnography, I have used the term "critical" often without defining it, but hopefully by evidencing a particular practice of being critical to which autoethnography depends. In defining or offering the parameters of critical engagement, I often turn to the important work of D. Soyini Madison (2005) as she writes about the nature of "critical" through the framework of "critical social theory" applied in ethnographic practices. In her discussion she states:

> As ethnographers, we employ theory [critical theory] at several levels in our analysis: to articulate and identify hidden forces and ambiguities that operate beneath appearances; to guide judgements and evaluations emanating from our discontent; to direct our attention to the expression within different interpretive communities relative to their unique symbols, systems, customs, and codes; to demystify the ubiquity and magnitude of power; to provide insight and inspire acts of justice; and to name and analyze what is intuitively felt.
>
> *(p. 13)*

Can you see how the work that I have provided you meets or responds to these aspects of *critical* in autoethnographic processes? Can you see how in my offered letter to my father I am engaged in a deep process of excavating meaning in my relationship to/with him in the tension of our being and becoming? Can you see how I negotiate or even vitiate my own power to construct him through both the tensiveness of a son remembering himself to his father, and as an academic making sense through a critical process of knowing, writing, research, and publication (across the presumed distance between his Ph.D. and his father's fourth grade education)? Can you see my attempt at inspiring an act of justice and reconciliation with my father, while providing the reader (and audience) with a template of sociality in their own processes of family autoethnography? I often see the *critical intentions of autoethnography* as being sutured to a *passion of purpose* – to critically relive lived experience as an active process of recovery, renewal, and reconciliation with self and the other.

Activity: Additional Questions to the Reader

Consider the following questions. Write about them. Reflect on the chapter as you respond to the questions. Write about them in researcher memos or your researcher journal.

1. What is your orientation to doing autoethnography?
2. What do you seek to discover or uncover in the memory of your lived experiences?

3. How do you invite students to critically revisit aspects of their past as a means to address both their present and their possible futures? How do you then value and validate such exploration as critical to the curriculum, as a quest for knowledge and a demonstration of knowing (that is personal, political, and pedagogical)? How do you see such an approach inviting the articulation and exploration of diverse perspectives and lived cultural experiences?
4. How do you see autoethnography as *cultural studies*?
5. How do you plan to use the *insights of discovery* and the *critique of possibility* through autoethnography toward emancipatory ends for self and others?

Notes

1 This essay draws from Alexander, B. K. (2013a).
2 See Alexander, B. K. (2000); Alexander, B. K., Moreira, C. & Kumar, H.S. (2012); and Alexander, B. K. (2013b)
3 See Fat Albert and the Cosby Kids: https://en.wikipedia.org/wiki/Fat_Albert_and_the_Cosby_Kids.
4 See Fred G. Sandford, "Sandford and Sons," https://en.wikipedia.org/wiki/Fred_G._Sanford.

References

Adams, T. E., & Holman Jones, S. (2008). Autoethnography is queer. In N. K. Denzin, Y. S. Lincoln, & L. T. Smith (Eds.), *Handbook of critical and indigenous methodologies* (pp. 391–405). Thousand Oaks, CA: SAGE.

Alexander, B. K. (2000). Skin flint (or the garbage man's kid): A generative autobiographical performance. *Text and Performance Quarterly, 20*(1), 97–114.

Alexander, B. K. (2009). Autoethnography: Exploring modalities and subjectivities that shape social relations. In J. Paul, J. Kleinhammer-Tramill, & K. Fowler (Eds.), *Qualitative research methods in special education* (pp. 277–306). Denver, CO: Love.

Alexander, B. K. (2010). Critical/performative/pedagogy: Performing possibility as a rehearsal for social justice. In D. Fassett & J. T. Warren (Eds.), *Handbook of communication and instruction* (pp. 315–340). Thousand Oaks, CA: SAGE.

Alexander, B. K. (2013a). Teaching autoethnography and autoethnographic pedagogy. In T. Adams, C. Ellis, & S. Holman-Jones (Eds.), *The handbook of autoethnography* (pp. 538–556). Walnut Creek, CA: Left Coast Press.

Alexander, B. K. (2013b). Standing in the wake of my father's silence (an alternative eulogy). In S. Malhotra & A. Carrillo Rowe (Eds.), *Silence and power: Feminist Reflections at the edges of sound* (pp. 230–238). London, UK: Palgrave Macmillan.

Alexander, B. K. (2022a). Reading *(to/for)* dádēē: a performative address for first generation college students as an activist critical performative pedagogy. In B. K. Alexander, M. E. Weems, D. C. Hill, & D. M. Callier (Eds.), *Performative intergenerational dialogues of a black quartet* (pp. 67–78). New York, NY: Routledge.

Alexander, B. K. (2022b). Exploring self with/for others. In B. K. Alexander & M. E. Weems (Eds.), *Collaborative spirit-writing performance in everyday black lives*. New York, NY: Routledge

Alexander, B. K., Moreira, C., & Kumar, H. S. (2012). Resisting (resistance) stories: A tri-autoethnographic exploration of father narratives across shades of difference. *Qualitative Inquiry, 18*(2), 121–133. doi: 10.1177/1077800411429087. (On Line First)

Aronowitz, S., & Giroux, H. (1991). *Postmodern education: Politics, culture & social criticism.* Minneapolis, MN: University of Minnesota Press.

Conquergood, D. (1985). Performing as moral act: Ethical dimensions of the ethnography of performance. *Literature in Performance, 5,* 1–13.

Denzin, N. K. (1997). *Interpretive ethnography: Ethnography practices for the 21 century.* Thousand Oaks, CA: SAGE.

Denzin, N. K., & Lincoln, Y. S. (Eds.) (2000). *The SAGE handbook of qualitative research* (3rd ed.). Thousand Oaks, CA: SAGE.

Ellis, C., Adams, T. E., & Bochner, A. P. (2010). Autoethnography: An overview. *Forum Qualitative Sozialforschung/Forum: Qualitative Social Research, 12*(1), Art. 10. Retrieved from http://nbn-resolving.de/urn:nbn:de:0114-fqs1101108.

Gingrich-Philbrook, C. (2005). Autoethnography's family values: Easy access to compulsory experiences. *Text and Performance Quarterly, 12*(4), 297–314.

Giroux, H. A. (2001). Cultural studies as performative politics. *Cultural Studies<->Critical Methodologies, 1*(1), 5–23.

Hamera, J. (2007). *Dancing communities: performance, difference and connection in the global City* (p. 23). London, UK: Palgrave Macmillan.

Holman Jones, S. (2005). Autoethnography: Making the personal political. In N. K. Denzin & Y. S. Lincoln (Eds.), *The Sage handbook of qualitative research* (3rd ed., pp. 763–791). Thousand Oaks, CA: SAGE.

Madison, D. S. (2005). *Critical ethnography: Methods, ethics, and performance.* Thousand Oaks, CA: SAGE.

Madison, D. S. (1998). Performance, personal narratives, and the politics of possibility. In S. J. Dailey (Ed.), *The future of performance studies: Visions and revisions* (pp. 276–286). Annandale, VA: National Communication Association.

McLaren, P. (1999). *Che Guevara, Paulo Freire, and the pedagogy of revolution.* Lanham, MD: Rowman & Littlefield.

Muñoz, J. E. (2006). Stages, queers, punks, and the utopian performative. In D. S. Madison & J. Hamera (Eds.), *The Sage handbook of performance studies* (pp. 9–20). Thousand Oaks, CA: SAGE.

Tamas, S., & Tamas, R. (2021). Conscripted collaborators: Family matters in autoethnography. *International Review of Qualitative Inquiry, 14*(2), 296–301.

6

CRITICAL, DE/COLONIAL, AND CONTEMPLATIVE APPROACHES TO QUALITATIVE INQUIRY

Kakali Bhattacharya

Critical, De/colonial, and Contemplative Approaches to Qualitative Inquiry

As a transnational academic in the United States of America, who was born in India and completed high school and undergraduate education in Canada, I am Nayyirrah Waheed (2013, p. 54) when she says:

> i am a child of three countries.
>
> the water.
>
> the heat.
>
> the words.

At the time of this writing, the world is crumbling under the attack of various strains of the COVID-19 virus, with an inequitable distribution of vaccines across the globe creating vaccine apartheid (Joseph & Dore, 2021). To make matters worse, local, national, and international heads of state creating politicized narratives for this public health issue have prolonged divisive rhetoric that has contributed to millions of deaths and permanently destroyed families (Halverson, Yeager, Menachemi, Fraser, & Freeman, 2021). When I traveled to India in April 2021 due to a death in the family, fully vaccinated, I was filled with both guilt and gratitude. I have the geographical privilege of being a US citizen. Yet, in India, thousands of people were dying around me due to a lack of vaccines, a completely collapsing medical system, and complicated regional and national politics that failed to bring care and relief to the virus-stricken patients and their families.

DOI: 10.4324/9781003126621-8

By the time my elderly mother and I arrived in Kolkata, the pandemic had reached such a level of destruction that frequent lockdowns were imposed to limit its spread. Densely populated cities like Kolkata are highly vulnerable to the virus's attack. Maa and I fled to a rural mountain resort in Darjeeling, fully aware of the privilege that allowed us some reprieve from the virus, given our immunosuppressed conditions. We knew of breakthrough cases even among those who were fully vaccinated, so we chose to leave for the mountains where Maa could rest and I could complete some writing projects.

I open with this narrative because if we are to consider qualitative research, whose history is grounded in inquiry about people's lived experiences, then we must make space for embodied theorization that incorporates diverse perspectives, disrupting the normalized understanding of who can author and create scholarly theories and philosophies of being and knowing in qualitative research. Following this argument, the traditional methodological moves qualitative researchers make in collecting narratives of people's experiences must also be disrupted in favor of culturally situated practices of relationality.

Having traveled to India in the midst of developing a keynote workshop informed by the title of this chapter: my embodied theorization of qualitative inquiry, our ethical orientations, and the need to understand the enormity of the privilege with which first-world scholars engage in research have become salient. In this chapter, I return to my travel narrative to underscore this saliency, and as such, the chapter will deviate from the norms of scholarly writing in various ways. I use my travel to India to ground theoretical and methodological arguments. By offering narratives of my critical historicity, I invite readers to conceptualize their own theoretical and methodological pathways that intersect multiple characteristics of critical, creative, contemplative, and disruptive approaches.

Critical Historicity: Deepening the Practice

I understand historicity as documenting events and people's lives as part of social and cultural history unfolding. Critical historicity, to me, investigates the narrative of these events and lives unfolding as shaped by local, national, and global structures of oppression. I consider locating one's critical historicity to be a crucial practice that deepens our understanding of positionality in qualitative research.

During my trip to India, while I was in Darjeeling, I journaled the following:

> I am at a rural tea estate in Darjeeling, India. It is April 2021. Three new mutant variants of the Coronavirus are in the air and have created devastation and deaths that I had never seen in my lifetime. Whole families are dying within days of each other. Diasporic Indians are flying back from the world to tend to parents and other family members who are sick and then become ill themselves, and ultimately dying – various relief groups

filled with people begging for oxygen, medicine, and beds for their loved ones. And the most forgotten people in this rampage are the transwomen, migrant workers, Dalit garbage pickers, custodians, Adivasi (Indigenous) tribes, unhoused HIV +ve folks battling the virus with little to no support or priority of care.

In the midst of all this, I cannot miss the privilege of being isolated in a tea estate trying to write a text about critical and contemplative approaches to qualitative research. If this is the time I must write this text, then I am marking this time as one of global urgency and critical interconnectivity. We are interconnected. The saint and the sinner. The privileged and the oppressed. The Us and the Other. And while we might have different stations in life, if we have chosen to engage with critical qualitative research, then we must understand this interconnectivity as well as our need to be in a community with groups and people where we feel supported, nourished, and nurtured.

(Bhattacharya, April, 2021)

For most of my life, I have struggled with issues of belongingness, having been born in India, continuing my high school and undergraduate work in Canada, and landing in the US for my graduate studies and employment. These physical movements were accompanied by cognitive, emotional, and spiritual movements in which I shuttled between *here and there*, and perhaps also through a middle, third space. It has taken me a long time to understand why I could not identify who "my people" were.

I conceptualized "my people" as more than an essentialized identity category, since I naturally see the world and its people in complex and interconnected ways. I tend to understand that our relations and practices with people and affinity groups are ways to enrich a matrix of connections. In that connectivity, we can see each other in our vulnerabilities and strengths, with unconditional positive regard, so we can continue to build complex frameworks of interconnectivity. In doing so, we blur binaries, soften oppositional stances, and reimagine qualitative research – and by extension, higher education – with a framework that exceeds restrictive boundaries imposed by disciplines, theories, and methodologies.

Perhaps with these intentions to blur binaries, I started imagining de/coloniality as a state of hybridity and movement by slashing the words de/colonial and de/colonizing (Bhattacharya, 2009a, 2009b, 2013a, 2021, Online first). I explained that there is no pure space in our current material existence that is devoid of coloniality. But we have dreamspaces and aspirations that allow us to imagine a utopian future devoid of colonial forces of oppression. When we engage in such dreaming and existing in multiple realities, we shuttle back and forth, creating a hybrid, fluid form of existence. The slash embodies the middle space – the bridge, the gap, the liminality – in which we pause, contemplate, and negotiate how we cross the thresholds of each of our worlds and engage in actions in those worlds.

Early on in graduate school, Linda Tuhiwai Smith (1999) taught me to recognize the imperialistic nature of research. Explaining the philosophy of inquiry informed by imperialism, she stated, "Western ideas about the most fundamental things are the only ideas to hold, certainly the only rational ideas, and the only ideas which can make sense of the world, of reality, of social life, and human beings" (Smith, 1999, p. 56). This understanding of imperialistic inquiry reinforces a western intellectual superiority while erasing the knowledge and wisdom traditions of numerous non-western cultures.

For Indigenous people, Smith (1999) explained, "research" was a dirty word that referred to a violent and exploitative act. And yet, western research across the globe has been accepted as a benchmark for goodness and superiority, simultaneously normalizing and erasing the effects of colonization. Smith (1999) elaborated on the imperialistic nature of research:

> It is an approach to Indigenous people which still conveys a sense of innate superiority and an overabundance of desire to bring progress into the lives of Indigenous peoples— spiritually, intellectually, socially, and economically. It is research which from Indigenous perspectives, "steals" knowledge from others and then uses it to benefit the people who "stole" it.
>
> *(p. 56)*

Given that the history of colonialism affects most nations globally, it is difficult to ignore the thievery associated with that history. From my lineage, India was a prosperous nation before suffering 300 years of British colonization. During those years, the British stole our resources, knowledge systems, precious stones, and much more, relegating us to a "Third World" nation.

Within the field of qualitative research, I have witnessed culturally situated ideas of interconnectivity and materiality co-opted into discussions within post-qualitative discourses that deploy so much obscure language that it begins to resemble a disciplinary gatekeeper, a move that is predominant within the history of colonization. This gatekeeping creates an insider/outsider binary in which the privileged insider is situated as the theoretically and philosophically sophisticated scholar (read: civilized). In contrast, those on the outside conducting empirical work using other modes of theoretical and philosophical framing are viewed as less sophisticated theoretically and philosophically (read: backward/uncivilized). On the other hand, positivist and post-positivist discussions continue to create disciplinary boundaries for qualitative research, leading to numerous incongruences with the way participants live and make sense of their lives. In both of these moves, there is a notion of superiority that erases, minimizes, or co-opts various communities. Smith explained the implications of such superiority and erasure:

> Some Indigenous and many minority group researchers would call this approach simply racist. It is research thoroughly imbued with an "attitude"

and a "spirit" which assumes certain ownership of the entire world and which has established systems and forms of governance which embed an attitude in instructional practices.

(p. 56)

It is not surprising that those with colonial lineages also create colonizing structures of knowledge creation and inquiry, continuing to situate themselves hierarchically above all others and establishing entire systems of imperialistic approaches to inquiry.

Smith's (1999) bold assertion began to dislodge my faith in the systems that presented research as ahistorical, acultural, and value neutral. I no longer fetishized notions of objectivity or tried to argue with my colleagues who championed positivist or post-positivist ideas to benchmark the goodness of qualitative research. I unsubscribed from the practices that falsely legitimize what counts as research.

My journey and subsequent academic endeavors focused on disrupting, in any way I could, the western superiority of knowledge systems, despite confronting multiple forms of challenge and resistance. I began to center communities whose knowledge was stolen and commodified. I questioned the need to privilege the next new term, the latest theoretical or methodological move, made by the most privileged people in academia when they did not incorporate the colonizing history of the world or challenge the settler-colonial knowledge systems – and when they engaged in incestual citational politics that upheld the binary relationship between those considered insiders versus outsiders.

I understood that knowledge lives everywhere (Bhattacharya, 2009b) and that the most disenfranchised people, who are not in academia, know how to theorize and create knowledge. It is just that they use language differently and connect to the wisdom of their body, ancestors, and experiences. With this understanding, I altered my citational practices and began to cite various sources outside academia, including singers, poets, novelists, and community wisdom keepers. I began to reclaim what I had forgotten or never learned and to be rooted in my cultural history, which a colonizing system of education rendered invisible and irrelevant.

It is not surprising that those with colonial lineages also create colonizing structures of knowledge creation and inquiry, continuing to situate themselves hierarchically above all others and establishing entire systems of imperialistic approaches to inquiry.

I noted that Rey Chow (1992) offered us cautionary notes as we navigated oppressive systems and created knowledge around our histories. She explained, "The task that faces Third World feminists is not simply that of 'animating' the oppressed women of their cultures, but of making the automatized and animated condition of their own voices the conscious point of departure in their intervention" (Chow, 1992, p. 111). This call for introspection about how our voices have been automatized and how we animate ourselves with such automatization became an impetus for un/learning much of what I was taught in colonizing educational systems (Bhattacharya, 2013b).

It is no coincidence, then, that my dissertation focused on border crossings, and my subsequent scholarship can best be described as interdisciplinary work grounded in higher education's social and cultural foundations, informed by de/colonizing ontoepistemologies and transnational, postcolonial feminisms. Embedded in each of these framings are arguments of interconnectivity, complexity, fluidity, and complicated complicities. By tracing the multiply interlocked subject positions I occupy, my scholarship has focused on how I negotiate the complicated complicities of being a Brown woman academic in the US and yet still being perceived as a *Third World broker*, whose scholarship is always vulnerable to exoticized readings.

Elaborating on these ideas, I wrote:

> Simply put, informed by Western discourses, it is easy for me to become automatized and essentialize oppression, liberation, and agency through/ with/against my de/colonizing epistemologies and methodologies. As a transnational scholar in training in the US, I am painfully aware of my complicated positioning in researching other female Indian graduate students. I realize that despite my best intentions to de/colonize my work, I cannot remain neutralized in what I produce because it is always already colonized through my British/Indian/Canadian/U.S. upbringing, training, and presentation of my work in the colonizer's language to Western academia.
>
> Put another way, I write in English to capture the experience of people whose language of communication is a hybridized form of Hindi and English already in its colonized package. I write to translate the cultural productions of "Others," unwittingly taking on the role of a "Third World" broker in a format acceptable in Western academic gatekeeping. These complicated situations and actions continue to create im/possibilities in which I exist, function, interrogate, and abandon thoughts, beliefs, and epistemologies.
>
> *(Bhattacharya, 2009b, p. 108)*

It is through negotiating these moments of impossibilities and complexities that I am convinced that a transnational existence like mine must be forged with solidarities that are grounded in softening binaried relationships, challenging essentialized understandings and performance of identities, and disrupting the exoticization of scholarly work from those who identify as part of the Global majority.

Thus, when I was in India – tormented by mass cremations, seeing families destroyed by the minute, terrified of breakthrough cases, while being mindful of my interconnected privileges – bearing witness to the suffering due to vaccine apartheid, especially when India helped to produce the vaccine, was gut-wrenchingly painful. I witnessed failures of local, national, and international leadership, leading the people of India to realize that no one was coming to save them. No infrastructure existed to alleviate the mass deaths and subsequent cremations, and no time or resources could be spared to appeal to the goodness of various levels of leadership to do better by their people.

Grassroot organizations sprung up, taking care of each other in ways that further reinforced the power of interconnected solidarities. These solidarities were established to mitigate suffering by offering a reprieve from the innumerable challenges or nearly every household faced with COVID-infected individuals. Caste, class, political party, neighborhood, and religious boundaries were crossed with a deep understanding of and commitment to the collective good.

During this global humanitarian crisis, community-based organizations created a space that survived on the idealism of the greatest good for all people. When the government and relief agencies forgot about the cremation workers, people worldwide and within India joined forces to collect funds to offer this most neglected group of people some relief. Granted, more needed to be done due to the devastation caused by the virus and limited access to resources. Yet bearing witness to the support that poured in from people and organizations from within and outside the country reminded me that border crossings and interconnectivity are just relational practices that can be highlighted in critical and de/colonial qualitative research. Nurturing and strengthening this interconnectivity reconfigured power, rejecting the oppressor's model of hierarchical power relations. Grassroots organizations focused on the sanctity of human lives, especially those quickly forgotten by various agencies and organizations that uphold multiple interlocked social structures of domination.

This trip, taken during my 16th year as a faculty member, prompted me to interrogate not only how we understand philosophies of inquiry, but also who gets to create philosophical discourses and tenets in the first place. In my academic training, I questioned why I have not read philosophers who work from justice-oriented perspectives and identify as being multiply marginalized. I noted that scholars such as bell hooks, Toni Morrison, Alice Walker, James Baldwin, W.E.B. Du Bois, and Trinh Minh-ha have written critical philosophical texts, but not from within the discipline of philosophy. I remembered the problematic terrain of philosophy (Bhattacharya, 2020, online first), rife with discriminatory practices and exclusivity.

I no longer felt obligated to understand the philosophical nature of inquiry from the perspectives of scholars who failed to interrogate their privileges yet still constructed narratives about knowledge, reality, rationality, and human existence. My border crossing desires sprung up, and I began to trace the historicities of my ontoepistemologies. The critical question I asked myself was: *Who influences your thoughts about being, knowing, doing, thinking, feeling, existing, resisting, collaborating, and connecting?* I marked these moments as pivotal to my journey as an academic.

Tracing these pivotal moments, I noted that critical and de/colonial qualitative research, for me, have become means of documenting relationalities and practices within and beyond academia (Bhattacharya, 2009b). In Darjeeling, I wrote in my journal:

> These people are failed by local, national, and global leadership. I hope to set their experiences as the context to understand criticality, de/coloniality, and contemplation and their implications in qualitative inquiry. In doing so, maybe I can become a bit stronger and wiser in sharing stories with as much courage and honesty as those living them.
>
> *(Bhattacharya, April 2021)*

I want to underscore that relationality and practices in qualitative research are primary gateways for initiating inquiry organically. Therefore, the orientation toward exploration would be guided by the ethics of the relationality and practices established before any western standards and expectations of inquiry are imposed. In my journaling, I noted that the relationalities and practices would allow me to understand the courage and honesty required for people to navigate their lives during a humanitarian struggle in which their moves for survival are grounded in intercommunal solidarity. This is indeed courageous when the world around us, and in India, continuously incentivizes oppositional discourses to keep communities at odds with each other, discouraging them from creating alliances that would disrupt power hierarchies.

Contemplative Practices, Journeying, and Performances in Qualitative Inquiry

I have been a contemplative practitioner for a long time (Bhattacharya, 2009b, 2019b, 2020b; Bhattacharya & Payne, 2016). I understand contemplative practices as a series of reflective activities that allow me to explore deeply my relationship with myself, others, animate and inanimate objects in this world, and energies beyond this world. I engage in writing, meditation, bearing witness, artmaking, deep listening, compassion, and perspective-taking to deepen my experience (Bhattacharya, 2021b).

Through my academic journey, I shuttled between two primary archetypical identities in their hyphenated form as the warrior-monk (Bhattacharya, 2021a). While my warrior side was battle-ready, I also craved contemplation and inner journeying, cultivating spiritual nourishment of my being to navigate my material realities. Shadow work (Bhattacharya, 2009b) became a powerful tool of inner journeying. I excavated my repressed pain from my position at the receiving end of multiple societal, interpersonal, and familial forces of oppression (Bhattacharya, 2018b).

In this context, Gloria Anzaldúa's (1999) shadow and healing work became instructive. Anzaldúa stated:

> Yes, all you people wound us when you reject us. Rejection strips us of self-worth; our vulnerability exposes us to shame. It is our innate identity you find wanting. We are ashamed that we need your reasonable opinion, that we need your acceptance. We can no longer camouflage our needs, can no longer let defenses and fences sprout around us. We can no longer withdraw. To rage and look upon you with contempt is to rage and be contemptuous of ourselves. We can no longer blame you nor disown the white parts, the male parts, the pathological parts, the queer parts, these vulnerable parts. Here we are weaponless with open arms, with only our magic. Let's try it our way, the *mestiza* way, the Chicana way, the woman way.
>
> *(Anzaldúa, 1999, p. 110)*

This acceptance of our internalized oppressive narratives, along with Chow's (1992) reminder to consciously depart from automatizations and animations, fueled me with the courage needed to trace detrimental narratives and their relationship with multiple social structures of oppression. I understood the complicated hybridities and liminalities in which I exist as a transnational academic in the US. I understood that these hybridities also produce complicities that might be forever entangled and messy. The messy methodologies that support such insight-generating activities almost inevitably involve an engagement in critical historicities and tracing and excavating wounds.

I began to write autoethnographically (Bhattacharya, 2014, 2018a, 2019a), because I was committed to doing my homework before engaging in any further empirical work in qualitative research. By doing autoethnographic work, I theorized complex frameworks that can be culturally situated and cross boundaries to create entry points for cultural outsiders. Additionally, I demonstrated the myriad ways in which being marginalized has always been a produced condition designed to benefit the oppressor.

As I began to un/learn, I questioned how oppositionality is incentivized in academia, leaning on AnaLouise Keating's (2013) work on post-oppositionality. Keating explained post-oppositionality as a form of thinking and theorizing that extends beyond binaried relationships and creates generative possibilities to engage in academic work beyond oppositional discursive practices. She noted:

> I interrogate some of the diverse forms that binary-oppositional thought can take while resisting the (very strong) temptation to react oppositionally. I aspire to offer viable additions and alternatives to the oppositional states of consciousness and politics that currently drive social-justice theorizing, activism, and academic disciplines. I develop nonoppositional theories and relational methods that insist on a real politics of hope and the possibility of planetary citizenship.
>
> *(Keating, 2013, p. ii)*

Keating's (2013) thinking aligned well with my need for multifaceted solidarities that cross borders with a globalized sensibility that does not privilege only western intellectual contributions. She was appealing to my monk side when my warrior side was becoming battle-fatigued. In this way, I was no longer positioning my warrior and monk sides in opposition to each other, but instead honoring the urge to fight, challenge, and disrupt oppressive practices while also cultivating a sensibility of equanimity, generosity of spirit, and expansiveness.

Contemplative practices allowed me to soften some of my knee-jerk tendencies toward oppositionality. Simultaneously, I engaged in first-person awareness of presence, bearing witness, cultivating relationalities across differences, and engaging in rituals that bring pause and introspection. These rituals included art-making, writing, beholding, perspective-taking, and practicing unconditional positive regard for others, even in unpleasant situations. I began to recognize the power of healing such practices had in my own journey and those of my students. These practices translate into pedagogies and forms of inquiry for me.

Further, I leaned on my cultural and wisdom traditions to deepen these practices as they rooted me, reminding me of forgotten knowledge. I was able to model the intersectional nature of creativity, criticality, and contemplation for colleagues and students and repeatedly break academic traditions of scholarship (Bhattacharya, 2013b, 2020a; Bhattacharya & Payne, 2016). Tracing power relations, I excavated local and situated knowledge against national and global discourses and materialities. These discussions led me to understand how I located myself in my complex complicities in border-crossing work.

I utilized creativity and interrogation as modes of inquiry to break established rules of thinking, writing, and publishing in academia. Such space-making becomes expansive, allowing other similarly located scholars and graduate students to do their own space-making, creating a vast academic terrain that is friendly to disruptive and non-traditional work. These inner journeys prompted me to argue for the necessity of healing as integral to any kind of interrogative, critical, and de/colonial work (Bhattacharya, 2015).

Given the centrality of white scholars in qualitative research, these moves provided ways to create culturally and communally situated approaches to inquiry, something that was deemed by colonizing/racist/biased spaces of qualitative research as too agenda-driven, valueless research with personalized subjectivities. In doing this work, I positioned community and cultural insiders as having legitimate authority to speak about themselves and their community, to create scholarly and activist agendas without having to worry about the western intellectual gaze every time they decide to forge their own paths and possibilities of inquiry.

During my trip to India, I noticed how social media spaces were becoming sites for community building and resource sharing. I shared these spaces with understanding an embodied interconnectivity during my keynote workshop at the Advanced Methods Institute at The Ohio State University. I invited attendees to engage in an inner journeying to trace these complex intersections using an example from my trip to India. I offer one such example (see Figure 6.1) to elaborate.

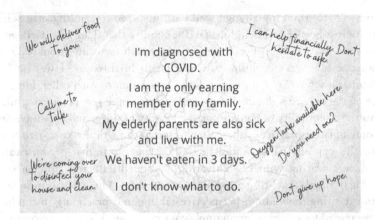

FIGURE 6.1   Community Gathering Around Each Other Through Grassroots Efforts

Note: Slide presented at 2021 keynote workshop for Advanced Methods Institute.

A woman in India shared that along with her parents, she was recently diagnosed with COVID. They were all living under the same roof. They did not have anything to eat for three days, and she was too unwell to take care of anyone. Immediately, the community gathered around the woman and offered help via food delivery, financial relief, companionship, and supplying medical necessities.

I shared this example during my workshop for the Advanced Methods Institute. The attendees understood their interconnectivity to this woman's suffering, the community that gathered around her to offer relief juxtaposed against multiple national and global structures of oppression. By reflecting on this woman's experience, the attendees understood that the message many people worldwide have received from their leaders is that family destruction, death, and intergenerational suffering are acceptable consequences for them.

In contrast, the community grassroots support neutralized this dehumanization via actions that upheld the sanctity of human lives. We discussed our locations during such a crisis and our multilayered complicities. Since privileges and oppression intersect our complex identities, none of us are perfect victims of oppression, thereby entangling our liberation and resistance.

Seeing how community grassroots organizations sprung up with aid for people in need demonstrated that they did not require the government, leadership organizations, or existing infrastructure to act as saviors. People became their own saviors, reconfiguring the unequal power relations maintained by those who exploited a public health issue for individual or political gain. Those on the margins did not need to convince the "center" of anything. The models of possibility existed at the margins.

These models of possibility offered resources, community, and life-saving support systems amidst a pandemic. I am not the first person to acknowledge the possibilities that lie at the margins, as various scholars, poets, and philosophers before me have offered wiser insights than mine (Anzaldúa, 2002; hooks,

1994; Lorde, 1984; Valdivia, 2002). However, experiencing the synergy between what I read and witnessed reinforced the notion that power is an unbound force that can move multi-directionally, even when people create power hierarchies with divisive intentions. For a critical and de/colonial qualitative researcher, it is essential not just to locate oneself when conducting inquiry, but also to fully understand one's relationship with power based on one's past, present, and aspirations for the future. Such critical historicity can disrupt the center/margin binaried relationships, liberate us from the master's house, and materialize models of possibility wherever members of the Global majority might find themselves.

Jatra: Methodological and Theoretical Moves

> When reviewers asked for more positivistic criteria of goodness in my work, I simply stated, "My work is not informed by positivism as a philosophy of inquiry. Instead, I am driven by different philosophies of inquiry, whose criteria for goodness exceed positivism. To do what you [ask?] would make me fall out of alignment with my ontoepistemologies and theoretical and methodological frameworks. This misalignment would compromise the quality of my work, and I would be vulnerable to criticism from colleagues who are insiders to my discipline."

Jatra is a multivalent word in Bangla that means a journey or community theater performance. In this section, I describe how engaging with the works of scholars who identify as part of the Global majority influenced my approaches to qualitative inquiry.

As I continued to unsubscribe from detrimental narratives and colonizing assumptions, I began to use theorizing as a liberatory praxis and grounded such theorizing in de/colonial ontoepistemologies. I then argued for methodological and representational moves from my disruptive frameworks and ontoepistemologies to justify why my work needed to look and feel different from traditional expectations. Utilizing this strategy, I legitimized culturally situated, folk, and ancestral ontoepistemologies as framing devices for qualitative inquiry.

When reviewers asked for more positivistic criteria of goodness in my work, I simply stated:

> My work is not informed by positivism as a philosophy of inquiry. Instead, I am driven by different philosophies of inquiry, whose criteria for goodness exceed positivism. To do what you ask would make me fall out of alignment with my ontoepistemologies and theoretical and methodological frameworks. This misalignment would compromise the quality of my work, and I would be vulnerable to criticism from colleagues who are insiders to my discipline.

I did not know how to language this justification until I began an un/learning journey. Also, my need to legitimize my work for an academic audience shifted. I benchmarked my work with a continuous interrogation of the question, *For whom is this work?* My ethics, writing, research design, and representation continued to change as I moved away from creating legitimacy for a western gaze that continuously engaged in the exoticized reading of my narratives. I wrote, instead, for the people with whom I worked in conducting qualitative research (Bhattacharya, 2019b).

These moves allowed me to create a liberatory methodological terrain in qualitative inquiry divested from certain culturally and spiritually incongruent practices. I developed frameworks for determining the purpose of our being in this world and then aligned that purpose with our academic agendas (Bhattacharya, 2019c). I curated culturally situated South Asian transnational sensibilities from my research and the works of and conversations with other like-minded scholars and community members.

I called these sensibilities Par/Des(i) ontoepistemologies and identified six aligned theoretical tenets. Desi is a contested term that denotes those from the homeland, including multiple South Asian nations. Pardesi refers to someone foreign to the mainland. These ontoepistemologies situate the transnational shuttling of being from *here and there* and occupying a third, liminal space. The slash in the middle blurs any essentializing purist notion of here and there, insider and outsider, due to the diasporic migrations and ubiquitous influence of western culture crossing boundaries via multiple mediums.

Having lived outside of India for decades, I am in many ways considered a hybrid version of Par/Desi when I am in India. I wanted to use this theorization to language the cultural existence of transnational South Asian people navigating and negotiating their/our lives. The theoretical tenets are not unique to this community. However, they offer a cultural resonance when we engage the tenets while still containing ideas that could be relevant for cross-community dialogues.

These liberatory moves allowed me to mentor junior scholars and doctoral students to work from a purpose-driven space without fragmenting themselves for academia. Instead, being empowered with purpose, one could justify the relevance and importance of their work and explain why they have to break some of the established rules and protocols to situate their work. Consequently, new paths are continuously being created, and the criteria for the goodness of qualitative research are being reconsidered and reconfigured (Crawford, 2017).

Three broad categories of information – positionalities, relationalities, and awareness – must be considered in disrupting existing practices and constructing new possibilities through critical, de/colonial, creative, or contemplative practices. Positionality considerations need to be mapped across one's identity as a researcher, community member, and member of academia and society. Such a mapping would reveal hybridities, liminalities, and complex responsibilities. A natural progression following these mappings would include reflecting on how one engages in relations and practices concerning their work with self, others, community, nation, and the world. These considerations foster an understanding of multipart frameworks of interconnectivity.

Awareness considerations require inner journeying and contemplations that help us trace our energetic investments in resistances, detrimental internalized narratives, wounds and healing, ways we understand interconnectivity, and how we orient ourselves with humility towards our work. The notion of humility is critical here because western intellectualism teaches us that researchers are data extractors and participants are data repositories. Inquiry, then, becomes an act of extracting data from participants as a form of entitlement, authorized by specific paperwork signed to indicate consent.

I have argued elsewhere that informed consent is not always a culturally-situated ethical practice and has its own critical history of harm when marginalized communities sign paperwork (Bhattacharya, 2007). Instead, I have proposed that we enter a research relationship first by investing in the relationship without any transactional motives and then co-construct lines of inquiry with the community members. In such a scenario, the researcher's role should be that of a learner, practicing humility and expressing gratitude for what they receive from the generosity of community members who participate in inquiry (Bhattacharya, 2009b, 2021b).

These methodological moves would then guide one's process of gathering information, commonly known as data collection. I will not offer a laundry list of what such information-gathering methods might look like because they would be generatively created with community members. Such procedures could include, but are not limited to, sister circles, walking and talking, hanging out, community picnics, and wisdom talks from community elders. Our ethical orientation emerging from critical, de/colonial, and contemplative perspectives should focus on journeying together with community members, creating organic relationships, and documenting information gathering in ways that honor these relationships. The freedom created by a theoretically liberatory praxis could guide how we gather and analyze information and how we represent the relationships in which we engage.

The Last Word

The primary question I ask myself when I engage in critical, de/colonial, and contemplative work is: *How are you creating and expanding possibilities with your work?* In this chapter, I described my approaches to softening binary relationships by slashing terms that are oppositional to each other. I discussed the value of engaging in ontoepistemologies that are located beyond the privileging of western intellectual superiority. I advocated for embracing disruptive, culturally situated ontoepistemologies. To do so, I argued that we must cultivate curiosity and remind ourselves that our posture as researchers should reflect the humility of a learner invited to witness someone else's experiences, relationships, triumphs, and losses, and to observe how they make sense of such events.

In doing such work, we must be mindful of how we locate and situate ourselves in relation to the participants, our interiority, and the world at large. Our work can carry local, national, and global implications, so we must understand these tentacles emerging from our work as invitations for complex intersectional solidarities that cross borders. In doing so, we make it possible to hear, know, understand, and make space for each other, which extends an invitation to healing. Any justice-oriented work should incorporate healing as a critical component of such work. As qualitative researchers, we need to cultivate healing practices as we bear witness to others. Finally, when we choose to inscribe these experiences into existence through our writing, we create critical historicity representing the people with whom we work, entangled in our current moment with our liberation and resistance. In doing so, we enact a complex framework of solidarity that defies boundaries, inviting nuanced and comprehensive ways of being in community with one another.

Activities

I list some activities for the reader to consider. Remember, there are no right or wrong answers, but instead opportunities for contemplation, interrogation, and perspective-taking. I offer three prompts for you to ponder. You will need to journal about these prompts. I find that journaling by hand brings out information in a different way than typing, so I invite you to try both and see what might be most illuminating for you.

1. Free write for at least 15 minutes in response to the following prompt. When you've finished, highlight words and phrases that draw you in or have some kind of powerful connection for you, without analyzing why. Just trust your intuition and instinct. Once you have selected these words and phrases, put them in a separate space and begin to consider what kind of philosophies of inquiry (academic or non-academic) would best align with you.
   The question: Who influences your thoughts about being, knowing, doing, thinking, feeling, existing, resisting, collaborating, and connecting?
2. Behold the image in Figure 6.1. By beholding, I mean just look at it. Read the words slowly. Notice what comes up for you. How does your body feel? How does your heart feel? What is happening to your breath? What is happening to your jaw – is it clenched? Soft? What emotions arise? Journal about everything that arises for you. Pay attention to how you understand your relationship with self, others, and the world. In what ways do you want to show up in the world? What do you want to respond to?
3. Make sure you complete the first two activities before initiating the third. For this final activity, hold the following question in your mind and go for a walk in whatever way your ability allows. Do not force an

> answer but simply become aware of a witness consciousness within you. Witness the world around you as you walk with a question in your mind. Witness the grass, the sky, the streets, and anything else you notice. When you return from the walk, reflect without any judgment or censorship on everything that comes up for you in response to the following question: *How are you creating and expanding possibilities with your work?*

Use these three activities to craft your positionality, choice of research topic and design, relationship with participants, reciprocity, and ethics in qualitative research.

References

Anzaldúa, G. (1999). *Borderlands la frontera: The new Mestiza.* San Francisco, CA: Aunt Lute Books.

Anzaldúa, G. (2002). Now let us shift … the path of conocimiento … inner work public acts. In G. Anzaldúa & A. Keating (Eds.), *This bridge we call home: Radical visions for transformation* (pp. 540–577). New York, NY: Routledge.

Bhattacharya, K. (2007). Consenting to the consent form: What are the fixed and fluid understandings between the researcher and the researched? *Qualitative Inquiry, 13*(8), 1095–1115.

Bhattacharya, K. (2009a). Negotiating shuttling between transnational experiences: A de/colonizing performance ethnography. *Qualitative Inquiry, 15*(6), 1061–1083.

Bhattacharya, K. (2009b). Othering research, researching the Other: De/colonizing approaches to qualitative inquiry. In J. Smart (Ed.), *Higher education: Handbook of theory and research* (vol. xxiv; pp. 105–150). Dordect, The Netherlands: Springer.

Bhattacharya, K. (2013a). Performing gender as "Third-world-Other" in higher education: De/colonizing transnational feminist possibilities. *Creative Approaches to Research, 6*(3), 30–47.

Bhattacharya, K. (2013b). Voices, silences, and telling secrets: The role of qualitative methods in arts-based research. *International Review of Qualitative Research, 6*(4), 604–627.

Bhattacharya, K. (2014). Cirque de silence: Acrobatics of transnational female academic. *Critical Studies ↔ Critical Methodologies, 14*(2), 209–213.

Bhattacharya, K. (2015). Diving deep into oppositional beliefs: Healing the wounded transnational, de/colonizing warrior within. *Cultural Studies ↔ Critical Methodologies, 15*(6), 492–500. https://doi.org/10.1177/1532708615614019

Bhattacharya, K. (2018a). Coloring memories and imaginations of "Home": Crafting a de/colonizing autoethnography. *Cultural Studies ↔ Critical Methodologies, 18*(1), 9–15.

Bhattacharya, K. (2018b). Walking through the dark forest: Embodied literacies for shadow work in higher education and beyond. *The Journal of Black Sexuality and Relationships, 4*(1), 105–124.

Bhattacharya, K. (2019a). Migratory patterns of a fish doodle. *Departures in Critical Qualitative Research, 8*(1), 31–41. https://doi.org/10.1525/dcqr.2019.8.1.31

Bhattacharya, K. (2019b). Theorizing from the streets: De/colonizing, contemplative, and creative approaches and consideration of quality in arts-based qualitative research. In N. Denzin & M. Giardina (Eds.), *Qualitative inquiry at a crossroads: Political, performative, and methodological reflections* (pp. 109–125). New York, NY: Routledge.

Bhattacharya, K. (2019c). (Un)settling imagined lands: A Par/Des(i) approach to de/colonizing methodologies. In P. Leavy (Ed.), *The Oxford handbook of methods for public scholarship* (pp. 175–215). Cambridge, UK: Oxford University Press.

Bhattacharya, K. (2020a). Connecting with water spirits: An autoethnography of home and higher education. In R. Boylorn & M. Orbe (Eds.), *Critical autoethnography: Intersecting cultural identities in everyday life* (Second ed., pp. 103–107). New York, NY: Routledge.

Bhattacharya, K. (2020b). Superheroes and superpowers: Contemplative, creative, and de/colonial approaches to teaching qualitative research. In P. Leavy (Ed.), *The Oxford handbook of qualitative research* (Second ed., pp. 1163–1182). Cambridge, UK: Oxford.

Bhattacharya, K. (2020, online first). Rejecting labels and colonization: In exile from post-qualitative approaches. *Qualitative Inquiry, 27*(2), 179–184.

Bhattacharya, K. (2021a). Becoming a warrior monk: First, second, and third shifts in academia. *Journal of Autoethnography, 2*(1), 123–127.

Bhattacharya, K. (2021b). Embedding critical, creative, and contemplative data analysis in interview studies. In C. Vanover, P. Mihas, & J. Saldana (Eds.), *Analyzing and interpreting qualitative research: After the interview* (pp. 371–390). Thousand Oaks, CA: Sage.

Bhattacharya, K. (2021, Online first). De/colonizing educational research. In *Oxford Research encyclopedia of education*. Cambridge, UK: Oxford University Press.

Bhattacharya, K. (April, 2021). *Darjeeling diary*.

Bhattacharya, K., & Payne, R. (2016). Mixing mediums, mixing selves: Arts-based contemplative approaches to border crossings. *International Journal of Qualitative Studies in Education, 29*(2), 1100–1117. https://doi.org/10.1080/09518398.2016.1201163

Chow, R. (1992). *Postmodern automatons*. New York, NY: Routledge.

Crawford, B. (2017). *Lights up when plugged in, the superpower of disability: An arts-based narrative*. Manhattan, Kansas: [Kansas State University].

Halverson, P. K., Yeager, V. A., Menachemi, N., Fraser, M. R., & Freeman, L. T. (2021). Public health officials and COVID-19: Leadership, politics, and the pandemic. *Journal of Public Health Management and Practice, 27*, S11–S13. https://doi.org/10.1097/phh.0000000000001281

hooks, b. (1994). Theory as liberatory practice. In W. Kolmar & F. Bartkowski (Eds.), *Feminist heory: A reader* (pp. 28–33). Mountain View, CA: Mayfield Publishing.

Joseph, S., & Dore, G. J. (2021). Vaccine apartheid: A human rights analysis of COVID-19 vaccine inequity. *Social Science Research Network* (June 30, 2021). https://doi.org/http://dx.doi.org/10.2139/ssrn.3876848

Keating, A. (2013). *Transformation now! Toward a post-oppositional politics of change*. Chicago, IL: University of Illinois Press.

Lorde, A. (1984). *Sister outsider: Essays and speeches by Audre Lorde*. Berkeley, CA: The Crossing Press.

Smith, L. T. (1999). *Decolonizing methodologies: Research and indigenous peoples* (2nd Ed.). London, UK: Zed books.

Valdivia, A. N. (2002). bell hooks: Ethics from the margins. *Qualitative Inquiry, 8*(4), 429–447.

Waheed, N. (2013). *salt* [e-book]. Scotts Valley, CA: CreateSpace Independent Publishing Platform.

7

INTERSECTIONALITY AS A LENS IN QUALITATIVE RESEARCH

Possibilities, Problems, and Practices

Antonio Duran, Susan R. Jones

Since its coining in the late 1980s by critical legal scholar Kimberlé Crenshaw, intersectionality has gained prominence as a framework intended to identify how systems of oppression overlap to create unique forms of marginalization for those at the intersections of minoritized identities. Described as a traveling theory (Said, 1983), intersectionality has transcended disciplinary boundaries as individuals strive to interrogate the nature of systemic injustices within various social institutions. Now taken up in fields like education (Tefera, Powers, & Fischman, 2018), political science (Smooth, 2016), and public health (Bowleg, 2021), intersectional theorizing has been key to advancing novel perspectives on how oppression functions in visible and invisible ways in different contexts. To do the work of mobilizing intersectionality is difficult given the wide spectrum of how people operationalize the framework (Cho, Crenshaw, & McCall, 2013). As scholars have named the complexity involved with using intersectionality as a lens (Carastathis, 2016; Collins, 2015, 2019; May, 2015), one central question that persists is: *how can intersectionality be employed when engaging in research?*

In fact, in recent years, increasing numbers of scholars are wrestling with what it means to utilize intersectionality when designing studies, especially in qualitative research (Bowleg, 2008; Duran & Jones, 2019; Esposito & Evans-Winters, 2022; Haynes, Joseph, Patton, Stewart, & Allen, 2020). For instance, researchers have pondered how they can practice proper stewardship of intersectionality in their projects and move toward actualizing the framework's focus on social change (Moradi & Grzanka, 2017). Others have presented strategies for how to engage in data collection and analysis sensitized by an attention to intersectional forms of oppression (Duran & Jones, 2019; Esposito & Evans-Winters, 2022). Consistent across this body of scholarship is the need to honor intersectionality's rich histories and traditions in manners that are congruent with qualitative research approaches, leaning into the complexities and messiness of the work.

DOI: 10.4324/9781003126621-9

This chapter contributes to the growing literature by illustrating how to apply intersectionality in qualitative research studies and presenting strategies that scholars across disciplines can follow. We begin our chapter with providing a brief overview of intersectionality as a framework, describing its potential as an analytical tool intended to expose systemic inequities. We then turn our attention to the possibilities that exist in employing intersectionality within qualitative research, before discussing the problems that people should be mindful of in the process. We conclude with practices that readers can tangibly apply to their own work, guided by the insights that we have obtained over the course of our careers. Throughout, we integrate exercises that readers can participate in to consider how our recommendations translate to their own work. It is our hope that this chapter may serve as a primer for those interested in exploring the nuances of intersectionality and how they translate to empirical studies.

Overview of Intersectionality's Analytical Potential

Though an expansive examination of intersectional scholarship is beyond the scope of this chapter, we find it necessary to provide an overview of where intersectionality's analytical potential lies. People frequently associate the concept of intersectionality with the work of Kimberlé Crenshaw, who introduced the term in 1989, which was then followed in 1991 with an article that built upon her initial conceptualization. In these texts, Crenshaw (1989, 1991) described how Black women, and Women of Color broadly, experience the overlapping effects of racism and sexism. In her 1989 article, Crenshaw showcased how court systems failed to understand the nature of oppression that Black women faced because of their use of frames that accounted for race-based *or* gender-based discrimination, but not the intersection of the two. In 1991, Crenshaw expanded upon her arguments to showcase how oppressive systems intersect with one another to shape how violence against Women of Color operates. These foundational articles have now led to what some refer to as a field of intersectionality studies (Cho, Crenshaw, & McCall, 2013), in which a number of individuals have added their own nuance and depth for mobilizing the framework. However, it is important to note that even as scholars extend the use of intersectionality, the framework must be considered as part of a larger lineage of activism and academic theorizing.

Genealogies of Intersectionality

Though Crenshaw (1989, 1991) is often credited with advancing the language of intersectionality in the academy, scholars regularly acknowledge that Crenshaw's coining of the term is part of a larger tradition of Women of Color naming the need to examine the compounding effects of systems of oppression. For example, in her intellectual history of intersectionality, Hancock (2016) described intersectionality's emergence as a product of centuries of activism conducted by Black women specifically, as well as Women of Color. Both Hancock (2016) and Crenshaw (1989) acknowledge how individuals like Sojourner Truth and Anna Julia Cooper inter-rogated the racism and sexism that Black women faced in the era of chattel slavery. Hancock (2016) also named how Women of Color activists during the period of the 1960s and 1970s similarly advocated for a nuanced way of understanding inter-secting forms of oppression. Additionally, the work of Crenshaw should be read alongside other Women of Color feminists who made key interventions into fem-inist and ethnic studies that failed to engage the intersections of these disciplines (e.g., García, 1997; Lorde, 1984; Min-Ha, 1989; Moraga & Anzaldúa, 1983).

Although many contend that intersectionality should be understood within broader activist and academic projects, it is also not fair to suggest that Crenshaw offered nothing new when she advanced the notion of intersectionality within critical legal studies. Addressing this point specifically, Carastathis (2016) exam-ined the theories that inevitably created the foundation for intersectional-ity's unique form of analysis, but that themselves were conceptually distinct. Specifically, intersectionality evolved from those who named the need to see oppression from the perspective of double jeopardy (Beal, 1970), triple jeopardy (TWWA, 1970), and interlocking systems (Combahee River Collective, 1983). Double jeopardy and triple jeopardy took additive approaches to understanding inequity, with the former examining racism and sexism and the latter incorpo-rating an attention to classism. Conversely, Combahee River Collective, 1983) statement argued that systems of oppressions were in fact overlapping, honing in on racism, sexism, classism, and heterosexism. Another of Crenshaw's contem-poraries, Patricia Hill Collins (1990/2009), advanced the concept of a matrix of domination, leveraging a sociological approach to understanding how people experience marginalization uniquely based on their social location. What must be underscored is that in order to employ intersectionality with a proper sense of responsibility in research (Moradi & Grzanka, 2017), individuals need to com-prehend how it is situated within a wider history of theorizing while also high-lighting its distinctive contributions.

Operationalizing Intersectionality

Given the extent of intersectionality's travels, scholars have consistently warned of its misuse and misapplication, largely attributed to the lack of specificity that the framework offers (Davis, 2008). In particular, scholars like Collins (2015) have named how intersectionality is a "an overarching knowledge project whose changing contours grow from and respond to social formations of complex social inequalities" (p. 5). Its ever-evolving contours are both the greatest strength and perhaps the biggest weakness in operationalizing intersectionality as a framework. Given these criticisms, it is imperative to return to Crenshaw's original conceptu-alization of intersectionality, which may lend itself to its use in research designs.

In her initial 1989 article, Crenshaw offered a couple of analogies that reveal the potential that intersectionality holds as an analytical framework: a traffic intersection and a basement. Her traffic intersection analogy positions a person who experiences multiple forms of oppression at the center of multiple roads. As Crenshaw (1989) described, when this individual experiences an accident, it is difficult to truly know which lane (in which these roads represent discrimination) the crash occurred. What this metaphor exposes is that it is impossible to think of oppression in such a way that is easy to parse where racism occurs versus sexism. Consequently, marginalization is complex and cannot be understood in additive ways. In an often-forgotten metaphor (Carastathis, 2013), Crenshaw (1989) also painted the picture of a basement in which those who experience more forms of oppression are placed at the bottom away from a hatch in the ceiling that allows people into the house. Those who hold more privileged identities are consequently closer to the hatch/exit and have a greater opportunity to escape the basement. This analogy is meant to symbolize how social reproduction and hierarchies are maintained in place, systematically denying those with multiple minoritized identities important access and resources. Both the basement and the traffic intersection reveal the multifaceted arguments that Crenshaw (1989) embedded in her coining of intersectionality.

In her 1991 article, Crenshaw illustrated three ways in which those with multiple minoritized identities encounter intersectional forms of oppression, naming these as structural, political, and representational intersectionality. Explaining how Women of Color experience different kinds of violence, this article sheds light on the explicit and implicit ways in which marginalization occurs. Specifically, structural intersectionality describes how social institutions create laws and policies that erase the needs and realities of those with multiple minoritized identities, further disenfranchising them. Political intersectionality explores how social movements intended to advocate for marginalized communities frequently center those with the most majority identities. Political intersectionality brings to life the basement metaphor by showcasing how individuals cater toward those closest to the hatch instead of centering those at the bottom of the basement. Finally, representational intersectionality explicates how groups in power produce insidious messages and images about those with multiple minoritized identities. Thus, representational intersectionality calls attention to how dominant ideologies manifest and produce forms of othering for certain communities. Read together, people can utilize these forms of intersectionality to actualize the potential of the analytical framework. We explain below how these ideas related to intersectional theorizing can be tangibly translated into qualitative research.

> Structural intersectionality describes how social institutions create laws and policies that erase the needs and realities of those with multiple minoritized identities; political intersectionality showcases how individuals cater toward those closest to the hatch instead of centering those at the bottom of the basement; representational intersectionality explicates how groups in power produce insidious messages and images about those with multiple minoritized identities (Crenshaw, 1991).

Possibilities of Intersectionality in Qualitative Research

As noted above, scholars have increasingly sought to understand what it means to fully integrate an intersectional lens throughout a project (e.g., Bowleg, 2008; Duran & Jones, 2019; Esposito & Evans-Winters, 2022). The reason behind this rising intrigue in intersectional qualitative approaches stems from the possibilities that this framework provides those committed to eradicating societal inequities. In particular, in response to the question of "What does intersectionality allow us to do in qualitative research?" some answers include that it offers a means to analyze overlapping structures of oppression, shine a light on the complexities within minoritized groups, and move toward equitable and liberatory futures.

Central to intersectionality is a focus on how oppressive systems constitute one another to create the marginalization that those at the intersections experience in their day-to-day. As scholars Chun, Lipsitz, and Shin (2013) bluntly put it, the framework "primarily concerns the way things work rather than who people are" (p. 923). Its focus on critiquing structural realities defines the tradition of intersectional theorizing, which is why many worry that it is increasingly applied to symbolize intersecting identities and not intersecting systems of marginalization (May, 2015). Therefore, to invoke intersectionality means to name a commitment to looking beyond individuals and instead engaging the policies, discourses, and movements that shape how people move through the world. For qualitative researchers hoping to take up this analytical tool, it is in this attention to structures that intersectionality holds the most possibility. This lens can be applied to various spheres such as understanding why trans People of Color experience disproportionately low and inadequate access to social services (e.g., health care, housing), why Women of Color encounter unsupportive environments in STEM (Science, Technology, Engineering, and Mathematics) fields, and why low-income individuals with disabilities may not be able to obtain sufficient mental health counseling.

Related to its attention to how power operates in both explicit and implicit manners with society, intersectionality also holds substantial utility for researchers hoping to shed light on the multifaceted nature of minoritized communities. In particular, intersectionality necessitates an attention to within-group differences that exist in marginalized groups (Dill & Zambrana, 2009). Different from its theoretical predecessors (e.g., Combahee River Collective, 1983; Beal, 1970; TWWA, 1970), people have applied intersectionality across all forms of oppression (e.g., racism, ableism, sexism, heterosexism; Collins, 2015). What is at the core of the analytical framework in understanding how all these systems overlap to affect those who hold multiple minoritized identities. Consequently, intersectionality should prompt researchers to reflect on what they mean when they invoke certain identity categories (e.g., Women of Color), because the framework encourages individuals to identify who is most marginalized within social groups. To leverage intersectionality, especially in qualitative research, means to utilize a lens that interrogates the complexities of marginalized groups – one of its greatest strengths.

Finally, another possibility that intersectionality allows qualitative scholars is to not only learn how to identify social inequities, but to take steps to challenge and push back on these oppressive structures. Other scholars have named this as one of the central outcomes of intersectional qualitative research (e.g., Duran & Jones, 2019; Moradi & Grzanka, 2017). The reason is that intersectionality's genealogies include legacies of activists who actively tried to transform society in the hopes of centering the needs of those with multiple minoritized identities (Hancock, 2016). Consequently, in this tradition, intersectional scholars should be able to answer the question of how their work engages visions of social change. However, how researchers may integrate these histories of activism into their studies leads us to reflect on some problems that scholars frequently run into while using this framework in their projects.

Problems Involved in Mobilizing Intersectionality in Research

Although intersectionality offers possibilities in the study of how inequity functions across various social institutions, scholars hoping to actualize the framework in their scholarship must consider potential pitfalls and problems that they may encounter along the way. For this reason, this section seeks to answer the question: *what should scholars be mindful of when applying intersectionality in qualitative research?* In particular, we cover the following: navigating epistemological questions, wrestling with who is an intersectional subject, working within and beyond the contours of intersectionality, and questioning how to enact goals of social change.

Navigating Epistemological Questions

One of the central tasks of a qualitative researcher is to establish congruence across their study, especially as it relates to their epistemological foundations and the chosen theoretical framework (Jones, Torres, & Arminio, 2014). The epistemology of a study represents the theory of knowledge in which people are grounding their research. In our own scholarship, we have located intersectionality under the umbrella of a critical epistemology (Duran & Jones, 2019; Jones, Torres, & Arminio, 2014), naming it as a framework intended to focus on the identification and eradication of social inequalities. However, increasingly, we have seen researchers pair intersectionality with other frameworks that may or may not fall under a critical epistemological stance. For instance, scholars have paired queer theory and intersectionality together (e.g., Duong, 2012) or in our own research, we have sought to pair intersectionality with a constructivist epistemology (see Duran & Jones, 2019). Such decisions, however, require researchers to plan for what this form of blending means for the underlying nature of knowledge present in a project.

Put plainly, pairing intersectionality with another framework and/or epistemology necessitates intentional reflection on the part of the researcher to understand how this will inform their study design. Individuals will need to examine
how intersectionality complements the other framework and/or epistemology,
but most importantly, they will need to be mindful of how they conflict with
one another. Comprehending the points of divergence and convergence must
then translate to other decisions made in the project. For example, if queer theory seeks to challenge the construction of identity categories and intersectionality presupposes examining oppressive systems on the basis of identity categories,
how can researchers employ them both? How does this affect data collection
and analysis? These example questions reflect the intention that researchers must
demonstrate when using intersectionality as they seek to align the framework(s)
with the epistemological foundations of a study. To help contextualize the process of blending frameworks and/or epistemologies, we encourage readers to
conduct the activity below.

Individuals will need to examine how intersectionality complements the
other framework and/or epistemology, but most importantly, they will also
need to be mindful of how they conflict with one another.

Activity 1: Considering the Blending of Intersectionality with other Frameworks and/or Epistemologies

To reveal the tensions and possibilities that result from using intersectionality
in conjunction with other frameworks and/or epistemological foundations,
reflect on the following prompts:

1. What is another framework and/or epistemology that is commonly used
   in your discipline or that you regularly employ in your own scholarship?
2. Create a table where you list out intersectionality in one column heading
   and the other framework/epistemology in the other.
3. Under these column headings, write down what you perceive to be the
   historical lineages of the framework/epistemology and how scholars have
   operationalized these concepts.
4. Write a memo (a memo is an analytic strategy used in qualitative research
   whereby the researcher documents their thinking, their actions, their
   hunches, their quandaries) where you identify the strengths and limitations of each framework/epistemology. Moreover, name what it means
   to use them together. Describe what this reflective exercise means for
   your scholarship.

Wrestling with Who Is an Intersectional Subject

In addition to navigating one's epistemological foundations, another challenge that scholars face in working with intersectionality as a framework is deciding whether or not it is appropriate in their studies on certain populations. In fact, a common debate within the field of intersectionality studies has become who is intersectionality for and about (Nash, 2019). This question inevitably translates to the practice of qualitative research as individuals wonder if intersectionality is appropriate to use with their population of interest. Whereas some assert that intersectionality was created by and for the study of Black women, other intersectional scholars have named the importance of thinking expansively about intersectionality's range (Collins, 2015). It is in fact the broad nature of the framework that has led to its popularity and its use to interrogate the nature of oppression across disciplines, but it has also resulted in the misappropriation of intersectional scholarship (Davis, 2015).

However, if scholars are to apply intersectionality beyond the study of Black women and Women of Color, they must be explicit in how these genealogies that have informed the framework have found their way in the scholars' studies. For instance, researchers should engage with the questions of: *(a) What does it mean to use a theory grounded in Black feminism, as well as Women of Color feminism broadly and how does this then inform my use of the framework? and (b) What is it about intersectionality that necessitates my utilization of it in this project?* The answers to these questions are important to consider, so as to avoid simply using intersectionality for the sake of invoking a framework that has gained recognition and popularity in a discipline. Furthermore, reflection upon what intersectionality uniquely offers versus another framework is imperative as researchers seek to use it responsibly. Though numerous other perspectives exist about who constitutes a subject of intersectionality (see Nash, 2008, 2019 for a description of these debates), what we implore individuals to do is participate in a thorough examination of the field of intersectionality studies before deciding to use it in their research.

Working Within and Beyond the Contours of Intersectionality

Discussed in an earlier section, intersectionality as a field of study has expanded far beyond Crenshaw's initial conceptualization in her 1989 and 1991 articles. As a result, qualitative researchers must reflect deeply on what is signified when they say that they have invoked intersectionality in their study. Far too often researchers name the use of intersectionality in their work. However, as illustrated in a content analysis conducted on articles published in the higher education discipline, the term is rendered a buzzword as researchers fail to engage it meaningfully throughout their design (Harris & Patton, 2019). Citing the works of Crenshaw and other intersectional theorists is an important *first* step, but we would be reckless if we named it as the *only* step in the creation and implementation of a study.

In her manuscript on intersectionality's definitional dilemmas, Collins (2015) argued that there are oftentimes similarities in how people conceptualize the framework, but that these are ever-changing and also require close reading to understand the differences in these contours. For those seeking to utilize intersectionality in their research, they must be willing to do the work to ground their own studies in specific traditions and ways of knowing intersectionality. In our previous article (Duran & Jones, 2019), we offered the examples of Collins and Bilge (2016), Dill and Zambrana (2009), and May (2015) who each had their own description of intersectionality's guiding characteristics. The question then becomes: *what does it mean to take up Collins and Bilge's perspectives on intersectionality versus May's?* We assert that researchers should examine scholars' defining of intersectionality by putting it in their disciplinary contexts and by naming how the conceptualization of the framework is unique. Otherwise, individuals run the risk of using intersectionality in imprecise and general ways that do not honor the wide landscape of intersectional scholarship.

Enacting Social Change

Described above, one of the unique possibilities that intersectionality creates is the ability to design a study that not only identifies how oppressive systems operate, but also that intentionally engages methods and tools that change the social realities in which multiply minoritized populations find themselves (Moradi & Grzanka, 2017). However, as we have examined previously (Duran & Jones, 2019), enacting goals of social change within one's traditional academic parameters is quite difficult if scholars stick to the habits with which they are most familiar. For example, most qualitative research finds its way into academic journal articles, book chapters, and books. Although these have the potential to impact readers' understandings and practices, other opportunities exist to challenge social equities. As a result, researchers who hope to use intersectionality in their study design must wrestle with the question: *how am I hoping to better the lives of the participants in my study and the communities in which I am focusing my scholarship?*

Though not applicable for all, one of the ways that qualitative researchers are answering this question is by using methodologies in which they work intimately among individuals to engage in the process of designing the study and engaging in action with one another based on their findings. In particular, participatory action research (PAR) is one such tradition that scholars have utilized in conjunction with intersectionality (see Fine, Torre, Oswald, & Avory, 2021; Wheeler, Shaw, & Howard, 2020). PAR methodologies insist upon researchers collaborating with the communities that are affected by a given social phenomenon to center their voices throughout the project. Moreover, PAR scholars are deeply invested in developing relationships with groups in order to learn how they can contribute to advocacy efforts in the process. Rather than design the study prior to connecting to participants, PAR asks scholars to work with communities to establish a problem statement. When viewed from an intersectional lens, PAR projects emphasize that "research should never be severed from action" (Fine et al., 2021, p. 348), making it a useful approach to employ in conjunction with intersectionality. Albeit one example, PAR reveals how scholars committed to an intersectional framework should establish a commitment to not only the study design process, but in conceptualizing what comes after a project concludes and when communities still face social injustices.

Practices When Employing Intersectionality in Research

Although the use of intersectionality in qualitative research requires great attention and care to avoid the problems identified previously, there is great promise that the framework offers for scholars broadly. To assist those who are interested in mobilizing intersectionality in their projects, we offer a few practices that have been helpful in our own research as we have sought to interweave an intersectional lens throughout a study design. Namely, we discuss ways that intersectionality should inform the recruitment and selection of participants, creation of interview questions, processes of analysis and interpretation, and practices of critical reflexivity.

Recruiting and Selecting Participants

When using intersectionality as a framework, the recruitment and selection of participants is changed. The connection between the framework of intersectionality and this part of a study is imbedded within intersectionality's ability to reveal the complexities of minoritized communities (Dill & Zambrana, 2009). As scholars like May (2015) have argued, it is important to avoid the trap of viewing oppression from a double-axis perspective, in which individuals simply focus on two forms of marginalization (e.g., racism and sexism) for the sake of simplicity. Such an approach is analytically incongruent with intersectionality, resembling the earlier framework of double jeopardy (Beal, 1970). Instead, researchers must bring attention to within-group differences in their work on multiply minoritized communities.

An example may be a qualitative researcher who is hoping to understand how the academy negatively affects the career opportunities of low-income Women of Color. Such a topic might lead a scholar to solely consider the intersections of classism, sexism, and racism as they design their study. However, this point of view may lead the person conducting the project to overlook the presence of ableism or how heterosexism similarly plays a role in how low-income Women of Color are disproportionately impacted by career opportunities. Consequently, employing an intersectional lens in this type of study would require remaining open to the systems of oppression shaping the career opportunities of low-income Women of Color.

What this means in the context of recruiting and selecting participants is that researchers must be mindful of the various identities and experiences that are represented in their pool. In our research, we have navigated this practice by using demographic forms in which we ask participants which identities are most salient to them across a range of categories (e.g., ability, sexuality, gender, worldview). Collecting this type of information is then valuable as we select individuals across the list of interested participants. Although we find it necessary to say that there will never be a perfect participant pool, intersectionality has sensitized us to question how we are illustrating the within-group differences that may exist in a given community. If we were conducting the research project on low-income Women of Color, we may resist the inclination to only select those who are also able-bodied, heterosexual, and who identify with a Christian denomination. Those looking to actualize intersectionality should use similar considerations as they recruit and select participants, in order to not flatten the ways that various forms of oppression shape the lives of people; instead, intersectionality necessitates recruiting for within-group differences.

Designing Interview Questions

To integrate intersectionality in a qualitative research design means to honor it at all stages of a project, including in how one develops questions. Qualitative scholars interested in crafting intersectional studies have honed in on interview questions as a particularly difficult, yet necessary, element of a research design that people should critically approach (Bowleg, 2008; Duran & Jones, 2019; Esposito & Evans-Winters, 2022). For example, Bowleg (2008) described the difference between asking additive and intersectional interview questions in research. An additive question renders people's identities, and the forms of oppression that impact them, as being siloed. For instance, in a study centered on Jewish women, a researcher may ask: *how do you experience oppression based on your gender? What about your worldview?* These types of questions thus render sexism and anti-Semitism as discrete concepts without understanding that they are intricately connected for individuals. What results from these additive questions is what Bowleg (2008) termed, an additive answer.

Conversely, if people are interested in understanding the interconnections between forms of oppression, they must instead write their questions to allow for this comprehension. In the aforementioned example, the questions may then look like: *(a) how do you experience oppression tied to your gender, worldview, and other identities? (b) In what ways do you experience these oppressions as interrelated? and (c) What are the structures in your lives that lead you to say this?* Though this example is quite simple for instructive purposes, it reveals the necessity to resist additive approaches when developing interview questions. Although some participants may offer reflections that sound additive, or researchers may find use in asking the occasional additive question, we encourage scholars to lean into the complexities of people's experiences by asking intersectional questions.

When designing interview questions, this is also an opportunity to attend to which traditions of intersectionality a person is utilizing in their project. Named above in the section on working with the contours of the framework, scholars should seek to establish congruence amongst their conceptualization of intersectionality and the kinds of questions they develop relative to their project. To help readers think through this process, we provide a brief activity below that one can engage in relative to designing interview questions.

Activity 2: Designing Interview Questions Informed by Intersectionality

As explained above, crafting interview questions that allow participants to speak to intersecting and overlapping forms of oppression is a complex art. Select a population with whom you work and who holds multiple minoritized identities.

For the purposes of this activity, you are designing a study to understand how these groups experience disproportionate access to healthcare.

Write out interview questions that approach this phenomenon from an additive standpoint. Then, write out questions that are informed by intersectionality. Have a trusted colleague review both sets of questions and provide feedback.

Analyzing Qualitative Data and Addressing Matters of Representation

Once a researcher has collected their data, they are then faced with another opportunity to honor the framework of intersectionality as they interpret, analyze, and describe participants' stories. The matter of designing an analytical strategy is an expansive one that should include attending to a methodological tradition and the selected conceptual/theoretical framework in a study (Jones, Torres, & Arminio, 2014). Consequently, researchers should establish an analysis plan that also aligns with their given methodology, such as narrative inquiry or grounded theory. However, regardless of what methodological guidance one is following, they must also ensure that they honor intersectionality's attention to systems of oppression in their analysis. For instance, if a grounded theorist is coding the data in a line-by-line fashion, the question becomes how they are coding in accordance with a lens sensitized to power and oppression. Conversely, a narrative inquiry scholar must be able to demonstrate how they are understanding the elements of participants' stories from this intersectional perspective.

When taking an explicitly critical stance in one's data analysis, a concern that may result is the difference in interpretation that may be experienced by the researcher relative to the one from the participant themselves. Given intersectionality's overarching focus on social inequities, it may be possible that a participant does not perceive the influence of oppressive systems on their lives, but the researcher does. This then leads to what some term a crisis in representation (Denzin, 1997). Put simply, how does one deal with how they represent a person's reality, especially if the participant has a vastly different interpretation? Although there is no perfect solution to this issue, a scholar's navigation of this scenario should align with intersectionality's focus on advancing social change, as well as its attention to structural inequities and not individuals' experiences. For example, researchers may see this as an opportunity for a debriefing conversation with participants, offering them the chance to provide their thoughts on the differing interpretations. When writing up the findings from the project, a person should consider writing about these differences and how the actors involved came to a resolution, if any. Such a process could even serve to bolster the trustworthiness of a research project, as it reveals the steps that a scholar took to consider all theoretical possibilities of the data. What is evident in these comments is that researchers must be prepared to deal with the epistemological questions that intersectionality generates, especially when it comes to data analysis and representing people's narratives.

Practicing Critical Reflexivity

Finally, as intersectional researchers seek to expose how social institutions affect those with multiple minoritized identities, it is imperative that researchers consider how their potential ties to the academy, as an institution, shape their engagement in a research process. Moreover, recognizing that one may hold numerous identities and roles that afford them privilege relative to the communities they are studying requires researchers to critically reflect on their own self throughout a project. For this reason, we echo previous intersectional theorists who have argued that attention to the self before, during, and after a project is critical (Esposito & Evans-Winters, 2022; Moradi & Grzanka, 2017).

Consequently, we offer up the practice of critical reflexivity as a tool that qualitative researchers can use as they engage in the creation of their scholarship. Critical reflexivity represents a turn to move beyond simply examining who one is as it relates to their social identities, positions, and background; instead, it requires individuals to understand what these facets of their identities mean within larger systems of privilege and oppression, especially as it relates to how this affords them power in a research project (Gemignani, 2017). In a project informed by intersectionality, it is of vital importance that scholars see critical reflexivity as a continuous process that they must attend to honor the framework. We offer an example of a potential activity that people can engage in at the beginning of a project.

Activity 3: Engaging Critical Reflexivity from the Beginning of a Study

Noted above, the practice of critical reflexivity is imperative to the implementation of a research project that utilizes intersectionality as a central framework.

For the purpose of this activity, write memos about how you are positioned relative to a project that you are currently designing or hope to conduct in the future. Here are some questions that may guide your thinking:

1. Who am I in relationship to my intended study?
2. How do I hold positions of power that will inform my connection to the communities I hope to work alongside?
3. How do I address the answers to these previous questions when I make initial contact with participants and as I design the study?

Engaging in this type of exercise could be one way to be critically reflexive. Scholars should also consider having conversations with participants (if they are willing) about these very inquiries – in order to bring them into the complexities of qualitative research. As intersectionality is committed to understanding how power and oppression functions in society, it is imperative that researchers constantly reflect on how these very systems find their way into the research process.

Conclusion

In its travels, intersectionality has captured the minds of scholars, practitioners, and policymakers across disciplines interested in exposing how social institutions produce and maintain systemic inequalities. Offering a unique lens to make meaning of how systems of oppression overlap to affect those with multiple minoritized identities, individuals can leverage this framework to engage visions of social change when used appropriately. To pay respect to the larger field of intersectional theorizing, however, is no easy task, a reality illustrated in this chapter applying its analysis in qualitative research specifically. To prevent its misuse and misapplication means to be a responsible steward (Moradi & Grzanka, 2017) of its genealogies and its nuances. Researchers must be able to do so while ensuring the congruence of a study design from its inception to the conclusion of a project. It is only when a scholar approaches this work with intention and care that they can successfully identify and challenge overlapping forms of oppression through their scholarship.

References

Beal, F. M. (1970). Double jeopardy: To be Black and female. In T. Cade (Ed.), *The Black woman: an anthology* (pp. 90–100). New York, NY: Signet. (Original work published in 1969)

Bowleg, L. (2008). When Black + lesbian + women ≠ Black lesbian woman: The methodological challenges of qualitative and quantitative intersectionality research. *Sex Roles, 59*(5–6), 312–325.

Bowleg, L. (2021). Evolving intersectionality within public health: From analysis to action. *American Journal of Public Health, 111*(1), 88–90.

Carastathis, A. (2013). Basements and intersections. *Hypatia, 28*(4), 698–715.

Carastathis, A. (2016). *Intersectionality: Origins, contestations, horizons.* Lincoln, NE: University of Nebraska Press.

Cho, S., Crenshaw, K. W., & McCall, L. (2013). Toward a field of intersectionality studies: Theory, applications, and praxis. *Signs: Journal of Women in Culture and Society, 38*(4), 785–810.

Chun, J. J., Lipsitz, G., & Shin, Y. (2013). Intersectionality as a social movement strategy: Asian immigrant women advocates. *Signs: Journal of Women in Culture and Society, 38*(4), 917–940.

Collins, P. H. (2009). *Black feminist thought: Knowledge, consciousness and the politics of empowerment.* London: Routledge. (Original work published 1990)

Collins, P. H. (2015). Intersectionality's definitional dilemmas. *Annual Review of Sociology, 41*(1), 1–20.

Collins, P. H. (2019). *Intersectionality as critical social theory.* Durham, NC: Duke University Press.

Collins, P. H., & Bilge, S. (2016). *Intersectionality.* Cambridge: Polity Press.

Combahee River Collective (1983). The Combahee River collective statement. In B. Smith (Ed.), *Home girls: A Black feminist anthology* (pp. 264–275). New Brunswick, NJ: Rutgers University Press. (Original work published in 1979)

Crenshaw, K. (1989). Demarginalizing the intersection of race and sex: A Black feminist critique of antidiscrimination doctrine, feminist theory, and antiracist politics. *University of Chicago Legal Forum, 8*(1), 139–167.

Crenshaw, K. (1991). Mapping the margins: Intersectionality, identity politics, and violence against women of color. *Stanford Law Review, 43*(6), 1241–1299.

Davis, K. (2008). Intersectionality as buzzword: A sociology of science perspective on what makes a feminist theory successful. *Feminist Theory, 9*(1), 67–85.

Denzin, N. K. (1997). *Interpretive ethnography: Ethnographic practices for the 21st century.* Thousand Oaks, CA: Sage.

Dill, B. T., & Zambrana, R. E. (2009). *Emerging intersections: Race, class, and gender in theory, policy, and practice.* New Brunswick, NJ: Rutgers University Press.

Duong, K. (2012). What does queer theory teach us about intersectionality? *Politics and Gender, 8*(3), 370–386.

Duran, A., & Jones, S. R. (2019). Using intersectionality in qualitative research on college student identity development: Considerations, tensions, and possibilities. *Journal of College Student Development, 60*(4), 455–471.

Esposito, J., & Evans-Winters, V. (2022). *Introduction to intersectional qualitative research.* Thousand Oaks, CA: Sage.

Fine, M., Torre, M. E., Oswald, A. G., & Avory, S. (2021). Critical participatory action research: Methods and praxis for intersectional knowledge production. *Journal of Counseling Psychology, 68*(3), 344–356.

García, A. (Ed.). (1997). *Chicana feminist thought: The basic historical writings*. London: Routledge.

Gemignani, M. (2017). Toward a critical reflexivity in qualitative inquiry: Relational and posthumanist reflections on realism, researcher's centrality, and representationalism in reflexivity. *Qualitative Psychology, 4*(2), 185–198.

Hancock, A.-M. (2016). *Intersectionality: An intellectual history*. Oxford: Oxford University Press.

Harris, J. C., & Patton, L. D. (2019). Un/doing intersectionality through higher education research. *The Journal of Higher Education, 90*(3), 347–372.

Haynes, C., Joseph, N. J., Patton, L. D., Stewart, S., & Allen, E. L. (2020). Toward an understanding of intersectionality methodology: A 30-year literature synthesis of Black women's experiences in higher education. *Review of Educational Research, 90*(6), 751–787.

Jones, S. R., Torres, V., & Arminio, J. (2014). *Negotiating the complexities of qualitative research in higher education: Fundamental elements and issues* (2nd ed.). London: Routledge.

Lorde, A. (1984). *Sister outsider: Essays and speeches*. Berkeley, CA: Crossing Press.

May, V. M. (2015). *Pursuing intersectionality, unsettling dominant imaginaries*. London: Routledge.

Min-Ha, T. T. (1989). *Women, native, other: Writing post-coloniality and feminism*. Bloomington, IN: Indiana University Press.

Moradi, B., & Grzanka, P. R. (2017). Using intersectionality responsibly: Toward critical epistemology, structural analysis, and social justice activism. *Journal of Counseling Psychology, 64*(5), 500–513.

Moraga, C. L., & Anzaldúa, G. E. (1983). *This bridge called my back: Writings by radical women of color* (2nd ed.). Latham, NY: Kitchen Table/Women of Color Press.

Nash, J. C. (2008). Re-thinking intersectionality. *Feminist Review, 89*(1), 1–15.

Nash, J. C. (2019). *Black feminism reimagined: After intersectionality*. Durham, NC: Duke University Press.

Said, E. W. (1983). Traveling theory. In E. W. Said (Ed.), *The world, the text, and the critic* (pp. 226–247). Cambridge, MA: Harvard University Press.

Smooth, W. G. (2016). Intersectionality and women's advancement in the discipline and across the academy. *Politics, Groups, and Identities, 4*(3), 513–528.

Tefera, A. A., Powers, J. M., & Fischman, G. E. (2018). Intersectionality in education: A conceptual aspiration and research imperative. *Review of Research in Education, 42*(1), vii–xvii.

TWWA. (1970). *Triple jeopardy: Racism, imperialism, sexism* (Third World Women's Alliance Records, 1971–1980). Northampton, MA: Sophia Smith Collection, Smith College.

Wheeler, J., Shaw, J., & Howard, J. (2020). Politics and practices of inclusion: Intersectional participatory action research. *Community Development Journal, 55*(1), 45–63.

8

good kid, m.A.A.d. research

Culturally Sustaining Research and Calling Out the White Gaze in Our Epistemologies

Casey Philip Wong

Introduction

When considering what it means to do education research *otherwise*, and to call out the White gaze in our epistemologies,[1] I begin with the thinking of scholars like Jarrett Martineau (2015), Coulthard, Simpson, and Walcott (2018). They remind us that our ideas are only made possible and given life and meaning by the constellations of co-resistance around us (Simpson, 2017). Operating from Nishnaabewin ways of knowing, Simpson (2017) argues that each of us has our own constellations of relations that support our "flight path[s] out of darkness" (Simpson, 2017, Ch. 12, para 9). These constellations serve to help us triangulate how we know each other, how we know the world, and what we value as we deliberate on what it means to gather, interpret, and share knowledge in the interest of collective freedom (Simpson, 2017; see also Bang & Vossoughi, 2016; Wong, 2021).

In this chapter, I conceptualize the White gaze, sustenance, and relevance in relation to a constellation of intellectuals including, but not limited to, Toni Morrison (1998), Gloria Ladson-Billings (2021), Amanda Tachine (2021), Tim San Pedro (2018), and Django Paris and H. Samy Alim (2017). In relation to Hip Hop, from the title of this chapter it should come as no surprise that I'm celebrating and centering the philosopher, artist, and activist, Kendrick Lamar (2011; 2012; 2015),[2] and the assemblage of elders, youth, and artists who have informed his projects. I'm directly building upon the work of Jeff Chang (2016) and *We Gon' Be Alright*, and Bettina Love (2016) and her paper that also enters into conversation with Kendrick Lamar (2012) and his album *good kid, m.A.A.d city*. Of course, important for this chapter, I'm thinking about a constellation of theorists ruminating on what it means to move toward collective freedom. I'm specifically reflecting upon the offerings of Sylvia Wynter (2003), Katherine McKittrick (2006),

DOI: 10.4324/9781003126621-10

James Baldwin (1963), Michel-Rolph Trouillot (1995), Nick Estes (2019), Eve Tuck (2009), Kim Tallbear (2018), Cedric Robinson (1983/2000), Barnor Hesse (2016), Jonathan Rosa (2019), Nelson Flores (2013), Kaba and Hassan (2019). You will hear these names reverberating across this chapter, alongside their words, works, and conceptualizations.

Grounding the chapter in this constellation of thinkers, and in turn, locating why I specifically focus on the work of Kendrick Lamar, I call upon a quote by Aimé Césaire (1945), "Poetic knowledge is born in the great silence of scientific knowledge" (p. 157). I want us to reflect upon how Lamar is engaging in gathering, interpreting, and sharing knowledge, what we might call research, and how he's doing so in ways that call out the overrepresented ways of narrating the world as determined by what Sylvia Wynter (2003) has referred to in our current problem-space as Man2. That is, Wynter has pointed out how there has been a dominant European-descended vision of being a "human" (currently "Man2," as moving from "Man1") that has come to overdetermine why and what it means to do research, and how and what it means to come to an understanding of the world around us (Wynter & McKittrick, 2015). Lamar invites us to know this through poetic knowledge.

Relating to poetic knowledge, it's important to understand Lamar's lyrical narration of the world through stories. As Brayboy (2005) reminds us, "Stories are not separate from theory. They make up theory" (p. 439). Brayboy (2005) encourages us to see how stories are the building blocks of learning, as human beings across the world have come to understand how and why things are the way they are. When we're speaking about "theory," that's all we're talking about, right? We're talking about how we have to have a reason why we think the things that we think.

With that said, the purpose of this chapter is to ruminate on what can be learned about calling out the White gaze in our epistemologies by bringing the aesthetic intellectualism of Kendrick Lamar into conversation with that of culturally relevant/responsive/sustaining/revitalizing researchers and theorists of collective freedom.[3] This chapter begins by exploring the hegemonic project of education research within the larger academic-industrial complex, which I refer to as "m.A.A.d research." Building specifically on the works of Lamar (2012) and Flores (2013), Hesse (2016), Robinson (1983), Rosa (2019), Trouillot (1995), Tuck (2009), and Wynter (2003) to conceptualize m.A.A.d research, I consider how education research, and research more broadly, is dominated by White supremacist and colonial ways of knowing. These hegemonic ways of knowing regularly take for granted that racial categories (e.g., Black, Asian, Native American, Latinx, White), languages (e.g., English, African American Language, Spanish) and cultures (e.g., Chinese culture, Mexican culture, Black culture) are always, already constituted (Rosa, 2019).

I follow intellectuals, artists, and activists who interrogate how well-intentioned "social justice" education research is often still epistemically invested in supporting teachers within compulsory state-sanctioned schooling to erase, replace, and/or supplement home languages, cultures, and knowledges on the way to what is decided upon as needed to maintain and reform the dominant U.S. White settler colonial-capitalist cisheteropatriarchial order (Alim, Paris, & Wong, 2020). These intellectuals, artists, and activists examine how responsive, relevant, sustaining, revitalizing, and otherwise strength-based teaching and research often comes to be *maddeningly* misinterpreted and misapplied (Ladson-Billings, 2021) in service of unquestioningly "including" and "integrating" youth into existing society without questioning how compulsory state-sanctioned schooling operates through "modern-colonial practice[s] of violence, assemblage, subordination, exploitation, and segregation ... demarcating the colonial rule of Europe over non–Europe" (Hesse, 2016, p. vii; Rosa, 2019).

I then conceptualize what I am referring to as, "G.o.o.d.K.i.d. research," which Lamar and so many folks are challenging us to move toward. G.o.o.d.K.i.d. research does not take for granted the epistemologies, ontologies, and axiologies undergirding m.A.A.d research. G.o.o.d.K.i.d. research interrogates how White perceiving/listening subjects (Inoue, 2006; Rosa, 2019) have created categories and stereotypes that allow particular people and ways of knowing, being, speaking, and valuing to be positioned as "non-White," and in turn, to exist or not exist. In this way, G.o.o.d.K.i.d. research has little interest in offering data and analysis on who should and should not be a part of always, already existing categories – and does not seek to expend energy justifying "the right" to exist. These efforts too often empower "reform" at the expense of abolition and decolonization, and support research that aims to locate better ways to advance compulsory state-sanctioned schooling. This m.A.A.d research is left unquestioned as a structural mechanism for building up the U.S. White settler colonial-capitalist cisheteropatriarchial order (Wong, 2021). Instead, G.o.o.d.K.i.d. research focuses upon how to dismantle and build past contemporary and historical power formations that elevate and maintain systems of oppression (Hesse, 2016; Rosa, 2019). This is what Lamar is inviting us to do with his framing of "good kid, m.A.A.d city," which refuses the hegemonic and controlling normative understanding of Black and marginalized youth in U.S. schooling: m.A.A.d kid, good city (Love, 2016). I build upon Lamar's (2012) re-framing in this chapter to help us meditate on what it means to engage social justice as education researchers: Good kid, unjust society. Not bad kid, just society.

K-Dot's[4] Epistemic/Ontological/Axiological Shift: Moving from Bad Kid, Just Society to Good Kid, Unjust Society

The primary work that I reference is Lamar's (2012) album, *good kid, m.A.A.d city*. This album is widely recognized as one of the best Hip Hop concept albums of all time. A concept album links an idea or theme across the duration of a musical project. In the case of his album, Lamar (2012) thematically outlines what it means to be colonially/racially constituted (Hesse, 2016) as a Black boy where he grew up: Compton, California. Lamar retells a highly impactful day in his life.

He locates how Black boyness has come to be a historically and institutionally constituted subject formation within his community, and how Black peoples (read: not a homogenous category!) are more broadly re-narrating and building new forms of knowing, being, speaking, and valuing outside of the U.S. White settler colonial-capitalist order.

This chapter centrally explores the ways that Lamar (2012) could be said to epistemically sum this up within the title of his album, which also could be said to be the thesis and running thread through his larger oeuvre as a Hip Hop artist. Relatedly, I'd like to note that this chapter closely references Lamar's (2011; 2012; 2015) works *Section.80* and *To Pimp A Butterfly*. I see these preceding (i.e., *Section.80*) and subsequent (i.e., *To Pimp a Butterfly*) works as enveloping, grounding, nuancing, and extending the thesis and arguments he puts forth in *good kid, m.A.A.d city* as an intellectual, activist, and artist.

Reflecting upon this title/thesis – *good kid, m.A.A.d city* – Lamar challenges the deficit-based and damage-centered frames that position poor and working-class Black and marginalized youth as *mad* (i.e., mad/bad/superpredator kid), U.S. society as fundamentally defined by goodness (i.e., good/just city), and education research as therefore needing to support teachers in finding ways to incorporate *mad* kids into an otherwise socially just and *good* society. Instead, Lamar says there's no such thing as the White perceiving/listening subject's (Inoue, 2006; Rosa, 2019) colonially/racially constituted "superpredator," "bad," and/or "m.A.A.d" Black and marginalized kid in the mythic "urban" city (i.e., m.A.A.d as representing "my Angels on Angel dust"). K–Dot invites us to think about how there are *good kids* within *mad cities* dominated by systemic injustices. He epistemically, ontologically, and axiologically challenges the foreclosure of the "human" as a mythological and boundaried subject formation inhabited by White bodies and their constructed ways of knowing, being, speaking, and valuing (Wynter, 2003). Lamar positions himself and his peers as human beings, and human beings that do things for a reason – especially harm and violence. He situates the harm and violence as being made possible by anti-Black and White supremacist institutions and structures managing Black and marginalized populations within the racial capitalist and settler colonial context of Compton.[5] Lamar appeals for his audience to engage in projects of social justice, enacting forms of personal responsibility that are tied to transforming the public sphere, and to end the systemic injustices taking place in what he calls the m.A.A.d city.

Lamar's (2015) music video for "Alright" from *To Pimp a Butterfly* represents Lamar's bold epistemic/ontological/axiological re-framing of Blackness, which challenges White ways of conceptualizing/controlling Blackness inside and outside of the academic-industrial complex. The cinematographic sequence that follows the music video's opening portrait of Black life – beginning at 1:54 minutes into the video – could be said to exemplify what I refer to, in conversation with Lamar, as m.A.A.d research. With three other Black men listening to music, finding joy, and seemingly cruising through the city in an old car, the zoomed in camera finds Lamar rapping beside them in the driver's seat. The music video

visually and aurally depicts an enunciation of Black maleness that is often crim-
inalized, disciplined, and policed from the streets, to the classroom. In the context of academic and education research, such scenes depicting Black men and
boys are often deployed as invitations to consider how "they" could be "fixed,"
made to be "productive," given "capital," taught to "codeswitch," told how to
dress and speak "right," and how to orient themselves around (Povinelli, 2002)
and/or inhabit White ways of knowing, being, speaking, and valuing. But in
this cinematographic sequence, the camera begins to zoom out and engages in
imaginative justice work. Expressed through his larger and ongoing aesthetic,
intellectual, and activist vision, Lamar (2015) not only invites us to see a fuller
picture, and what is happening amongst people racialized as Black within his life,
he also invites us to radically contemplate and reimagine what it might mean to
enact social justice.

Lamar (2015) zooms out to show us the fuller picture. He symbolically shows
White police officers engaging in the transformation of society, beginning to
take responsibility for their historical and institutional role in maintaining White
settler colonial-capitalist domination and anti-Black violence. They carry the
car with Lamar and three Black men through the streets; as they're expressing
all the joy of *being* as they want to *be*. There is no policing by the police of the
Blackness in the vehicle. Also noticeable in this scene is the tension from which
Lamar grapples with revenge versus justice, and what it might mean for each
of us to give up our power and take responsibility for moving societies toward
visions of collective freedom. Are the police officers being punished for what
they've done, or are they voluntarily taking up the vehicle of justice to answer
for their participation in state-sanctioned violence? Following the lead of Lamar,
this wondering exemplifies one of many points of concern within what I refer to
as G.o.o.d.K.i.d research.

> Lamar positions himself and his peers as human beings, and human beings
> that do things for a reason: especially harm and violence. He situates the
> harm and violence as being made possible by anti-Black and White suprema-
> cist institutions and structures managing Black and marginalized populations
> within the racial capitalist and settler colonial context of Compton.

And of course, this isn't a perfect project, which should be stated in the context
that there can be no such thing as a perfect project (i.e., in spite of White supremacist claims to perfection; Baldwin, 1963). Lamar's (2012) framing of "mad"
should and does not grapple with dis/ability, nor does it seriously think about
contemporary and historic cisheteropatriarchy as an interlocking institutional
and relational power formation that has arguably been one of the most significant obstructions to anti-colonial and freedom movements since the 1960s. But
this too is in part recognized by Lamar, who in fact re-narrates a world where

mistakes are not feared, but are confronted with courage, vulnerability, and honesty, in the name of interlocking personal and societal growth. This is an overarching theme prominently expressed through Lamar's (2012) grappling with harm and violence through Black renderings of Judeo-Christian understandings of sin, forgiveness, and righteousness (i.e., Judeo-Christian hegemony could also be said to be unquestioned within Lamar's larger oeuvre). Lamar (2012; 2015) invites us to epistemically move past Westernized frames of "critique," to something else entirely. He asks us to refuse goodness and badness as something that we can "be" or "become," and instead to move toward forms of community responsibility that acknowledge the role of society in constraining and expanding our agency; and accordingly, to enact accountability based on our actions, in spite of whatever may be our intentions.

Methodological Liner Notes

This chapter emerges from a purposefully multimodal Advanced Methods Institute keynote workshop presentation with audio and video clips. This presentation included semiotically rich visuals and lyrics, which in our current technological moment, are not able to be aesthetically and expressively represented in the medium of a printed book chapter. In this way, many of these cues and messages appear as written text, which in particular, do not do justice to Lamar's (2011; 2012; 2015) aesthetic intellectualism. (See presentation at https://u.osu.edu/quallab/advanced-methods-institute/).

Relatedly, my intention, as much as possible, is to present Lamar's conceptualizations in his own words, alongside and in conversation with direct excerpts from texts of education researchers and theorists of collective freedom. Notably, I do not claim to know how and if Lamar would interpret his aesthetic intellectualism in the ways I do here, which also goes without saying for the other thinkers referenced: this chapter is an offering which reflects my own lifeways and constellations, and my own shifting epistemologies, ontologies, and axiologies.

I would also like to note that I begin the two primary sub-sections of this chapter modeling an epistemic practice emerging from predominantly African diasporic peoples and knowledges, which I have learned and used to theorize, make sense of, and get feedback about ideas as part of my life as a Hip Hop artist. It's common among folks engaged with Hip Hop to expressively and joyfully process viewpoints, observations, and thoughts in ways that do not involve writing notes, making an outline, creating interpretative hierarchies of codes, theming, and/or other European-rooted modes of knowledge interpretation and production. In this case, I summoned and wrote verses.[6] Writing verses is an affective and spiritual process of expressive summoning that I would do, and continue to do, alongside high school students in my Hip Hop programming. I wrote the two verses below seeking to unpack and consider the epistemologies undergirding education research. This verse writing was also just me having fun with poetics and finding possibility and generativity through aesthetically demanding narration. This was an *otherwise* way of me w/rapping my mind around what m.A.A.d research and G.o.o.d.K.i.d. research denotes and means for us, for me. *Let's go!*

m.A.A.d research

> **m**ythologies of Man2 are maintained
> **A**ccumulation-based theories of change,
> institutions rearranged, or kept the same,
> with an approach all-consuming
> **A**ssuming and ahistorical,
> bound to lose the intersectional,
> insurrectional, and omnidirectional,
> stereotypically wound around the
> **d**amage-centered and deficit-based,
> deconstituted, overdetermined, eliminated,
> and erased

Mythologies of Man2 Are Maintained

One of the epistemic anchors of Lamar's (2012) project – *good kid, m.A.A.d city* – is a track that bears one half of the album's name, "m.A.A.d city." Lamar grounds how he arrived at his worldview:

> Fresh outta school 'cause I was a high school grad
> Sleeping in the living room of my momma's pad
> Reality struck I seen the white car crash
> Hit the light pole two n***** hopped out on foot and dashed
> My Pops said I needed a job I thought I believed him
> Security guard for a month and ended up leaving
> In fact I got fired 'cause I was inspired by all of my friends
> To stage a robbery the third Saturday I clocked in
> Projects tore up, gang signs get thrown up
> Cocaine laced in marijuana
> And they wonder why I rarely smoke now
> Imagine if your first blunt had you foaming at the mouth
> I was straight tweaking the next weekend we broke even
> I made allegiance that made a promise to see you bleeding
> You know the reasons but still won't ever know my life
> Lamar AKA Compton's human sacrifice
>
> (Lamar, 2012, excerpt from "m.A.A.d city")

What does Lamar reveal within this excerpt? And how does this help us think about the ways that we conceptualize education research from what education is supposed to do? Lamar situates the myth of U.S. schooling. *Just go to school, that's what they tell us, right? You're supposed to go to school. If you do well, you graduate. If you graduate, you do well. You're supposed to get a job. That job is supposed to sustain you and your loved ones. That job is supposed to help you materially take care of yourself, and make it possible for you to have a family, buy a house, live happily ever after, and be included into the U.S. nation state.*

Lamar's autoethnographic examination dispels this myth of U.S. schooling through detailing and situating his subject formation in Compton (Haile, 2018). Lamar graduates high school. His dad helps him get a job as a security guard, because his schooling did not support his realization of any other job, even though it was promised to him. That low paying job leads him to depression, and entrance into an alternative economy where Black and marginalized populations have to find ways to survive by dispossessing and eliminating to accumulate in the face of their own ongoing exploitation and erasure (Robinson, 1983). Lamar exposes this lie and showcases the violence of this lie, and the consequences for youth racialized as Black who do not get that promised inclusion into U.S. society.

So to think about what Lamar is vividly narrating, I enter into conversation with Wynter (2003), who offers theory to explain this mythology, this idea of man. So what Wynter theorizes (2003) is that, when we say man (e.g., "that's one giant step for man, one giant leap for mankind"), that invoked "man" is not a neutral personhood. This "man" is a naturalized representation of a European-descended model of personhood. This genre-specific vision of "man" gets over-represented as the only way to be "human." So Wynter (2003) points out that when we say human, when we say man, the unquestioned normative interpretation is to assume this "man" and "human" means everybody, all people. And Wynter points out how we're currently in the era of the version of man, Man2 (Wynter & McKittrick, 2015).

So when Wynter (2003) is talking about "Man1" and "Man2," this is just notation she created to talk about how that one overdetermined vision of humanity, which European-descended people have tried to overrepresent as belonging to all humans, has changed over time. Wynter argues that it started off in the Renaissance with European populations defining man/humanity (i.e., Man1, *homo politicus*) by whether they were a "rational"/"civilized" political subject and belonged to a nation-state (i.e., with European models of nation-statehood/governance being the exclusionary measure of who got to be human and less-than-human; citizens vs. slaves/migrants/barbarians; Wynter, 2003).

Wynter (2003) says this changed in the 18th century with Darwin and the rise of biological sciences (i.e., Man2, *homo oeconomicus*). The origin story of humanity suddenly moved to revolve around this idea that we evolved through processes of natural selection (i.e., into "races" that were racialized as naturally inferior or superior), which defined who deserved to rule and not rule over the natural world (i.e., White supremacy through its esteemed projects of racial capitalism, liberal democracy, cisheteropatriarchy, etc.). By means of Darwin's story of human evolution, among other emerging European ways of knowing the world, there came to be hierarchies of being and existing. And these European-descended hierarchies came with modes of classification that were conceptualized and applied during a time period where European colonialism was starting to expand and take over the world. Evolution and natural selection, which were constructed as favoring White cishetero able-bodied men from Western Europe, came to be seen as "objective" and "empirical" naturally occurring processes that could justify the rule of Europe over all of non-Europe (Hesse, 2016; Rosa, 2019). European-descended ways of being, seeing, valuing, thinking, teaching, and learning came to be naturalized as superior/useful, which all humanity needed to abide by, for all time.

This also became the case with education, and understandings of what got to be teaching and learning, what got to be seen as education research, and more broadly what could and could not be research (see Wong, 2021). This was crucially the case with the compulsory state-sanctioned school, developed by European-descended people in the 19th century, which has continued to carry out the genre-specific purposes of Man2-as-human (i.e., descent of Mann/ Dewey, Wong, 2021). Man2's vision for schooling differentially has come to incorporate populations in ways that make sense to the overdetermined vision of the respective representatives of the European-descended colonial order within a specific geopolitical context, the embodied ideological appointees of European-descended man, which in the U.S. nation-state came to declare themselves as "White."

And just to return back to where Lamar (2012) took us, in conversation with Wynter, he questioned this idea that schooling *is* education, and that education *equals* inclusion. And for education researchers, this interrogates the primary purpose of normative and naturalized "education research," which is supposed to support schooling in that mythological inclusion. Lamar (2012) invites us to question these assumptions as Man2's mythology, and to call out the White gaze that epistemically presupposes the purpose of schooling and education research.

Accumulation-Based Theory of Change

Another aspect of m.A.A.d research is this concern with accumulation-based theories of change that undergird what, how, and why we research (Rosa, 2019). On his track "Money Trees," Lamar (2012) summons his memories from his time in high school, where he dreamed of becoming a rapper. His dreams were based upon lessons he had learned from then popular Bay Area rapper, E-40 (i.e., Earl Stevens). Lamar elucidates the ideology that E-40 propagated: the idea that if you just work hard and get better at rapping, and accumulate more and more skills at rapping and selling your work, that the result will be steadily increasing material compensation by means of a lucrative rapping career where you can sustain yourself and incorporate yourself into the U.S. nation-state.

Instead, what Lamar finds is that he engages in this process of accumulating rapping skills and selling his work, only to still end up being poor. His uncle Tony gets killed. E-40's theory of accumulation does not result in change for him. Lamar calls attention to the "racial" foundation of capitalism and his colonial subject formation in Compton (Robinson, 1983): *You don't become a rich by working hard and accumulating skills at rapping and doing "business," no matter how good you are at rapping, or how closely you follow directions on how to become rich.* Lamar reveals how becoming rich requires access, racialized access, to already stolen capital, and/or the means to use existing societal institutions created by White settlers to steal and accumulate from racialized "others." Lamar is eventually granted access to a large corporation (i.e., "label"), which grants him the institutional means to accumulate capital if he substantially gives back to that corporation, and abides by a positionality that is legible to the liberal multiculturalist democratic order (Povinelli, 2002; Rose, 2008).[7] Lamar questions widely propagating accumulation-based theories of change that overlook how the larger racial capitalist mechanisms determine whether you will or will not receive material compensation for your respective work. He calls this out based upon reflections on how he applied this theory of change, and how it has affected young Black kids who want to become rappers.

While Lamar elucidates how this logic plays out in the realm of music and expressive practice, this logic moves across our society, including in schooling and education. It's similarly imagined that all educators need to do is find ways to prepare young people to have more European ways of knowing, being, valuing, and speaking, and that will result in inclusion and success in U.S. society. This logic undergirds the idea of code switching. Code switching presumes that regardless of your body, all you need to do is continually accumulate White ways of existing, and know how to "switch," and the result will be incorporation into the U.S. society. And while educators and education researchers can point out how there are opportunities to strategically squeeze through and find your way through White supremacy and systems of domination, this does not result in success for most Black and non-White identified peoples. The ways that institutions and structures exist mean that certain populations are racially/colonially constituted (Hesse, 2016) as existing for specific services and labor for the larger U.S. White settler capitalist-colonial project. Exceptions are permissible (i.e., especially when they benefit the dominant liberal democratic order), but only as long as they don't change the fundamental desired stratified composition of U.S. society and White supremacy's vision of the world.

As an example for education researchers, Rosa and Flores (2017) point out how this accumulation-based theory of change plays out to make possible an "ideology of languagelessness" within U.S. language instruction. They illuminate how an ideology of languagelessness makes it so a Latinx person who speaks two varieties of language can be what they call a "non-non," and how particularly Latinx children across the U.S. can be ontologically framed as deficient in Spanish *and* English regardless of their perceived proximity to standardized norms. *No matter how much language you accumulate, you are not as fluent, because of racial stigmatization.* So Rosa (2019) says the aim is not redistribution and/or accumulation, but decolonization and abolition of White supremacy and systems of domination that structurally exclude and attach racial stigmatization to whatever non-White identified populations *do.*

Assuming and Ahistorical

> And you ask, "Lift up your shirt" cause you wonder if a tattoo
> Of affiliation can make it a pleasure to put me through
> Gang files, but that don't matter because the matter is racial profile
> I heard them chatter: "He's probably young but I know that he's down"
> Step on his neck as hard as your bullet proof vest
> He don't mind, he know we'll never respect, the good kid, m.A.A.d. city
> (Lamar, 2012, excerpt from "good kid")

Another aspect of m.A.A.d research: it's often assuming and ahistorical. m.A.A.d research regularly doesn't question it assumptions, and it doesn't approach research within the context of history. Let's consider how Lamar helps us think about this.

So Lamar (2012), in the anecdote that he's shared in the above excerpt, is talking about an experience where he encounters a police officer. He reflects upon how the police officer perceives him through the White gaze. Lamar examines and returns the gaze to the officer, who could simultaneously be said to be acting as a researcher. Lamar evaluates the officer as a researcher who was institutionally prepared by White supremacist systems of domination that naturalize "racecraft" (Fields & Fields, 2014). That is, in this instance, the anti-Black practice of policing creates the illusion that peoples racialized as Black are biologically, socially, and/or culturally pre-disposed to criminality. This racecraft leaves unquestioned how policing and mass incarceration are historically and institutionally rooted in anti-Blackness, and ongoing attempts to subjugate Black laborers and communities in the interest of advancing the White settler colonial-capitalist cisheteropatriarchal order (Fields & Fields, 2014). In the case of Lamar, the officer is looking for gang members. This officer accesses his knowledge on what a gang member "looks like," and through his unquestioned position as a White perceiving/listening subject determines/profiles (Rosa, 2019): Lamar must be a gang member. The police officer is looking for gang members as he patrols the communities of Black boys and men walking through Compton, and he finds what he's looking for when he sees Lamar. That assumption of what models and stereotypes of personhood can inhabit and exist as a "gang member" allows the officer, through his institutional participation within a larger White epistemological project, to find and see Lamar in this way. *When you have assumptions, and you're not prepared to question them and how they're related to systems and power, your viewpoints default to the naturalized position that is ratified by whatever systems of domination you are operating within.*

How do we see this taking place in education research? An example can be seen in what was once the popular, which is still widely propagating in many circles, so-called language or "word gap" (Avineri et al., 2015). Researchers engaged in a study and made the claim that kids in poverty – with racial capitalist processes constraining particularly marginalized Communities of Color – spoke

30 million less words than affluent kids by the age of three (Hart & Risley, 1995). Since they noticed that particularly kids in poverty were saying less words than this elevated and boundaried affluent group, it must be a relevant and important gap to literacy. That 30 million "word gap" must be the reason why they're not doing well in compulsory state-sanctioned schooling. They argued that we needed to change schooling and society to make it so kids in poverty could have opportunities to learn more words and catch up with their affluent (read: superior) peers.

As developed and invoked by Eve Tuck (2009), damage-centered research "operates, even benevolently, from a theory of change that establishes harm or injury" in order to achieve reparation or justice (p. 413). Damage-centered, and more broadly deficit-based approaches, presume that the job of the researcher is to share research that can convince those in power to fix recognized damage done to the marginalized "other."

What is revealed when you take a closer look at the assumptions undergirding this research? As education researchers and linguistic anthropologists like H. Samy Alim, Django Paris, Ana Celia Zentella, Jonathan Rosa, and Nelson Flores have pointed out (Avineri et al., 2015), this research is grounded in White supremacist and racial capitalist ideologies. The researchers looked at predominantly White affluent children, counted the words that they spoke, and argued that all kids needed to do what they were doing. They made White affluent kids the standard against which to measure every child (i.e., White supremacy and racial capitalism quite literally being enacted). Following culture of poverty arguments and logics (Lewis, 1965), they assumed that U.S. society was fundamentally just, with communities left in "cycles of poverty" due to damaged and "bad culture." But literacy "gaps" have much more to do with what is constructed as needed by the dominant structures and ideologies within a society, than the marginalized populations being "measured" for their presumed deficits. And of course, we know from years of literacy research, that literacies are measured in a variety of ways across communities seeking to prepare youth to read texts and the world. The number of words you speak has little to do with your communicative competency. And it goes without saying for folks out there in the world, who come from communities who did not abide by many of these naturalized White affluent norms and turned out just fine: *you know this is a myth.* But these are assumptions that continue to go unquestioned by large numbers of influential educators and researchers (Avineri et al., 2015).

Another challenge to a widely prevailing assumption that Lamar offers in this verse, which is shared by a variety of linguistic anthropologists and like-minded intellectuals, is that form does not equal function (Rosa, 2019). Young people like Lamar can position themselves as appearing to follow the sovereignty of, say, a gang, but not actually be affiliated. This is often a strategic practice for survival to negotiate locally powerful alternative institutions, which are often formed to deal with circumstances that have been made possible by systems of domination like racial capitalism and liberal democracy. Those alternative institutions, like "gangs," assert control at the same time as more wide-ranging and powerful institutions of the U.S. nation-state – and particularly Black and Latinx populations within these constrained contexts have to find ways to survive. Lamar illuminates in his work how he wasn't gang affiliated, but all the same often had to know and/or abide by sets of cues and acts to negotiate multiple overlaying and contradicting sovereignties (Rosa, 2019; Wong, 2018).

This, of course, is related to historicity (Estes, 2019; Trouillot, 1995). When we don't look at the context of how and why acts happen and operate without an understanding of how sociohistorical circumstances are situated within ideologies of modernity, the assumption is what we see is wholly the expression and responsibility of whoever is in front of us (Scott, 2004). Violence can become completely the fault of whoever is directly committing such violence, and goodness can be ascribed as entirely the manifestation of those peoples who engage in it. And this of course obscures the ideological history that made the constructs of "violence" and "goodness," which are not divorced from their ontological beginnings (Estes, 2019). In this way, it becomes possible for researchers to look at the contemporary circumstances facing Black adults and youth in Compton, and not consider the historical segregation and racialized constraints violently positioning possibilities for Black populations. Researchers can miss how specific populations have been historically and institutionally exploited and refused opportunities, and accordingly, pushed toward developing institutions and engaging in acts that would otherwise be unnecessary (Trouillot, 1995).

We can think about how historicity is often something that education researchers evade and/or overlook; situating, describing, and drawing conclusions from "data" without an understanding of what made such data possible through time and space. When we undertake de-contextualized and ahistorical approaches to interpretation and analysis, it's possible to begin with the assumption that compulsory state-sanctioned schools have always existed and certain populations are predisposed to not "valuing" education. Understandings of what is "good" teaching and learning, and what is "achievement" and success, are transformed when we consider that state-sanctioned institution, the school, has only been around in its current formulations since the rise of the "common school"; the idea of the common school being developed primarily by Horace Mann in the context of the U.S. through European-descended pathways from specifically Germany, England, and Western European models of education. That school is not always where education has taken place, alike to how gathering, interpreting, and sharing knowledge has not always taken place within those feudal structures we now call colleges and universities (Wong, 2021). In this way, some questions that we can take to our own research: what assumptions make your research possible? How do you consider history? Do you consider how history shapes what you understand as problems and issues within your research agenda?

Damage-Centered and Deficit-Based

This is perhaps the most important aspect of the m.A.A.d acronym: m.A.A.d research operates from damage-centered and deficit-based perspectives. As developed and invoked by Eve Tuck (2009), damage-centered research "operates, even benevolently, from a theory of change that establishes harm or injury" in order to achieve reparation or justice (p. 413). Damage-centered and more broadly deficit-based approaches presume that the job of the researcher is to share research that can convince those in power to fix recognized damage done to the marginalized "other." While arguing that "damage-centered" approaches are situated within broader deficit-based models that "emphasize what a particular student, family, or community is lacking to explain underachievement or failure," Tuck (2009) specifically invokes damage-centered research to specifically describe the epistemic approach of researchers who attempt to take a social justice-based perspective and to account for "historical exploitation, domination, and colonization" to explain brokenness.

But how do these often well-meaning deficit-based and damaged-centered attempts to address educational injustice, actually impact educational injustice? What happens in practice? These approaches come to rely upon one-dimensional narratives of pain and deficiency because the strongest argument becomes: there is nothing good about or happening among the people who are being harmed or injured. Research that presents more substantial and complete portraits of marginalized populations and contexts risk jeopardizing damage-centered and deficit-based arguments that seek to garner sympathy, resources, and reforms from folks who operate from positions of heightened structural power within existing society. These damage-centered and deficit-based approaches rely upon giving benefit of the doubt to peoples operating from institutionally elevated positions of power, presuming that they desire or can be convinced to give up power and make society more just.

But as researchers and intellectuals like Tuck (2009), Coulthard (2014), and Simpson (2017) have pointed out, rather, it is more common to find that the structurally powerful are invested in holding on to their power, and what they have inherited from ancestors who designed systems to benefit them and their visions for the world. Any "resources" or support that is agreed to be provided is rarely substantial enough to transform societal conditions and does not endanger their position in the order. Alterations to society are minor and seek to maintain the existing system as fundamentally "good." And in turn, what does this mean for damaged "others"? It results in the wretched of the research (Wong, 2021), those non-White identified colonially constituted subjects, not being given the benefit of the doubt.

This is what Lamar (2012) is enunciating as he's described his experiences driving through and walking as a young person through Compton. The presumption is that he's up to no good, he needs to be fixed, and that there's something wrong with him – and this perspective is not limited to police and visibly violent agents of the state; this is also enacted by education researchers, teachers, and educators. Through Lamar's (2011; 2012; 2015) ongoing project across his albums, including *good kid, m.A.A.d city, Section.80, To Pimp a Butterfly*, his repertoire of works tries to expose the fact that there are multiple different dimensions to his personhood. Lamar doesn't refuse any of those dimensions. He tries to explore them in the hopes of developing better ways to hold himself and others responsible for harm and violence committed, even as he also does not limit himself to those stereotypes and situates those acts as taking place in relation to systemic injustices. He opens and exposes the harm and violence of damage-centered and deficit-based perspectives, and invites us to conduct research, *otherwise*: what I am referring to as G.o.o.d.K.i.d. research.

G.o.o.d.K.i.d. Research

Generative, not critical for critical's sake,
overstanding, not missing power and anti-Blackness, in the wake,
opening otherwise, death dying, mutual arising, enacting
demonic grounds perspectives, denaturalizing descriptive statements,
Kin-making and cultivating non-biological kinfulness to create alternative arrangements,
introspective of our influence, interdependence, and displacements,
desire-based, devotional, and refusing xenophobia and strangeness, in favor of imagining mutually pleasurable engagements

Generative

This excerpt from "Sing About Me, I'm Dying of Thirst" can help us think about the importance of social justice-based and culturally sustaining research being generative:

You wrote a song about my sister on your tape
And called it *Section.80*
The message resembled "Brenda's Got a Baby"[8]
What's crazy was I was hearin' about it
But doubted your ignorance
How could you ever just put her on blast and shit?
Judgin' her past and shit?

(Lamar, 2012)

In this verse, Lamar is double voicing the sister of someone he rapped about in an earlier project that he did (i.e., "Keisha" from his album Section.80). And on that song, Lamar narrated Keisha's life as a sex worker, trying to garner sympathy for her by describing what happened to her. Following some critical self-reflection and analysis, Lamar came to realize sharing that story, in the ways that he did, was not helpful for sex workers, nor for Keisha or honoring her legacy. *What are you supposed to do with the violent damage-centered and deficit-based narrative that he shared about this woman's sister, Keisha? We are told to just critique, and make whole libraries of critique: but what does this critique actually do?* When we arrive at a position where we ask ourselves – "what can we do with this?" – and we don't like the answer(s), that's a problem. It's a sign we need to move away from White epistemic knowledge production, rooted in the academic–industrial complex, toward generative ways of knowing that come with honoring and furthering life. G.o.o.d.K.i.d. research pushes us to move past critique for critique's sake, and toward research thinking about sustaining and generating socially just worlds.

Overstanding

> Every day I'm hustlin'
> What else is a thug to do
> When you eatin' cheese from the government?
> (Guest verse by Jay Rock on Lamar, 2012, excerpt from "Money Trees")

The concept of overstanding blooms from within Hip Hop epistemologies. Within Hip Hop ways of knowing, being, valuing, and speaking, overstanding is about how when you are looking at some entity in the world, you aren't just trying to comprehend it of itself – you're situating that entity within understandings of power. Some folks in Hip Hop might refer to this as the "Fifth element" (Chang, 2005); a knowledge of self that seeks to understand the relation of your personhood, and position in the world, to how you know what you know.

This can be seen within Jay Rock's guest verse on Lamar's (2012) album. Jay Rock's verse provides an almost ethnographic snapshot of a set of circumstances surrounding Lamar and himself within Compton. Jay Rock illuminates how he, and so many peoples racialized as Black, is pushing and pulling against constraint in the context of the m.A.A.d city. Theft is happening. Violence is happening. Substances are being sold. But how does Jay Rock situate this illustration of social life?: "What else is a thug do/when you eatin' cheese from the government?" Jay Rock asks us to think about how folks in his sociohistorical context have been institutionally and structurally constrained in their lived possibilities: these are the acts that folks like him are often left to do in order to survive. This is overstanding. As we approach our projects of knowing as education researchers, what might it mean to operate from an epistemic approach of overstanding as we examine and interpret peoples, situations, and entities in our worlds?

Opening Otherwises

> Martin had a dream, Kendrick have a dream
> (Lamar, 2012, line from "Backseat Freestyle")

Crucial to Lamar's (2012; 2015) work is this idea about the need to suggest and open otherwises: Does your research help us think about and towards liberatory futures? How are you ontologically positioning yourself, and those whom you are studying, in relation to visions of collective freedom? Is your research concerned with ways we can start building educational institutions and/or establishing practices and processes that will allow us to arrive at visions of collective freedom? Lamar engages in this work within a silly and humorous piece that performatively interrogates Western rationality, "Backseat Freestyle," where he attempts to ontologically inhabit and produce otherwises through the Hip Hop practice of freestyle. That is, he spontaneously produces an expressive piece without the constraint of pre-assigned topic, which relies upon affective and embodied presence and orientations within the immediate circumstances; often guided by some beat-driven stimuli.

What he's pointing out within this episodic moment of freestyle, as he's spontaneously drawn to the topic of his own freedom, is that otherwise work is not free from the forces of systemic injustices. In spite of efforts to sculpt and cultivate worlds by peoples throughout movements for collective freedom, the possibilities for opening otherwises are often only made possible for particular elevated and/ or ratified "leaders" by agents and institutions of the dominant order. Lamar is calling this out: that often even in the context of social justice and struggles for collective freedom, we continue to valorize the visions of "rational" leaders who have been demarcated and endorsed by the U.S. nation-state (Povinelli, 2002). This hierarchical stratification of vision and imaginative work does not provide most folks engaged in struggle, especially those deemed most illegitimate in the eyes of authorities of the state, the opportunities to have their dreams heard, let alone enacted. Lamar's freestyle invites us to collectively reflect upon what it might mean to produce change in the world through centering the voices of everyday folks, the most marginalized on their own terms, and what that could mean for projects of knowing and being concerned with generating and making possible collective freedom (i.e., in part the concern of scholars and intellectuals of "intersectionality," who have sought to meditate on and propel those peoples most structurally relegated out of participation and representation within struggles for social justice; Cho, Crenshaw, & McCall, 2013; Evans-Winters & Esposito, 2019).

Demonic Grounds Perspectives That Denaturalize Descriptive Statements

I put Lamar's (2012; 2015) re-mapping work into conversation with Wynter (1990) and McKittrick's (2006) conceptualization of "demonic grounds." Wynter and McKittrick point out how geographies, all the spaces that we find ourselves in the world, are often overdetermined in our problem-space by Man2; that one representation of humanity has come to dominate who gets to exist on and give meaning to the past, present, and future lands we find ourselves on and traversing.

McKittrick (2006), in building upon Wynter (1990), thinks about how in computing there is this idea about the daemon, the demonic; how there are programs that can operate behind the actual user and operate without them knowing. McKittrick relates this to Wynter's (1990) theorizations around the Western world's larger understandings of the "demonic," the unexplained non-linear and seemingly ungeographic, the iterative understandings and stories that emerge outside of dominant overdetermined modernity; the White European-descended tradition. Specifically considering Black womanhood, Wynter and McKittrick (2015) appeal to us to ask how we can appreciate and reveal the demonic, and support those perspectives that emerge from what they call, demonic grounds.

Relatedly, when Wynter invokes the need to denaturalize "descriptive statements," she's theorizing how every version of humanity, inside and outside of European-descended traditions, has come up with "descriptive statements" to narrativize their respective origin story/ies as a type of human being; and what they're capable of and what they're able to know, do, and be (Wynter & McKittrick, 2015). Wynter challenges us not to only narrate our own stories, but to denaturalize the moments when certain stories[9] come to overdetermine and create stereotypes that construct certain people as not existing, or as existing outside of geographic and spatial-temporal possibilities.

In many ways, this is the project of *good kid, m.A.A.d city*, as Lamar seeks to redefine specifically Black boyness and the geographies of Compton through epistemologies emerging from African diasporic, Black peoples. The album charts Lamar's navigation across a variety of locales in Compton, within a minivan that serves as a literal and figurative vehicle to re-narrate space and re-constitute Blackness from the severing and destructive institutions and relations that he encounters. This is likewise what can be seen across his next album, *To Pimp a Butterfly*, particularly represented in his cinematic music video for his work "Alright." In the music video, Lamar supernaturalizes the ways we imagine the landscape of Blackness in the Bay Area, aurally and visually representing liberation through his flight through and defiance of metaphysics, and even the physics, of the anti-Black m.A.A.d city.

Kin-Making and Cultivating Non-Biological Kinfulness (Collective Responsibility and Co-Conspiracies)

> Sorry to hear what happened to your homeboy, but don't learn the hard way like I did, homie. Any n***** can kill a man, that don't make you a real n****. <u>Real is responsibility. Real is taking care of your motherfuckin family. Real is God, n*****.</u>

> (Guest interlude by Lamar's father on Lamar, 2012, excerpt from "Real"; emphasis is mine)

Within a crucial moment of *good kid, m.A.A.d city*, Lamar (2012) offers the relational knowledges of his father to show that there are different ways of existing together;

to establish an epistemic direction by which to approach what and how we should seek to know, in order to better *be in* the world. Lamar's father interrogates the logics of systems of domination as they have often played out in Compton, whereby your "realness" and prestige are established through your domination of others: in this case, by killing someone. In opposition to racial capitalist expressions of larger White supremacist politics that define life by domination, Lamar's father talks about moving toward a way of knowing and existing where responsibility is what defines us. That is, our responsibility to our families, to each other. While invoked from a Judeo-Christian perspective, Lamar's father is more importantly narrating the possibility of thinking about our broader connections to the universe. He's appealing for us to prioritize being in good relation to that universe, and our relatives in that universe – even outside of our immediate biological kin (i.e., those peoples outside the racial capitalist and cisheteropatriarchal constituted "nuclear family" that could be killed or dominated without concern) – and changing what we value, and therefore, what we decide is and is not worthy to know (Tallbear, 2018).

As education researchers, we can read this as an invitation to re-consider our too often unchallenged "empirical" and "objective" ways we epistemically understand our relations – particularly the naturalized figures of the "participant" and "subject." Does your research look at whom you are researching as objects, subjects, or kin, and what are the consequences? How might our findings change if we thought about our research as a process of engaging in kin-making and cultivating non-biological kinfulness?

Introspective of Your Influence and Interdependence

> I remember you was conflicted
> Misusing your influence
> Sometimes I did the same
> Abusing my power full of resentment
> Resentment that turned into a deep depression
> Found myself screaming in a hotel room
> I didn't want to self-destruct
> The evils of Lucy was all around me
> So I went running for answers
> Until I came home
> But that didn't stop survivors guilt
> Going back and forth
> Trying to convince myself the stripes I earned
> Or maybe how A-1 my foundation was
> But while my loved ones was fighting a continuous war
> Back in the city
> I was entering a new one, a war based on apartheid and discrimination
>
> (Lamar, 2015, excerpt from "Alright")

Lamar (2012; 2015) calls for taking up ways of knowing that are vulnerably situated within forms of relationality that acknowledge our interdependence; which is in alignment with what has been passed down within Black liberation theology and Black feminist traditions of love-politics, like that of James Baldwin (1963) and Toni Morrison (1998). He models a two-way critical reflexivity ("You" and "I did the same"), which pushes us to help each other see when, how, and why we have power in relation to whom we encounter. Through this two-way witnessing, Lamar appeals for knowers to honestly reflect and take responsibility when they abuse their power, or witness others abusing their power; acknowledging the context of how our agency is institutionally expanded and constrained by historical systems of domination. Lamar denaturalizes the dichotomous mythology of "good" and "bad" people through his own admittance of his own complicity in abuse. He locates justice not as an embodied position, but as the act of locating and being accountable for one's actions within the context of an unjust anti-Black and racist society.

Desire-Based and Devotional

Kendrick resists the individualist notion that the violence and harm we commit is wholly our fault, even as he acknowledges the need to take responsibility. He advocates for moving from individualist renderings of accountability, to community responsibility: *Fightin' for your rights, even when you're wrong.*

While m.A.A.d research is arguably anchored in its damaged-centered-ness and deficit-based-ness, we now consider the epistemic foundations of Lamar's (2011; 2012; 2015) work, in conversation with what Eve Tuck (2009) has named as a "desire-based approach." A desire-based approach "accounts for the loss and despair, but also the hope, the visions, the wisdom of lived lives and communities … [it] draws on Indigenous understandings of collectivity and the interdependence of the collective and the person rather than on the Western focus on the individual" (Tuck, 2009).

This is an undertaking Lamar (2015) commits to within his expressive and semiotic project for his song and video for "Alright." Lamar only provides verses and aesthetic visual renderings of oppression, as situated within the larger song and video showcasing unadulterated joy-making and thriving. This includes himself, as he portrays himself rapping, whispering, screaming, getting shot by the police, being carried by the police, smiling, frowning, rocking out with chosen kin, and flying through the setting within the California Bay Area – all within the same project, the same song. He concomitantly focuses on what it might mean to exist, live, resist, *and* move toward futures of thrivance without anti-Blackness and systemic oppressions.

And Lamar (2015) is literally and figuratively enunciating all this through expressive verses *and* film, right? He portrays himself as having the power and possibilities that White supremacist society imagined he cannot possibly have. While Hollywood films overwhelmingly showcase White cishetero male and female superheroes fighting to preserve the current order at all costs, Lamar presents himself as a Black liberatory superhero flying through the city: he's dancing on light poles, hovering and defying gravity, summoning elation, and enacting forms of being that suggest and point to hopeful possibilities and futures of collective freedom.

And closely relating to this desire-based perspective, Lamar calls for our projects of knowing to be devotional, and to honor the sanctity of our lives: what happens when we think about our research as needing to sustain and preserve the sacredness of life?

> **Fightin' for your rights, even when you're wrong,**
> And hope that at least one of you think about me when I'm gone
> Am I worth it? Did I put enough work in?
> When the lights shut off and it's my turn
> To settle down, my main concern
> Promise that you will **sing about me**
>
> (Lamar, 2012, excerpt from "Sing About Me,
> I'm Dying of Thirst"; emphasis mine)

Lamar (2012) engages a very similar politics to James Baldwin (1963). He reflects on how we are not born "evil," but shaped by the institutions and systems around us that both enable our cooperation and complicity with White supremacy and systems of domination, and support us in being responsible for and with each other. Lamar resists the individualist notion that the violence and harm we commit is wholly our fault, even as he acknowledges the need to take responsibility. He advocates for moving from individualist renderings of accountability, to community responsibility: *Fightin' for your rights, even when you're wrong.* Lamar suggests that we need to pursue a societal maturity, a growing up that links the personal to the public (Nash, 2013). He resists overdetermined White supremacist renderings of Judeo-Christian ideologies that suggest justice occurs by biologically and culturally assigning populations as "good" and "evil," and then disposing of the evil-doers.

Accordingly, a devotional approach to knowing the world, and each other, involves giving benefit of the doubt, as we seek to transform ourselves with the world. It involves having faith in our capacity for transformation, actively reflecting and acting upon the harms and violence we commit, and giving grace to and prioritizing justice for peoples who are most impacted by systemic harm and violence (Kaba & Hassan, 2019). It is crucially about transforming society such that those forms of harm and violence are no longer possible, or even imaginable (i.e., what has been rendered as a goal of "transformative justice," and as an aspiration for abolition; Kaba & Hassan, 2019). It is about not just expecting each other to know how to be responsible for each other, and punishing and shaming folks who don't know, but about supporting each other on that journey.

In this way, Lamar (2012) invites us to sing about him, and so many marginalized "others," who are disposed of within an anti-Black criminal punishment system (Kaba & Hassan, 2019). Lamar pleas for projects of knowing that do not refuse or cover up our responsibility for what we have done and will do. Instead, he pleas for us to help each other investigate where we have gone wrong and how we've been hurt. He asks us to situate our actions in the knowledge that we live within an unjust society that needs to be transformed, and in turn, to give each other grace and to operate by a faith in our possibilities for creatively pursuing, imagining, and enacting socially just ways of knowing and being with each other.

And it's important to note that Lamar (2012) is not saying *write about me if you can*, he's asking us to *promise to sing about him*. He's not saying to simply tell his story. This idea about singing about me, which he repeats here, is about a higher form of accountability in how we share knowledge about each other; characterized not by rational and distanced objectivity, but rather impassioned and interdependent collectivity: *will you sing about me?* That's the type of research that he suggests we should pursue, and how we should gather, interpret, and share knowledge. How can we as education researchers pursue knowledge that sings to and about our communities and folks that we're concerned with, which is devotional and shares knowledge in ways that invite us to witness and sustain each other as honored kin?

We Gon' Be Alright: Epistemic Joy and Escaping the Coloniality of Hopelessness

At the end of my talk, which became this chapter, I was asked a question that I didn't expect: *You had so much joy in this presentation, how do you maintain that?* While I hadn't intended to conclude on that question, it occurred to me, *maybe this gracious attendee was on to something which didn't make it into the acronym: G.o.o.d.K.i.d.* I thought about how, maybe, this was how this chapter was always supposed to end.

My first thought after their question: it's hard. Racial capitalist institutions and ideologies have aggressively pushed us to imagine joy as just an expression of laziness, as something that's easy, and even joy as irresponsible in the face of ongoing systemic injustices.

And it can seem hopeless to get there, especially while witnessing the daily atrocities of White supremacy and intersecting systems of domination. We've been increasingly put in positions where we're squeezed to the point where we're just trying to survive, right? But as folks like Bettina Love (2019) remind us, when we become defined by that ontological constraint – survival – and we don't give ourselves time to thrive, then we also don't give ourselves the opportunity to enact those futures that we're trying to strive for. Futures are not some ending that we've never seen, futures are now. So joy must always be now (Estes, 2019).

We have to think about how joy has always existed in the face of the greatest violence and oppression (Camp, 2002; Tuck, 2009). One of the most joyful varieties of musical and cultural production to ever emerge, Hip Hop, literally emerged in one of the most impoverished and anti-Black and oppressive contexts in the then U.S. We have to relatedly think about how even Whiteness might arguably be said to be in part defined by its colonial leeching off of and attempts to constantly steal the processes and practices of joy from among particularly Black peoples, and other peoples across the world, in order to give White identifying peoples opportunities to survive the nihilist, self-destructive soul work of White supremacy. Of course, joy cannot be possessed or stolen, because it's an earnest expression of the human spirit. That's how we arrive at White teens, depressed as they get, famous dancing to dances they didn't imagine, singing songs they didn't craft, and hosting parties imitating bodies they could never inhabit. The coloniality of joy, which is no joy at all.

While we have to give ourselves time to weigh and process emotions to survive, including all those violent attempts to steal our joy, we always have to make time for joy. As Joan Morgan (2015) reminds us, our presence with pleasure and hope, and the thrills of living, foreground all that is worth knowing and being. Since I got down to Los Angeles, I have a friend, Shena, and she'll probably see this chapter in print later, but she's someone who's a cultivator of communities and fun and life, and I've realized that. And when I arrived, she saw my spirit. *She was like I got to chill with Casey, and I was like I got to chill with Shena (#BadAPIs4Life).* She's going to make sure that I'm out here and I'm not just behind a computer or just marching and thinking about joy, instead of living it. And in all we've done together with our chosen kin, I've gained so many intuitive insights to the worlds that we want to create. And that's the radicality of it, that's getting to the root. That's how we generate and maintain joy. That's how we thrive and that's why we need to find community, right? In so many ways, laying the foundation for how and what we should know, Lamar's (2011; 2012; 2015) project is about claiming community and those moments of joy (Chang, 2016), even when we're told those moments shouldn't be the priority, they're wrong, and worst, that they're impossible. So not joy as reward or luxury, joy as epistemology.

We gon' be alright.

Activity

Critically reflect upon the assumptions undergirding your education research project(s):

1. What is the relation of your education research to the overrepresented monohumanist project of Man2?
2. How does your research further and/or question the project of Man2?
3. Is your research aiming to reform or transform education? How do you know?

4. Does your education research support what Wynter refers to as moving towards a "third event"? That is, as aesthetically and intellectually pursued by Lamar, does your research support humans across the world in moving towards narrating and creating their own origin stories, with their own ways of knowing, being, valuing, and speaking? In our case, for education and research?[10]

Notes

1 Significant for this chapter, I would also like to note how I use the terms epistemology, ontology, and axiology. Using these specific terms often means that you have to acknowledge the European-rooted origin stories of these terms, and consider the descent of European cishetero male thinkers from which they are accredited to and from which they emerge. However, I make use of these terms as semiotic placeholders. How do we talk about how we know what we know, and our ways of knowing? Epistemology. How do we talk about ways of being, and the beingness of the world around us? Ontology. How do we talk about how and why we value what we value? Axiology. I don't want us to get stuck on how these terms inevitably reference and point toward European-rooted traditions (see Wong, 2021). I only use these terms as widely circulating and iconic terminology for considering ways of knowing, being, and valuing. I hope to suggest that we only use these terms as needed within a *Chinua Achebe-ian* (1975) tradition of strategic intelligibility, as we move to enact *Ngugi wa Thiong'o-ian* (1986) visions of the world that build outside of these terms, and the worldviews that they indelibly come to structure and reflect.

2 Born Kendrick Lamar Duckworth. Following Hip Hop epistemologies, I do not cite him as "Duckworth," but by the chosen last name that he uses within media, performance, and discourse: Lamar.

3 This chapter was made possible in part by a generous Lyle Spencer Foundation grant with H. Samy Alim and Django Paris exploring culturally sustaining pedagogies.

4 Another name that Kendrick Lamar goes by inside and outside of his work.

5 While the Compton City Council voted to disband the Compton Police Department in July of 2000, as of the summer of 2020, Compton residents were paying $22 million per year to the Los Angeles Sheriff's Department (i.e., the most money per resident in Los Angeles County; Cannick, 2020). As a result of ongoing police brutality against particularly Black adults and youth, Aja Brown and Lamar marched with over 5,000 residents of Compton in one of the largest protests in the history of city.

6 What might be called "rapping," even though my work more closely resembles spoken word with Hip Hop aesthetics (i.e., not all spoken word is expressively linked to Hip Hop practice).

7 While obscured through "indie" mechanisms that E-40 deployed, this was also the case for E-40.

8 Referencing a well-known rap song by legendary rapper, Tupac Shakur.

9 Wynter and McKittrick (2015) are of course very much focused upon the version of humanity in the problem-space of the 19th, 20th and early 21st century, who has come to position itself and all of humanity as being in relation to a Darwinian/Malthusian narrative peculiarity: Man2.

10 Wynter calls for re-narrating the defining moments of the world such that the origin of the universe was the "first event," the explosion of all forms of biological life was the "second event," and the yet to be fully realized "third event" being the emergence of a world with genres of humans being that are defined by both their biology and own mythoi/storytelling. This vision of the "third event" is in opposition to the overdetermined biocentric/economic subject of Man2 (Wynter & McKittrick, 2015; Wong, 2021).

References

Achebe, C. (1975). *Morning yet on creation day: Essays*. Garden City, NY: Anchor Press.

Alim, H. S., Paris, D., & Wong, C. P. (2020). Culturally sustaining pedagogy: A critical framework for centering communities. In N. S. Nasir, C. D. Lee, R. Pea, & M. McKinney de Royston (Eds.), *Handbook of the cultural foundations of learning* (pp. 261–276). London, UK: Routledge. https://doi.org/10.4324/9780203774977-18

Avineri, N., Johnson, E., Brice-Heath, S., McCarty, T., Ochs, E., Kremer-Sadlik, T., & Paris, D. (2015). Invited forum: Bridging the "language gap.". *Journal of Linguistic Anthropology, 25*(1), 66–86.

Baldwin, J. (1963). *The fire next time*. New York, NY: Vintage.

Bang, M., & Vossoughi, S. (2016). Participatory design research and educational justice: Studying learning and relations within social change making. *Cognition & Instruction, 34*(3), 173–193.

Brayboy, B. M. J. (2005). Toward a tribal critical race theory in education. *Urban Review, 37*(5), 425–446. https://doi.org/10.1007/s11256-005-0018-y

Camp, S. M. (2002). The pleasures of resistance: Enslaved women and body politics in the plantation South, 1830–1861. *Journal of Southern History, 68*(3), 533–572.

Césaire, A. (1945). "Poésie et connaissance" [poetry and knowledge]. *Tropiques, 12* (January), 157–170.

Chang, J. (2005). *Can't stop won't stop: A history of the hip-hop generation*. New York, NY: St. Martin's Press.

Chang, J. (2016). *We gon' be alright: Notes on race and resegregation*. New York, NY: Picador.

Cho, S., Crenshaw, K. W., & McCall, L. (2013). Toward a field of intersectionality studies: Theory, applications, and praxis. *Signs: Journal of Women in Culture and Society, 38*(4), 785–810.

Coulthard, G. S. (2014). *Red skin, white masks: Rejecting the colonial politics of recognition*. Minneapolis, MN: University of Minnesota Press. https://doi.org/10.5749/minnesota/9780816679645.001.0001

Coulthard, G., Simpson, L. B., & Walcott, R. (2018). Situating indigenous and Black resistance in the global movement assemblage (video presentation). *Studies in Social Justice, 12*(1), 90–91.

Estes, N. (2019). *Our history is the future: Standing rock versus the Dakota access pipeline, and the long tradition of indigenous resistance*. London, UK: Verso.

Evans-Winters, V. E., & Esposito, J. (2019). Intersectionality in education research: Methodology as critical inquiry and praxis. In N. K. Denzin & M. D. Giardina (Eds.) *Qualitative inquiry at a crossroads: Political, performative, and methodological reflections* (pp. 52–64). London, UK: Routledge.

Fields, K. E., & Fields, B. J. (2014). *Racecraft: The soul of inequality in American life*. London, UK: Verso Trade.

Flores, N. (2013). Silencing the subaltern: Nation-state/colonial governmentality and bilingual education in the United States. *Critical Inquiry in Language Studies, 10*(4), 263–287.

Haile, J. B. III (2018). Good kid, mAAd city: Kendrick Lamar's autoethnographic method. *The Journal of Speculative Philosophy, 32*(3), 488–498.

Hesse, B. (2016). Counter-racial formation theory. In P. K. Saucier & T. P. Woods (Eds.), *Conceptual aphasia in black: Displacing racial formation* (pp. vii–xii). Lanham, MD: Lexington Books.

Inoue, M. (2006). *Vicarious language*. Berkeley, CA: University of California Press.

Kaba, M., & Hassan, S. (2019). *Fumbling towards repair: A workbook for community accountability facilitators*. Chicago, IL: Project NIA.

Ladson-Billings, G. (2021). *Culturally relevant pedagogy: Asking a different question*. New York, NY: Teachers College Press.

Lamar, K. (2011). *Section.80*. Top Dawg Entertainment.

Lamar, K. (2012). *Good kid, m.A.A.d City*. Aftermath.

Lamar, K. (2015). *To pimp a butterfly*. Top Dawg Entertainment.

Love, B. L. (2016). Good kids, mad cities: Kendrick Lamar and finding inner resistance in response to Ferguson USA. *Cultural Studies ↔ Critical Methodologies, 16*(3), 320–323.

Love, B. L. (2019). *We want to do more than survive: Abolitionist teaching and the pursuit of educational freedom*. Boston, MA: Beacon Press.

Martineau, J. (2015). *Creative combat: Indigenous art, resurgence, and decolonization* (Doctoral dissertation).

McKittrick, K. (2006). *Demonic grounds: Black women and the cartographies of struggle*. Minneapolis, MN: University of Minnesota Press.

Morgan, J. (2015). Why we get off: Moving towards a Black feminist politics of pleasure. *The Black Scholar, 45*(4), 36–46.

Morrison, T. (1998, March). From an interview on Charlie Rose: Public Broadcasting Service [video]. Retrieved from: http://www.youtube.com/watch?v=F4vIGvKpT1c

Nash, J. C. (2013). Practicing love: Black feminism, love-politics, and post-intersectionality. *Meridians, 11*(2), 1–24.

Paris, D., & Alim, H. S. (Eds.). (2017). *Culturally sustaining pedagogies: Teaching and learning for justice in a changing world*. New York, NY: Teachers College Press.

Povinelli, E. A. (2002). *The cunning of recognition*. Durham, NC: Duke University Press.

Robinson, C. J. (2000). *Black Marxism: The making of the Black radical tradition*. Chapel Hill, NC: University of North Carolina Press. (Original work published 1983)

Rosa, J. (2019). *Looking like a language, sounding like a race*. Oxford, UK: Oxford University Press.

Rosa, J., & Flores, N. (2017). Unsettling race and language: Toward a raciolinguistic perspective. *Language in Society, 46*(5), 621–647.

Rose, T. (2008). *The hip hop wars: What we talk about when we talk about hip hop—and why it matters*. New York, NY: Civitas Books.

San Pedro, T. (2018). Abby as ally: An argument for culturally disruptive pedagogy. *American Educational Research Journal, 55*(6), 1193–1232. https://doi.org/10.3102/0002831218773488

Simpson, L. B. (2017). *As we have always done: Indigenous freedom through radical resistance* (Kindle version). Minneapolis, MN: University of Minnesota Press.

Tachine, A. R. (2021). The moon will tell us when it will rain. In A. L. Ellis, N. D. Hartlet, G. Ladson-Billings, & D. O. Stovall (Eds.), *Teacher educators as critical storytellers: Effective teachers as windows and mirrors* (pp. 91–101). New York, NY: Teachers College Press.

Tallbear, K. (2018). Making love and relations beyond settler sex and family. In Clarke, A. E., & Haraway, D. J. (Eds.), *Making kin not population* (pp. 145–166). Chicago, IL: Prickly Paradigm Press.

Trouillot, M. R. (1995). *Silencing the past: Power and the production of history*. Boston, MA: Beacon Press.

Tuck, E. (2009). Suspending damage: A letter to communities. *Harvard Education Review, 79*(3), 409–428. https://doi.org/10.17763/haer.79.3.n0016675661t3n15

Wa Thiong'o, N. (1986). *Decolonising the mind: The politics of language in African literature*. Nairobi, Kenya: East African Educational Publishers.

Wong, C. P. (2021). The wretched of the research: Disenchanting Man2-as-educational researcher and entering the 36th chamber of education research. *Review of Research in Education, 45*(1), 27–66.

Wynter, S. (1990). Beyond Miranda's meanings: Un/silencing the "demonic ground" of Caliban's "woman." In C. B. Davies & E. S. Fido (Eds.), *Out of the Kumbla: Caribbean women and literature* (pp. 355–372). Africa World Press. https://trueleappress.files.wordpress.com/2020/04/wynter-beyond-mirandas-meanings-unsilencing-the-demonic-ground-of-calibans-woman-1.pdf

Wynter, S. (2003). Unsettling the coloniality of being/power/truth/freedom: Towards the human, after man, its overrepresentation: An argument. *CR: The New Centennial Review, 3*(3), 257–337. https://doi.org/10.1353/ncr.2004.0015

Wynter, S., & McKittrick, K. (2015). Unparalleled catastrophe for our species? Or, to give humanness a different future: Conversations. In K. McKittrick (Ed.), *Sylvia Wynter: On being human as praxis* (pp. 9–89). Durham, NC: Duke University Press. https://doi.org/10.1215/9780822375852-002

SECTION III

Quantitative and Mixed Methods Innovations

It has always been impossible for me to separate theory from method. How can there be such a thing as critical methods without critical theory or politics and political theory? Can't we embrace theory and politics in the field and work for social justice – out of which our methods are generated – without being accused of 'telling people what to do'? (p. 391).

~ *D. Soynini Madison* ~

Madison, D. S. (2008). Narrative poetics and performative interventions. In N. K. Denzin, Y. S. Lincoln, & L. T. Smith (Eds.), *Handbook of critical and indigenous methodologies* (pp. 391–405). Thousand Oaks, CA: SAGE.

DOI: 10.4324/9781003126621-11

9

USING COUNTERFACTUAL MODELING AND MACHINE LEARNING GENERATED PROPENSITY SCORES TO EXAMINE BLACK SOCIAL CONTROL AND MATHEMATICS

Odis Johnson, Jr., Jason Jabbari

Introduction

In this discussion, we share some of our work concerning the infrastructure of social control. This work is supported by the National Science Foundation and co-produced with my/Johnson's former graduate students who were affiliated with the Race, Gender, and Social Control in STEM Lab (RGSC-STEM). The lab was founded, in part, as a response to the killing of Michael Brown by law enforcement in Missouri and the Ferguson Uprising. We were not oblivious to the reality that the same social forces that led to Michael Brown's death in August of 2014, and Breonna Taylor's some years later, were the same social forces that shaped the school experiences of Black youth, and that determined a non-trivial extent whether they excelled in mathematics or not. Therefore, this work draws from theoretical perspectives particular to the sociology of law and order – primarily social control and justice – and broadening participation theory in science, technology, engineering, and mathematics (STEM; Powell et al., 2018) to understand educational institutions' Black social control technologies.

Yet the RGSC-STEM lab was also rooted in the reality that the United States has struggled for decades to broaden the participation of underrepresented racial groups in STEM. The groups that tend to be underrepresented in mathematics courses, degree programs, and professions are the same racial groups that tend to be overrepresented in school discipline statistics and the school-to-prison pipeline. Racial marginalization and systemic racism are the ties that bind social control and justice to mathematics inequity and stymied STEM workforce development.

As we will demonstrate later, there are many school components that facilitate social control, and together form a carceral ecosystem of risk for youth. In this discussion, we will summarize these colluding social forces and explain how

DOI: 10.4324/9781003126621-12

we have sought to research them using counterfactual modeling, and machine learning-generated propensity scores. We end this discussion with a summary of what the Race, Gender, and Social Control in STEM Lab have learned related to policymaking, research, and justice.

Social Control in Education and the Carceral Ecosystem

The concept of social control concerns how a society maintains social order. Social control is often accomplished via *internal group regulation* (Kirk, 2009) in which individuals adhere to and internalize shared norms (Durkheim, 1961). Others have noted social control acts as a *repressive moral code* (Massey, 1996) in which stigma, embarrassment, and the fear of ostracism lead individuals to conform to social norms. However, as Janowitz (1975) observed, "any social order, including a society with a relatively effective system of social control, will require an element of coercion" (p. 84), or what we call formal social control. Formal social control has been described as the actions of state apparatuses (Althusser, 1970) and their technologies (Foucault, 1979) that establish the institutional regulation of life (Lacombe, 1996), and the laws, government action, and institutions that arise in reaction to perceived deviance (Parsons, 1937).

Schools too are agents of formal social control since most of them are state institutions or regulated by the state. In schools, social control is used to secure and maintain a safe and orderly environment conducive to learning, socialize youth by supporting their character and moral development, and formalize the sorting and allocating of youth into adult roles for the purposes of reproducing the initial expression of social order in the U.S., (i.e., settler colonialism, patriarchy, cisgender domination, white racial supremacy, etc.). In this discussion, we are interested in what Foucault called the *technologies of social control*, meaning what are the mechanisms, tools, and actual technological equipment that societies and institutions use to compel conformity?

In the past, these conversations were framed by the "school-to-prison" (STP) pipeline concept, which typified the fear that school experiences were leading students to jail cells instead of college classrooms. However, we view the singular connection of the STP pipeline to incarceration as too narrow to capture the effects of social control on learning and other outcomes. In this discussion, I review seven of the most common components of social control that form a carceral ecosystem within schools with far-reaching consequences for mathematics learning, advanced math course taking, high school completion, college entry, and disciplinary actions.

The first is the *state and federal policy and statutory context*. The policy infrastructure of social control includes zero tolerance laws, which became widespread with the passage of the Gun-Free Schools Act of 1994. The law urged states to enact inflexible and mandatory triggers for expulsion when students were suspected of safety violations, such as assaulting school personnel or bringing a weapon to school (U.S. Congress, 1994; Skiba & Rausch, 2006). These mandatory triggers seem reasonable on the surface; however, they had the effect of eliminating the consideration of intent for youth, which is taken into account for adult suspects and can mean the difference between involuntary manslaughter and a first-degree murder charge.

For example, if a school administrator chose to break up a scuffle between students and stepped in the way of a punch that was not intended for the administrator, the offending student would be expelled despite having no intention of hitting a staff member. Under zero tolerance policy, it would not matter that the student was acting in self-defense at the time the school official intervened. As zero tolerance became wide-spread, states also reclassified what would otherwise be normative child and adolescent behavior into prosecutorial offenses. In 2017 for instance, a Missouri state law went into effect reclassifying fighting and causing emotional distress from misdemeanor offenses to class A felonies, punishable with up to four years in jail for age groups as young as 7 (Matos, 2017).

The next component of social control is *cultural policing*, and it extends from the school's task of supporting the moral and character development of students. This commitment to have students reflect the morals and character of dominant social classes is enshrined in district codes of student conduct, including dress codes. A school's dress code reflects the institution's preference for student apparel and hairstyle, among other cultural aesthetics, giving school personnel the authority to apply sanctions to perceived deviations from preferred social norms. While healthy and affirming schools often have dress codes in place to minimize possible distractions in the classroom, these standards of representation are often subjective, and oftentimes demand students conform to normative appearances that may not align with their identity.

The cases of Andrew Johnson and DeAndre Arnold stand as examples; both Black students were barred from school activities, and in the case of the latter, suspended, until they agreed to cut their dreadlocks (Ahmed, 2018; Griffith, 2020). Arnold's school claimed that the young man's hair length, not cultural style, was the reason why he was punished (Griffith, 2020). Implicit within this reasoning is the schools' preference for normative gender appearances, that is, boys and young men with shorter hair. Cultural policing of students' gender and sexual orientation expression occurs routinely, leaving them (especially gender nonconforming girls) with a greater likelihood of receiving harsh discipline roughly three times that of their heterosexual counterparts (Brückner & Himmelstein, 2011) and suffering similar attacks from peers (Hunt & Moodie-Mills, 2012).

The third facet of school social control is the *technologies of surveillance* they put in place to restrict the entry of potentially harmful contraband (i.e., weapons and drugs), and to identify threats of intrusion from individuals who are not authorized to be on school grounds. However, technologies are also used in detecting the perceived deviance of students, restricting liberties, and encouraging self-regulation (Foucault, 1979). Metal detectors, facial recognition programs, and security cameras are among the technologies that have been adopted and implemented in a growing number of schools (Addington, 2014; Ascione, 2019).

It is important to understand the power technology has in shaping social narratives of crime and deviance. For example, decades ago, Ditton (1979) argued that crime waves could in fact reflect innovations in our ability to detect perceived crime rather than changes in rates of offending, and therefore might more appropriately be called "control waves." Advances in technologies of control, an increased reliance on them, along with a hardening of behavioral standards may be critical components of a recent control wave that has taken place in our schools. Hence, institutional dynamics rather than increases in deviance might explain why the STP pipeline has flourished even as rates of school violence have remained stagnant (Johnson, 2015; Muschert, Henry, Bracy, & Peguero, 2014).

Law enforcement is the fourth aspect of social control in U.S. schools. Since the Columbine mass shooting in 1999, the funding of officers to remain on school premises during school hours has been a frequent policy response to enhance the safety of schools (Muschert et al., 2014). Data from the National Center for Education Statistics (NCES) found roughly 61 percent of U.S. high schools had security personnel on school grounds in the 2017–18 academic years (NCES, 2019). While steps should be taken to prevent horrifying school shootings, police officers on school premises are merely a treatment rather than a solution. In fact, we are aware of no research showing the rate of school shootings has declined as the percentage of schools with SROs has grown (Johnson, Jabbari, Williams, & Marcucci, 2019).

There is evidence, however, that the presence of law enforcement within schools leads to the criminalization of students, and particularly Black students. For example, schools with SROs have, on average, a 12.3 percent higher referral rate than schools without them; between 2015 and 2018, school-related arrests and referrals to law enforcement in U.S. schools have increased 5 and 12 percent, respectively (Office for Civil Rights, 2021). Black students are especially impacted by arrests and referrals; they constitute 28.7 percent of referrals to law enforcement, and 31.6 percent of school arrests despite being just 15.1 percent of total school enrollment (Office for Civil Rights, 2021). Outsourcing classroom management and school discipline to the authorities, and criminalizing normative adolescent behavior and creating more criminals in the process, are counterproductive to the goal of school safety.

Fifth, we include *punishment and punitive ideologies* as a vital component of social control. Rather than considering punishment as merely an outcome of social control, we should also understand it as an ideology and the labeling and self-fulfilling processes it occasions. Unlike discipline, punishment sanctions behavior without the steps necessary to secure students' internalization of moral objectives, oftentimes labeling students as "no good" and "trouble-makers" instead of reaffirming their potential, and the behavioral and attitudinal modifications they need to take to achieve their potential. Without attending to the internalization of codes of moral and character development, punishment may instead increase students' feelings of unfairness, resentment, and the likelihood of future norm violations. Or worse, students may begin to embrace those labels of low expectation, seek respect through problematic behavior, and consequently realize a self-fulfilling prophesy for educators (Ferguson, 2001; Rist, 1970).

Discipline in contrast is a process in which school personnel facilitates students' internalization of the moral objectives associated with social sanctions, possibly through modeling due process, and fair and consistent consequences, so that self-regulation will prevent future behavioral violations (Bailey, Meland, Brion-Meisels, & Jones, 2019).

Political economic neoliberalism is the sixth facet of social control. It supports the application of market principles to social objectives and problems, while purporting to decentralize government control over social services and increasing individual freedom of choice (Harvey, 2007; Lipman, 2011). The view of schools as the primary contexts of labor market skill development (Bowles & Gintis, 1976), and as particularly difficult to reform agents of adult role allocation within society's economic apparatus (Henig, Hula, Orr, & Pedescleaux, 2001), has set the stage for policymakers and economists to promote market approaches to educational change.

Yet, decentralization and the introduction of market principles have also advanced carceral education through the proliferation of "no excuses" charter schools. No excuses charter schools are a subgroup of charter schools that typically have, among other features, a highly regimented educational experience, and expansive zero tolerance policies that include penalties for minor infractions and personal movement (e.g., position of hands, walking with hands at side, etc.) (Golann, 2015; Advocates for Children, 2015). As a consequence, charter schools tend to have inordinately high suspension rates, like in New York City, where charter schools enrolled roughly 7 percent of the district's student population, but accumulated nearly 42 percent of its suspensions in 2014 (Joseph & CityLab, 2016). Investment in exclusionary disciplinary practices in no excuses charter schools like KIPP have led to high student attrition, in some schools reaching 50 percent – undoubtedly positively inflating the network's student test outcomes through selectively pushing out targeted students (Henig, 2008; Woodworth, David, Guha, Wang, & Lopez-Torkos, 2008).

The *neighborhood context* is the seventh and final component of social control. The disparate impact of carceral education on minoritized students is enabled by the unequal geography of punishment that concentrates social control devices within racially segregated cities and neighborhoods. The concentration of poverty within largely Black neighborhoods in the later quarter of the 20th century laid the foundation for "tough on crime" political decisions that enacted stiffer penalties and zero tolerance laws to supposedly gain control of those disadvantaged areas (Alexander, 2010).

There are three critical connections between neighborhood composition and social control. First, concentrated disadvantage also concentrates kids with the greatest educational needs in educational institutions with the greatest tendency to punish those needs. Housing instability (Ferguson, Bender, Thompson, Xie, & Pollio, 2012), food insecurity (Kleinman et al., 1998), among other poverty-related conditions became social determinants of both limited opportunities to learn and higher chances of being identified for punishment. Second, racial segregation and concentrated poverty are associated with a heavier police presence (Johnson et al., 2019), which contributes to higher neighborhood incarceration rates (Clear., 2007) and youth interaction with law enforcement (Shedd, 2015). Third, racially integrated neighborhoods enact social control strategies to contend with heterogeneity. For example, public schools hoping to keep their neighboring white middle-class students from leaving their schools for private options position white students and diversity as beneficiaries of disproportionately high Black suspension and expulsion rates. Stratification scholars have long observed that schools within neighborhoods with a larger presence of white middle-class families were among the most stratified because higher-resourced white families demanded it (Jencks & Mayer, 1990; Lofton, 2021) and were skillful at hoarding resources and opportunities (Lewis-McCoy, 2014).

Making the Connection to STEM

As we briefly mentioned earlier in this discussion, the Race, Gender, and Social Control in STEM Lab were led by the realization that the same forces at play in the police killings of Tamir Rice, Rekia Boyd, and many other people of color structure the social and racial climate of schools, and opportunities to learn mathematics. While linkages between social control and mathematics were not common within funded NSF work: we made the linkage convincing to program officers by hypothesizing the highly regimented educational structure and conformity-seeking school strategies (i.e., social control) to which certain race-gender groups[1] are disproportionately exposed, are related to lowered levels of the qualities that are known to support success in STEM, including collaborative problem solving, creativity, learning through discovery, engagement, and self-efficacy.

Similar questions of whether the highly regimented instructional approach of no-excuses charter schools, such as Achievement First, positions students as passive learners (Lopez Kershen, Weiner, & Torres, 2019) and lack the ability to cultivate students' ability to "think for themselves" (Taylor, 2018). Hence, the link between social control in school and STEM inopportunity extends beyond the higher probability that Black and Latinx students will be referred to authorities, to the risk that poorly and well-behaved students alike will have their potential to innovate stifled by schools that overemphasize the importance of order. In the end, NSF provided us the opportunity to show them that filling the STEM pipeline required schools to first drain the school-to-prison pipeline and decarcerate by reevaluating their social control strategies.

To address these possibilities, our research lab posed the following general questions:

1. What are the short-term (math outcomes) and long-term (college attendance) effects associated with attending a high social control school (HSCS) and how are these impacts related?

2. How do the effects associated with directly receiving a suspension differ from the spillover effects associated with attending a HSCS?

As we pursued answers to these questions, we first recognized that existing analyses of social control effects were of local samples, and that there was a need for generalizable knowledge about the experiences of the average high school student in the U.S. (Kinsler, 2013; Perry & Morris, 2014). Subsequently, our team decided to pursue answers with the most recent nationally representative longitudinal surveys of high school students available through the NCES, the Educational Longitudinal Study (ELS) of 2002 and the High School Longitudinal Study (HSLS) of 2009. Second, we also acknowledged attendance in these high schools was not random: kids are enrolled in schools due to their social background characteristics – namely, their SES, racial/ethnic background, residency, among others – which research has found significantly related to mathematics and discipline outcomes.

Research up to this point had yet to use statistical methods that addressed the problem of non-random selection into schools, and the biases that tend to weaken the inferences about the relatedness of social phenomena. We therefore elected to use a counterfactual framework based on machine learning-estimated propensity scores (i.e., the predicted probability that an individual with certain qualities will experience a treatment when assignment is essentially nonrandom) to limit selection bias in the estimation of treatment effects associated with attending HSCS.

Third, we also understood that social control could give rise to a carceral ecosystem made up of the constructs we have already reviewed in this discussion, and therefore individual, school, and residential factors would need to be considered to take into fuller account the structure of carceral education. Therefore, we combined the counterfactual model with a multilevel approach to control for any between-unit variation in schools and residential areas, as there may be notable difference among them (see Snijders & Bosker, 2011; Jabbari & Johnson, 2020b). Fourth, we focused on in-school suspension (ISS) as our preferred indicator of discipline since it is less often studied in relation to math and recent moratoriums on out-of-school suspension may have heightened the use of ISS (Jabbari & Johnson, 2020a).

Finally, we adopted critical theoretical lenses in which we: (a) named systemic racism as a likely instigator of discipline and mathematics inequity (Johnson & Jabbari, 2021a); (b) acknowledged the history of place-based discrimination as a force that gathered people of color involuntarily, for greater and more efficient exposure to high social control; and (c) pursued intersectional analyses to show how students who are simultaneously gendered and raced experience social control via the prism of multiple social locations (Johnson & Jabbari, 2021b). We do not assume systemic racism is something that must be proven via analysis – rather, it is a prima facie social default to be disproven in statistical work, and to note with curiosity and interrogate when found insignificant. In the section that follows, we provide a methodological overview of how the Race, Gender, and Social Control in STEM Lab modeled these relationships.

Counterfactual Modeling and Machine Learning Generated Propensity Scores

We used a quantitative-computational mixed methodology, advanced analytical techniques to strengthen statistical inferences, nationally representative longitudinal data, and stringent models that also considered measures
prior performance, average levels of social disorder, and multiple units of
analysis (i.e., individual, school, and neighborhood).

Our approach to the estimation of social control effects involved counterfactual modeling, in which we come closer to supportable causal inferences without utilizing random assignment. In our approach, we identified two treatment
conditions, HSCS and low social control schools (LSCS) as we would in an
experiment. Since we did not have the luxury of random assignment, propensity scores were used to weight these data, according to the background
characteristics of students, to adjust for uneven selection of students into the
treatment categories. "Inverse probability of treatment weights" (IPTW) represented the predicted probability that individuals with *certain qualities* would
experience a treatment when assignment to those conditions was essentially
nonrandom.

Using both the ELS and HSLS samples, we searched for measures of school-
level attributes that reflected features of the previously summarized carceral
ecosystem to identify treatment categories. These longitudinal studies did
not include information on all the ecosystem attributes, but we were able to
construct a treatment variable with each sample that reflected attendance at
a HSCS, as opposed to attending a LSCS. The restricted-use ELS data provided a wealth of measures about the schools' social control infrastructure,
primarily through its Facilities Checklist Survey. The HSCS treatment variable reflected surveillance, including a school average of the following administrator variables: having a metal detector; having random metal detector
checks; closing the campus for lunch; having random dog sniffs; having random contraband sweeps; having drug testing; requiring uniforms; enforcing
strict dress codes; requiring clear book bags; requiring identification badges
for students; requiring identification badges for faculty; and having security
cameras. Based on this measure, high schools were broken down into three
distinct groups, creating a range of school usage of surveillance strategies.
The highest third was operationalized as high-surveillance schools, while
the lowest third was operationalized as low-surveillance schools (the middle
third was dropped).

HSLS in contrast had few measures of school social control since it did not
field the Facilities Checklist like its predecessor, the ELS. Therefore, the HSCS
treatment in the HSLS analysis reflected punishment in the form of ISS instead

of surveillance. Using a student-level, self-reported measure of ISS within the previous six months a base-year student weight, a weighted mean of suspensions was created for each individual high school. This created a school-level measure of ISSs that was representative of both schools and the students attending them. Based on this measure, high schools were broken down into five quintiles of equal distributions, creating a range of school typologies based on suspensions. The highest quintile was operationalized as high-suspension high schools, while the lowest quintile was operationalized as low-suspension high schools. Together, the HSLS and ELS presented an opportunity to make distinctions between the impact of punishment in an analysis of high suspensions schools from the impact of attending highly surveilled schools in relation to mathematics and college entry.

Counterfactual Modeling

As explained in Johnson and Wagner (2017), counterfactual modeling provides an advance over traditional observational approaches to data analysis because it not only tests the primary hypothesis about potential HSCS effects, but the alternative educational experience or LSCS is also tested. In our counterfactual framework, the treatment and non-treatment participants have potential outcomes in both states: the state in which they are observed and the state in which they are not observed (Rubin, 2005). Thus, the average treatment effect (ATE) in this study can be considered the difference in the potential outcomes associated with attending either high or low-suspension schools for all students. By examining both treatments and meeting key statistical assumptions, counterfactual modeling can allow researchers to make inferences that can approach causality.

The strongly ignorable treatment assignment assumption is the first of these assumptions, and requires that conditional on observed covariates, treatment assignment is independent of potential outcomes (Rosenbaum & Rubin, 1983). By utilizing observed covariates of both the treatment and the outcome in the propensity score estimation model, as well as the main analytical models, we can reasonably assume that we will control for most major confounding variables. A second assumption, the stable unit value treatment assumption, requires that "observation on one unit should be unaffected by the particular assignment of treatments to the other units" (Cox, 1958). In this regard, we can reasonably assume that there are few interactions between students that receive different treatments, as their treatments occur in different physical spaces (schools) that are often separated by substantial physical distances. However, in our analyses – due to the fact the initial measure of math achievement test scores occurred within the treatment duration, as well as the fact that there was not an exact pre-treatment measure of college attendance – the nature of our counterfactual models does not allow for true causal claims, but rather associational claims that are less prone to selection bias.

Machine Learning Generated Propensity Scores

> In propensity score analyses, persons are not "assigned to a particular treat-
> ment." Rather, propensity scores either weight samples via propensity scores
> to equalize the probabilities of assignment given individuals' pre-observed
> assignment, or select the most similar case for comparison among individ-
> uals who have already experienced the treatment. Only in experiments can
> we assign people to treatments, whether covariates are used to inform that
> assignment or not.

Our studies used an eight-step method in estimating propensity scores, which
can be summarized as follows:

1. Select covariates that are theoretically related to selection into the treatments, the underlying treatment mechanisms, the outcomes associated with
   the treatments, and meet temporal assumptions
2. A propensity score was estimated based on the observed covariates of a specific treatment using generalized boosted regression models (GBM)
3. An IPTW was created based on the propensity score
4. Propensity score weights were multiplied by the necessary survey weights
5. Checks were completed to ensure observed covariates were properly
   balanced
6. Checks were completed to ensure normally distributed and adequately over-
   lapped scores
7. Weighted analyses of the specified treatment were completed
8. Sensitivity analysis was performed to ensure that unobserved covariates
   were not confounders

First, since we were unable to assume student selection into these treatments
occurred randomly, a set of observed covariates that are theoretically related to
selection into the treatments and the outcomes associated with the treatments in
our studies, were used in the propensity score estimation model. The inclusion of
these variables in the propensity score estimation models not only limited potential biases in treatment assignment (HSCS and LSCS) but also balanced students'
pre-dispositional characteristics related to the underlying treatment mechanisms,
as well as the characteristics that are known to impact the outcomes under study
(high school math achievement and college attendance). Variables that occurred
before treatment assignment were preferred to meet the temporal assumption
that the treatment occurred before the outcome.

In the second step, we estimated propensity scores using a machine learning
application, GBM. GBM was used because model misspecification errors have
been shown to bias estimates of treatment effects in other approaches, especially

in analyses with binary outcomes (see Drake, 1993; Freedman & Berk, 2008), while nonparametric modeling approaches, such as GBM, have been shown to reduce the chance of these errors (McCaffrey, Ridgeway, & Morral, 2004). GBM utilizes automated, data adaptive modeling algorithms to "predict treatment assignment from a large number of pretreatment covariates while also allowing for flexible, non-linear relationships between the covariates and the propensity score" (McCaffrey, Ridgeway, & Morral, 2004, p. 3). GBM repeatedly fits decision trees to improve the accuracy of the model. A decision tree is a tool that uses a tree-like flowchart of options, tests, and possible outcomes. For each new tree in the model, a random subset of all data is selected using the boosting method.

In the estimation of IPTWs for the treatment, this study utilized the TWANG – Toolkit for Weighting and Analysis of Non-equivalent Groups – package (Ridgeway, McCaffrey, Morral, Burgette, & Griffin, 2014) in STATA. In doing so, both mean effect sizes and max Kolmogorov-Smirnov (KS) statistics were used to assess covariate balance. Fourth, as recommended by DuGoff, Schuler, and Stuart (2014) for inferences on populations (as opposed to samples), we multiplied the propensity score weights by the provided survey weights within TWANG to preserve the representativeness of the samples.

We next viewed the results of the propensity score estimation to confirm that all treatment covariates were properly balanced; there was no significantly different treatment group means among our model covariates. In step 6, we confirmed that propensity scores for both treatment and control groups shared an adequate region of common support, which was also the case when looking at the distribution of propensity score survey weights. These checks supported our conclusion that participants with similar treatment covariates have a theoretical probability of being in either the treatment or control group (Rosenbaum & Rubin, 1983). In step 7, we ran the analysis in which, following Guo and Fraser's (2014) notation, the ATE weights for cases in the first treatment group (LSCS) reflected $w_i = 1/p(x_i)$, while the ATE weights for cases in the second treatment group (HSCSs) reflected $w_i = 1/(1-p(x_i))$. Last, we performed a sensitivity analysis as our final step in the process and found that our models were robust to unobserved covariates that could potentially confound our analysis.

Summary & Concluding Thoughts

Using these methods, the Race, Gender, and Social Control in STEM Lab has generated three studies demonstrating the connection of social control to STEM (Jabbari & Johnson, 2020a; Johnson & Jabbari, 2021a; Johnson & Jabbari, 2021b), and five additional ones using structural equation modeling, hierarchical linear modeling, or a combination of these methodologies (Barnes & Johnson, 2018; Ibrahim & Johnson, 2020; Jabbari & Johnson, 2020b; Ibrahim, Barnes, Butler-Barnes, & Johnson, 2021; Jabbari & Johnson, 2021). What we have learned during the course of our work has established social control as a societal force that operates in the profession of education as it has within the profession of policing – exacerbating the racialization of criminalization, and directly contributing to the underrepresentation of minoritized youth in STEM. Using a quantitative-computational mixed methodology, advanced analytical techniques to strengthen statistical inferences, nationally representative longitudinal data, and stringent models that also considered measures prior performance, average levels of social disorder, and multiple units of analysis (i.e. individual, school, and neighborhood), our analysis found the following.

High Suspension Schools Lower Average Math Performances and College Entry Rates

Our analysis of HSLS data defined HSCS as average rates of ISS, and revealed HSCS was related to lower than average student mathematics test performances and decreased odds of attending college; 43% chance versus a 57% chance for high and low suspension schools, respectively. We confirmed these spillover effects in HSCS on college attendance and math achievement are similar – and at times greater – than the direct effects associated with a student receiving an ISS. A larger share of Black students was enrolled in high suspension schools than in low suspension schools (Jabbari & Johnson, 2020a).

Surveillance in HSCS Has Negative Effects Net of the Punishment It Facilitates

Our analysis of ELS data investigated a second type of social control, surveillance, and revealed 12th grade math test scores was significantly lower in HSCS and remained so after considering prior mathematics performances and individual suspensions. Apparently, the impact of surveillance is not limited to the identification of students for punishment, implying that schools with both a pronounced surveillance infrastructure and high suspension rates might compound the negative impacts of high social control. This surveillance setback would be most acute for Black students since Black enrollment was greatest in HSCS; nearly a quarter of all Black students were enrolled at HSCS compared to only 6 percent at LSCS (Johnson & Jabbari, 2021b).

The implications of this work are far-reaching for STEM fields, policymakers, and educators, especially those who are questioning how they might act in an era in which mass incarceration and fatal interactions with police have become more prominent obstacles to racial justice. This discussion has argued that the social forces at work in the hyper criminalization of Black communities are also at work within schools and their approaches to discipline, with consequences for mathematics equity. These study results suggest that schools should consider alternative approaches to securing safe and orderly climates conducive to learning, including restorative practices and trauma-informed practices. As we have argued elsewhere, the most effective way to create safe school environments is to support feelings of belonging, school connectedness, and fairness with transparent due processes so that youth internalize a commitment to shared norms of character and morals, and institutional culture (Bailey et al., 2019).

It is also important to note an anti-bias/anti-racists commitment and tools to achieve it are essential, since neither trauma-informed practices nor restorative justice can be effective in organizations that simultaneously hold deficit and anti-Black perspectives about students (Johnson et al., 2019). Likewise, policymakers should consider reforms that implement moratoriums on out-of-school suspensions for subjective offenses, but also how ISS might be refashioned to mitigate the impact of disciplinary actions on mathematics performances instead of exacerbating those effects.

Our analyses suggest dual objectives of eliminating racial disparities in ISS and mathematics make Black females more likely and Black males equally likely to attend college as other race-gender groups (Johnson & Jabbari, 2021b). Therefore, a convincing rationale exists for repurposing ISS as an opportunity for intensive math interventions to accelerate student learning. Along with reform of ISS, other statutes and policies related to zero tolerance, disturbance statutes, and codes of conduct should be reviewed with a focus on racial and ethnic equity, using data on DMC rates and referrals as important indicators of evaluative impact. These reforms should engage the other arenas within the ecosystem, including policy agencies that place law enforcement on school grounds (Philadelphia School Diversion Program, 2017), and lawmakers that legislate statutes that criminalize and stiffen sanctions for perceived misbehavior.

This work also presents implications for research. First, it is unfortunate that NCES did not include the Facilities Checklist in the design of its HSLS longitudinal survey, and we hope that it will be included in the High School and Beyond Study of 2022. Identifying schools that relied heavily on surveillance technologies was only possible because the Facilities Checklist included measures about the presence of metal detectors, cameras, among others relevant school features. Since HSLS does not have this capability, the nation has become blind to possible changes in the use and impact of surveillance technologies within its high schools. Our findings suggest the NCES should not only restore these measures but include others that collect data about the use of AI (Buolamwini & Gebru, 2018), facial recognition software (Ropke, 2019), how those biometrics are used to maintain order, and their impact on racial equity. Second, our studies show that estimates generated without controlling for selection are artificially inflated (Jabbari & Johnson, 2020a), suggesting more analytical strategies to address selection need to be applied in social control research.

Finally, our work only addresses a small area of the much larger carceral ecosystem of education. More work is needed to address its other aspects – cultural policing, no excuses charter schools, among others – may have effects that relate to racial justice, math equity, and contribute to a fuller accounting of the infrastructure of social control.

Activity

The inequities revealed by the RGSC-STEM Lab suggest more research is needed to expand our knowledge about the racially disparate impact of social control within schools. The following exercise takes through the initial step of conceptualizing a counterfactual framework. Once this three-step conceptualization is completed, researchers will be better prepared to work with appropriate data and follow steps 1 to 8 in this chapter's propensity score estimation procedures.

1. Considering the seven most common social control components of the carceral educational system summarized in this chapter, identify at least three constructs per component that can be related to social control (e.g., dress code violations, teacher use of commands, etc.). In this stage of the activity, you should keep in mind the most appropriate constructs should reflect authority, power imbalances, and social norms of behavior.

State and Federal Policy/ Statutory Context	Cultural Policing	Technologies of Surveillance	Law Enforcement	Punishment and Punitive Ideologies	Political Economy	Neighborhoods
1.						
2.						
3.						

2. Confirm that each social control construct is a condition all units (e.g., teachers, students, classes, professional development sessions) have, in theory, a reasonable probability of experiencing, and on which they can be dichotomized as having experienced it or not. Keep in mind that dosage and the severity of the experience can also be segmented into treatment categories.
3. For each construct, select at least seven covariates that are theoretically related to a) selection into the treatments, b) the underlying treatment mechanisms, c) the outcomes associated with the treatments, and d) can meet temporal assumptions. For example, if the construct is no-excuses charter school, then residency would be important covariates since the distance of the school from home often determines enrollment and the quality of the neighborhood in which children live might relate to parents' appreciation of schools that stress order and safety. Finally, residency, for example, usually precedes enrollment, which meets pre-treatment temporal assumptions.

Note

1 Race-gender is "black female, white female, Asian trans, etc." whereas race and gender groups are "black, white, Latinx, male, female, non-binary ..."

References

Taylor, K. (2018, January 11). Achievement first. *New York Times*. Retrieved from https://www.nytimes.com/2018/01/11/nyregion/can-a-no-excuses-charter-teach-students-to-think-for-themselves.html

Addington, L. (2014). Surveillance and security approaches across school levels. In G. Muschert, G. Stuart Henry, N. L. Bracy, & A. A. Peguero (Eds.), *Responding to school violence: Confronting the columbine effect* (pp. 71–88). Boulder, CO: Lynne Rienner Publishers.

Ahmed, S. (2018, December 23). The cutting of a teenage wrestler's hair was a familiar act of violence for black athletes. *The Guardian*. Retrieved from https://www.theguardian.com/sport/2018/dec/23/andrew-johnson-high-school-wrestler-dreadlocks-cut.

Alexander, M. (2010.) *The new Iim Crow. Mass incarceration in the age of colorblindness*. New York, NY: The New Press.

Althusser, L. (1970). *Ideology and ideological state apparatuses: Notes towards an Investigation*. Lenin and Philosophy and Other Essays. Retrieved from https://www.marxists.org/reference/archive/althusser/1970/ideology.htm

Ascione, L. (2019). Is facial recognition in schools reassuring–or invasive? *eSchool News*. Retrieved from https://www.eschoolnews.com/2019/02/28/facial-recognition-in-schools

DuGoff, E., Schuler, M., & Stuart, E. (2014). Generalizing observational study results: Applying propensity score methods to complex surveys. *Health Services Research*, *49*(1), 284–303. https://doi.org/10.1111/1475-6773.12090

Bailey, R., Meland, E. A., Brion-Meisels, G., & Jones, S. M. (2019, August 21). Getting developmental science back into schools: Can what we know about self-regulation help change how we think about "no excuses"? *Frontiers in Psychology*, *10*(1885). https://doi.org/10.3389/fpsyg.2019.01885

Barnes, D., & Johnson, O. Jr. (2018). The influence of parent socialization and school environment on African-American adolescent males' mathematics self-efficacy and engineering career trajectory. *Frontiers in Education Conference (FIE)*, 1–7. https://doi.org/10.1109/FIE.2018.8658772

Bowles, S., & Gintis, H. (1976). *Schooling in capitalist America: Educational reform and the contradictions of economic life*. New York, NY: Basic Books.

Brückner, H., & Himmelstein, K. (2011). Criminal justice and school sanctions against nonheterosexual youth: A national longitudinal study. *Pediatrics*, *27*, 49–57. https://doi.org/10.1542/peds.2009-2306

Buolamwini, J., & Gebru, T. (2018). Gender shades: Intersectional accuracy disparities in commercial gender classification. *Proceedings of Machine Learning Research*, *81*, 1–15. Retrieved from https://proceedings.mlr.press/v81/buolamwini18a/buolamwini18a.pdf

Clear, T. (2007). *Imprisoning communities: How mass incarceration makes disadvantaged neighborhoods worse*. Oxford: Oxford University Press.

Cox, D. R. (1958). *Planning of experiments*. New York, NY: Wiley & Sons, Inc.

Ditton, J. R. (1979). *Controlology: Beyond the new criminology*. London: Palgrave Macmillian.

Drake, C. (1993). Effects of misspecification of the propensity score on estimators of treatment effect. *Biometrics*, *49*, 1231–1236. https://doi.org/10.2307/2532266

Durkheim, E. (1961). *Moral education: A study in the theory and application of the sociology of education.* New York, NY: Free Press.

Ferguson, A. A. (2001). *Bad boys: Public schools in the making of black masculinity.* Ann Arbor, MI: University of Michigan Press.

Ferguson, K. M., Bender, K., Thompson, S. J., Xie, B., & Pollio, D. (2012). Exploration of arrest activity among homeless young adults in four U.S. cities. *Social Work Research, 36*(3), 233–238. https://doi.org/10.1093/swr/svs023

Freedman, D., & Berk, R. (2008). Weighting regressions by propensity scores. *Evaluation Review, 32*(4), 392–409. http://dx.doi.org/10.1177/0193841X08317586

Foucault, M. (1979). *Discipline and punish: The birth of the prison.* New York, NY: Vintage Books.

Golann, J. W. 2015. The paradox of success at a no-excuses school. *Sociology of Education, 88*(2), 103–119. https://doi.org/10.1177/0038040714567866

Griffith, J. (2020, January 22). Black Texas teen told to cut his dreadlocks to walk at graduation. *NBC News.* Retrieved from https://www.nbcnews.com/news/us-news/black-texas-teen-told-cut-his-dreadlocks-order-walk-graduation-n1120731

Guo, S., & Fraser, W. (2014). *Propensity score analysis.* Thousand Oaks, CA: Sage.

Harvey, D. (2007). *A brief history of neoliberalism.* Oxford: Oxford University Press.

Henig, J., Hula, R., Orr, M., & Pedescleaux, D. (2001). *The color of school reform: Race, politics, and the challenge of urban education.* Princeton, NJ: Princeton University Press.

Henig, J. (2008, March 31). What do we know about the outcomes of KIPP schools? National Education Policy Center. Retrieved from http://nepc.colorado.edu/publication/outcomes-of-kipp-schools

Hunt, J., & Moodie-Mills, A. (2012, June 29). The unfair criminalization of gay and transgender youth: An overview of the experiences of LGBT youth in the juvenile justice system. *Center for American Progress.* Retrieved from https://cdn.americanprogress.org/wp-content/uploads/issues/2012/06/pdf/juvenile_justice.pdf

Ibrahim, H., & Johnson, O. Jr. (2020). School discipline, race-gender, and STEM readiness: A hierarchical analysis of the impact of school discipline on math achievement in high school. *The Urban Review, 52*(1), 75–99. http://dx.doi.org/10.1007/s11256-019-00513-6

Ibrahim, H., Barnes, D., Butler-Barnes, S., & Johnson, O. Jr. (2021). *Impact of in-school suspension on black girls' math course-taking in high school.* Social Sciences. https://doi.org/10.3390/socsci10070272

Jabbari, J., & Johnson, O. Jr. (2021). The process of "pushing out": Accumulated disadvantage across school punishment and math achievement trajectories. *Youth & Society.* https://doi.org/10.1177/0044118X211007175

Jabbari, J., & Johnson, O. Jr. (2020a). The collateral damage of in-school suspensions: A counterfactual analysis of high-suspension schools, math achievement and college attendance. *Urban Education.* https://doi.org/10.1177/0042085920902256

Jabbari, J., & Johnson, O. Jr. (2020b). Veering off track in US high schools? Redirecting student trajectories by disrupting punishment and math course-taking tracks. *Child and Youth Services Review, 109,* 104734. https://doi.org/10.1016/j.childyouth.2019.104734

Janowitz, M. (1975/1991). *On social organization and social control.* Chicago, IL: University of Chicago Press.

Jencks, C., & Mayer, S. E. (1990). The social consequences of growing up in a poor neighborhood. *Inner-City Poverty in the United States, 111,* 186.

Johnson, O. Jr. (2015). Responding to school violence: Confronting the columbine effect. *Contemporary Sociology, 44*(4), 539–541. https://doi.org/10.1177/00943061155884871l

Johnson, O. Jr., & Jabbari, J. (2021a). Suspended while Black in majority White schools: Implications for math efficacy and equity. In *The educational forum*. https://doi.org/10.1080/00131725.2022.1997312.

Johnson, O. Jr., & Jabbari, J. (2021b). *The infrastructure of Black social control: A multi-level counterfactual analysis of surveillance, punishment, and educational inequality*. American Educational Research Association. Retrieved from https://convention2.allacademic. com/one/aera/aera21/index.php?cmd=Online+Program+View+Session&selected_session_id=1706244&PHPSESSID=34e8gevbo75uhj31l7rv03o75g

Johnson, O. Jr., & Wagner, M. (2017). Equalizers or enablers of inequality? A counterfactual analysis of racial and residential test-score gaps in year-round and 9-month schools. *Annals of the American Academy of Political and Social Science, 674*(1), 240–261. https://doi.org/10.1177/0002716217734810

Johnson, O. Jr., Jabbari, J., Williams, M., & Marcucci, O. (2019). Disparate impacts: Balancing the need for safe schools with racial equity in discipline. *Policy Insights from Behavioral and Brain Sciences, 6*(2), 162–169. https://doi.org/10.1177/2372732219864707

Joseph, G., & CityLab (2016, September 16). Where charter-school suspensions are concentrated. *The Atlantic*. Retrieved from https://www.theatlantic.com/education/archive/2016/09/the-racism-of-charter-school-discipline/500240/

Kinsler, J. (2013). School discipline: A source or salve for the racial achievement gap? *International Economic Review, 54*(1), 355–383. https://doi.org/10.1111/j.1468-2354.2012.00736.x

Kirk, D. S. (2009). Unraveling the contextual effects on student suspension and juvenile arrest: The independent and interdependent influences of school, neighborhood, and family social controls. *Criminology, 47*(2), 479–520. https://doi.org/10.1111/j.1745-9125.2009.00147.x

Kleinman, R. E., Murphy, J. M., Little, M., Pagano, M., Wehler, C. A., Regal, K., & Jellinek, M. S. (1998). Hunger in children in the United States: Potential behavioral and emotional correlates. *Pediatrics, 101*(1), E3. Retrieved from http://pediatrics.aap-publications.org/content/101/1/e3.long

Lacombe, D. (1996). Reforming Foucault: A critique of the social control thesis. *The British Journal of Sociology, 47*(2), 332–352. https://doi.org/10.2307/591730

Lewis-McCoy, L. (2014). *Inequality in the promised land: Race, resources, and suburban schooling*. Stanford, CA: Stanford University Press.

Lipman, P. (2011). *The new political economy of urban education: Neoliberalism, race, and the right to the city*. London: Routledge.

Lofton, R. (2021). Plessy's tracks: African American Students confronting academic placement in a racially diverse school and African American community. *Race, Ethnicity and Education*, 1–20. https://doi.org/10.1080/13613324.2021.1924141

Lopez Kershen, J., Weiner, J. M., & Torres, C. (2019). Control as care: How teachers in "no excuses" charter schools position their students and themselves. *Equity & Excellence in Education, 51*(4), 1–19. https://doi.org/10.1080/10665684.2018.1539359

Massey, D. (1996). The age of extremes: Concentrated affluence and poverty in the twenty-first century. *Demography*, 33(4), 395–412. https://doi.org/10.2307/2061773

Matos, A. (2017, January 6). In Missouri, students who bully could be charged with a felony. *The Washington Post*. Retrieved from https://www.washingtonpost.com/local/education/in-missouri-students-who-bully-could-be-charged-with-a-felony/2017/01/06/0e71f17e-d1e2-11e6-945a-76f69a399dd5_story.html

McCaffrey, D., Ridgeway, G., & Morral, A. (2004). Propensity score estimation with boosted regression for evaluating causal effects in observational studies. *Psychological Methods, 9*(4), 403. https://doi.org/10.1037/1082-989X.9.4.403

Muschert, G. W., Henry, S., Bracy, N. L., & Peguero, A. A. (2014). *Responding to school violence: Confronting the Columbine effect. Boulder, CO*: Lynne Rienner Publishers.

NCES (2019). Percentage of public schools with security staff present at school at least once a week, by type of security staff, school level, and selected school characteristics: 2005-06, 2015-16, and 2017-18. Retrieved from https://nces.ed.gov/programs/digest/d19/tables/dt19_233.70b.asp

Office for Civil Rights (2021). *An overview of exclusionary discipline practices in public schools for the 2017–18 school year.* Department of Education. Retrieved from https://www2.ed.gov/about/offices/list/ocr/docs/crdc-exclusionary-school-discipline.pdf

Parsons, T. (1937). *The structure of social action.* New York, NY: McGraw-Hill.

Perry, B., & Morris, E. (2014). Suspending progress: Collateral consequences of exclusionary punishment in public schools. *American Sociological Review, 79*(6), 1067–1087. https://doi.org/10.1177/0003122414556308

Powell, A., Nielsen, N., Butler, M., Buxton, C., Johnson, O., Ketterlin-Geller, L., & McCulloch, C. (2018). *Broadening participation in K–12 STEM education: NSF insights and implications for policy and practice.* Education Development Center, Inc. Retrieved from http://cadrek12.org/resources/broadening-participation-policy-practice-brief

Ridgeway, G., McCaffrey, D., Morral, A., Burgette, L., & Griffin, B. (2014). *Toolkit for weighting and analysis of nonequivalent groups: A tutorial for the R TWANG Package.* RAND Corporation. Retrieved from https://www.rand.org/pubs/tools/TL136z1.html

Rosenbaum, P., & Rubin, D. (1983). The central role of the propensity score in observational studies for causal effects. *Biometrika, 70*(1), 41–55. https://doi.org/10.1093/biomet/70.1.41

Rubin, D. (2005). Causal inference using potential outcomes: Design, modeling, decisions. *Journal of the American Statistical Association, 100*(469), 322–331. https://doi.org/10.1198/016214504000001880

Rist, R. (1970). Student social class and teacher expectations: The self-fulfilling prophecy in ghetto education. *Harvard Educational Review, 40*(3), 411–451. https://doi.org/10.17763/haer.40.3.h0m026p670k618q3

Ropke, L. (2019). Facial recognition software on the rise in U.S. Schools. *Government Technology.* Retrieved from http://www.govtech.com/products/facial-recognition-software-on-the-rise-in-us-schools.html

Shedd, C. (2015). *Unequal city: Race, schools, and perceptions of injustice.* Russell Sage Foundation.

Skiba, R. J., & Rausch, M. K. (2006). Zero tolerance, suspension, and expulsion: Questions of equity and effectiveness. In C. M. Evertson & C. S. Weinstein (Eds.), *Handbook of classroom management: Research, practice, and contemporary issues* (pp. 1063–1089). Erlbaum.

Snijders, T. A., & Bosker, R. J. (2011). *Multilevel analysis: An introduction to basic and advanced multilevel modeling.* London: Sage.

Woodworth, K. R., David, J. L., Guha, R., Wang, H., & Lopez-Torkos, A. (2008). San Francisco Bay Area KIPP schools: A study of Early Implementation and Achievement. Final report. *SRI International.* Retrieved from http://www.kippbayarea.org/wp-content/uploads/2010/06/SRI-International-Report.pdf.

10

EXAMINING DISCIPLINE FROM AN INTERSECTIONAL LENS

Jamilia J. Blake, Siqi Chen, Naomi Ruffin, Lyric Jackson

Examining Discipline from an Intersectional Lens

The disparate impact of exclusionary disciplinary actions such as suspension and expulsion on youth of color is a systematic problem having significant consequences on students' life trajectories. The national trend known as the School-to-Prison pipeline describes policies and practices, including disciplinary actions, that increase the probability of adverse outcomes for students, disproportionately those of color and students with disabilities (Mendoza, Blake, Marchbanks, & Ragan, 2020; Skiba, Arredondo, & Williams, 2014). The outcomes associated with discipline disparities include academic failure, school dropout, and eventual criminal justice system contact (Marchbanks, Peguero, Varela, Blake, & Eason, 2018; Smith et al., 2020). Some argue that the implementation of discriminatory policies and practices throughout the United States educational system has essentially generated educational inequalities that result in the racial disparities in school discipline practices we have observed for decades.

Early studies dating back to the 1970s and 1980s examined the distribution of discipline in schools and found that Black students were more likely to be given exclusionary disciplinary sanctions, such as suspensions, compared to white students (Children's Defense Fund, 1975; Skiba, Peterson, & Williams, 1997; Wu, Pink, Crain, & Moles, 1982). Most recent research has supported past findings, suggesting that Black students continue to receive disproportionate rates of exclusionary disciplinary practices (Losen & Gillespie, 2012; Noltemeyer & Mcloughlin, 2010), even though Black students are no more likely to commit more or more serious offenses than White students (Skiba et al., 2011; Skiba, Michael, Nardo, & Peterson, 2002). During the 2015-2016 school year, Black students accounted for nearly half of enrolled students who received suspension and expulsion as disciplinary actions (U.S. Department of Education, 2018). Although Black students are identified as

DOI: 10.4324/9781003126621-13

the highest racial group to receive exclusionary discipline, gender differences between Black boys and girls also exist (Crenshaw et al, 2015; Morris & Perry, 2017; U.S. Department of Education, 2018).

The discipline gap between Black girls and white girls is wider than the gap between Black and White boys (Crenshaw et al, 2015; Morris & Perry, 2017; U.S. Department of Education, 2018). Black girls are suspended at a rate 5.3 times higher than White girls, whereas Black boys are only suspended at a rate 3.3 times higher than White boys (U.S. Department of Education, 2018). Although educational leaders have acknowledged the detrimental impact of disciplining school policies on Black students, most of the focus has been on Black males (Harper, 2015). Few researchers have paid attention to the impact of practices on Black girls (Blake, Butler, Lewis, & Darensbourg, 2011). However, within the last decade, research examining discipline disparities have adopted a racialized gendered lens, with increasing studies examining the discipline experiences of Black girls (Dillon, 2010; Lewin, 2012). Current research focused on Black girls has found that Black girls receive disciplinary sanctions at disproportionate rates compared to their peers of other races (Annamma et al., 2019; Blake, Butler, & Smith, 2015; Blake et al., 2011; Morris & Perry, 2017; Slate, Gray, & Jones, 2016) warranting scholars and practitioners to adopt an intersectional lens to the study of school discipline that considers the intersection of both race and gender not only for Black girls, but also for other marginalized populations (Blake et al., 2011; Crenshaw, 1989).

Measuring Discipline Disparities

Racial discipline disproportionality in US schools has been a concern of education policymakers, researchers, and practitioners for decades, and several methodological techniques have been employed to quantify and estimate the nature of the racial discipline gap between students of color and white students (Petrosino et al., 2017). Accurately evaluating trends and changes in discipline disparities is essential in determining if the gap is closing or widening as well as determining if initiatives are truly leading to desired change. In order to document and gather sound empirical evidence of the extent to which certain groups of students are overrepresented in discipline, specific sets of methodological techniques have been employed and have come to be the standard for assessing discipline disparities among racial/ethnic groups Three standard methods used in calculating discipline disparities are risk ratio, risk gap, and composition indices, which we outline below.

The risk ratio consists of the quotient of the target group's risk and the reference group's risk. When the calculated value is greater than 1, the target group is at a higher risk compared to the reference group. This is a commonly used metric that allows for comparison across contexts where enrollment sizes differ. Risk ratios' weaknesses include their sensitivity to small cell sizes and changes and the lack of information regarding the number of students affected (Curran, 2020). This risk ratio formula is also used in measuring racial disparities in special education placement.

Risk Ratio Formula:

$$\frac{\left(\dfrac{\#\ target\ group\ students\ disciplined}{\#\ target\ group\ students\ enrolled}\right)}{\left(\dfrac{\#\ reference\ group\ students\ disciplined}{\#\ reference\ group\ students\ enrolled}\right)}$$

Secondly, the risk gap represents the difference in risk indices between a target group and reference group (Osher et al., 2015). A positive value calculated from the risk gap formula indicates that students in the target group have a higher likelihood of receiving disciplinary action when compared with students in the reference group. The strengths of this approach include being less sensitive to small cell sizes or small changes, allowing for comparison across contexts, and appearing useful for measurement of high-frequency events. However, over time, it is relatively unreliable and does not communicate the relative magnitude of discipline rates between subgroups (Curran, 2020).

Risk Gap Formula:

$$\left(\frac{\#\ target\ group\ students\ disciplined}{\#\ target\ group\ students\ enrolled}\right) - \left(\frac{\#\ reference\ group\ students\ disciplined}{\#\ reference\ group\ students\ enrolled}\right)$$

The composition index describes the proportion of a group with a particular characteristic within a population. Comparing two composition indices is necessary to gather information regarding disproportionality (Petrosino et al., 2017).

Composition Index Formula:

$$\frac{Percentage\ of\ target\ group\ receiving\ a\ disciplinary\ action}{Percentage\ of\ target\ group's\ total\ enrollment}$$

The current metrics to assess racial/ethnic disparities serve an essential role in illuminating the nature of discipline disparities, monitoring changes in these disparities, and informing policy to reduce the disparities. However, recognizing how other individual and school-related factors may impact students' discipline outcomes is also crucial due to the capacity of these other factors to impact subgroups differently.

Racial disproportionality in school discipline is an issue that is not adequately explored by calculating metrics and is a dynamic problem involving multiple, reciprocating systems placing some students at more risk than others. While school discipline gaps have largely been viewed based on differences across racial groups, there is a need for an intersectional approach in calculating and interpreting school discipline disproportionality. Intersectionality reveals the interconnected nature of overlapping factors that contribute to disadvantages (Crenshaw, 1998). In the case of school discipline, the interaction between race and gender brings attention to the inequitable discipline experiences of Black girls in the schools and suggests that more nimble and sophisticated techniques are needed to capture this population's experiences.

> In the case of school discipline, the interaction between race and gender brings attention to the inequitable discipline experiences of Black girls in the schools and suggests that more nimble and sophisticated techniques are needed to capture this population's experiences.

New Approaches to Discipline Disparity Identification

The current leading techniques in discipline disparities metrics are descriptive in nature and allow for simplicity in calculation and general ease of interpretation. However, these techniques do not capture the full, nuanced nature of discipline disparities, which requires an intersectional lens that emphasizes gender dynamics. Discipline disparities impact student groups differently along the lines of both race and gender. Transitioning the school discipline disparity field of study to include more advanced methodological techniques within gender analyses across race will be critical to inform equity initiatives.

One of the most significant challenges that discipline disparity research faces are that there are always many individuals and school-related factors that might impact students' discipline outcomes. Thus, a simple risk ratio comparison cannot control all factors. To make this situation worse, the hierarchical structure of most educational data, for example, students nested within classrooms and schools, indicates some school characteristics might also influence students' discipline outcomes, which might lead to biased estimation of the risk factors.

Discipline scholars could use regression-based methods to estimate the effect of a risk factor on students' discipline outcome while controlling the baseline differences among groups. However, there are concerns about the regression-based methods. First, if the baseline difference between groups is too large, no adjustment is enough for direct comparison and risk factor effect estimation. Second, regression-based methods should inference to the region of covariance overlap, which means the prediction should only be drawn when there is covariance overlap. Nevertheless, regression-based methods extrapolate the prediction to the region with little information or data support, and their standard diagnostics do not involve checking the covariance overlap (Dehejia & Wahba, 1999; Glazerman, Levy, & Myers, 2003). Lastly, regression-based techniques, in general, assume a simple linear relationship among covariates, but in reality, the relationships among covariates are much more complex. Thus, we suggest that discipline scholars consider adopting a matching technique to adopt an intersectional lens in discipline disparity research.

> We suggest that discipline scholars consider adopting a matching technique to adopt an intersectional lens in discipline disparity research.

A matching technique could be beneficial to discipline disparity research because it has the potential to highlight areas of the covariate distribution where there not sufficient overlap between groups. When there is a lack of adequate overlap of covariates, the resulting risk-factor effect estimates would rely heavily on extrapolation. Matching methods have precise diagnostics by which their performance can be assessed. Matching could be broadly defined as any method that aims to equate (or "balance") the distribution of covariates in the risk groups. In matching, the data sample is divided into two groups by the "risk" factor: high-risk and low-risk. Then we match the high-risk and low-risk groups with the same or similar covariates. Finally, the difference in the school discipline outcome between the risk groups could be viewed as the effect of the risk factor. In this chapter, the risk factor is whether more than two full-time social workers are present on a high school campus. The high-risk groups are high school campuses with two or less full-time social workers and the low-risk groups are high school campuses with more than two full-time social workers.

More specifically, implementing matching could be broken down into four critical steps, defining a distance, implementing a matching algorithm, diagnosing the matching algorithm, and estimating the risk factor effect (see Figure 10.1).

Step 1: Define a Matching Distance

First, we need to define the "closeness," which is the distance measure used to determine whether individuals from risk groups are a good match. There are two types of distance we could use in Matching. The first type of distance is called Mahalanobis distance. Mahalanobis distance is the spatial distance between two points in the multivariate space.

$$D_{ij} = \left(X_i - X_j \right)' \sum^{-1} \left(X_i - X_j \right)$$

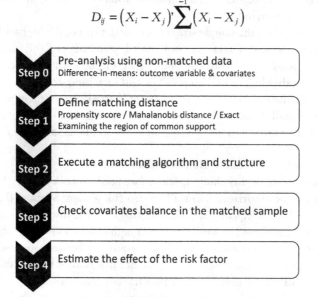

Step 0
Pre-analysis using non-matched data
Difference-in-means: outcome variable & covariates

Step 1
Define matching distance
Propensity score / Mahalanobis distance / Exact
Examining the region of common support

Step 2
Execute a matching algorithm and structure

Step 3
Check covariates balance in the matched sample

Step 4
Estimate the effect of the risk factor

FIGURE 10.1 Matching Technique Critical Steps

The propensity score is another type of distance. The propensity score could be viewed as the conditional probability of assigned one individual to the high-risk group. There are various ways to estimate the propensity score, especially with the rise of the machine learning technique. Traditionally, propensity scores are estimated using logistic regression models. Recently, increasing attention has been given to propensity score estimation methods that required less strict parametric assumptions, such as machine learning techniques.

$$D_{ij} = |e_i - e_j|$$

Step 2: Execute a Matching Algorithm and Structure

After choosing the matching distance, a matching algorithm that assigns low-risk individuals to the high-risk individuals using the defined matching distance should be selected. We can minimize individual distance using the greedy algorithm or minimize the overall distance using the optimal algorithm.

The greedy algorithm is quite similar to the forward stepwise regression model. We start with matching each high-risk and low-risk individual with the smallest matching distance, and then these matched individuals are removed from the eligible pool. We only consider the best match in the current step (Austin, 2011).

Instead of individual matching distance, the goal of the optimal algorithm is to minimize the overall distance by allowing broke previous matches and re-matched to achieve the overall minimal distance. Usually, an optimal algorithm is used in matching.

Sometimes, when the sample size is large, or the size of the high-risk and low-risk groups are quite different, we could do 1:k matching or a full matching. Full matching is usually used with the optimal algorithm with the intention to use every single individual in the sample. The full matching divides a sample into a collection of matched sets with any number of low risk sample members and minimizes the overall distance. Thus, full matching remedies the sample reduction problem of the prior methods by using all of the available samples.

Step 3: Check Covariance Balance after Matching

After implementing the matching algorithm, we need to check the matching quality by examining the covariance balance between risk groups. Suppose the matching algorithm has been adequately specified. In that case, the distribution of measured baseline covariates should be similar between high-risk and low-risk subjects in the matched sample, often referenced as balanced covariates between groups.

One of the widely used methods for balance diagnosis is the standardized difference. The means or prevalence of baseline covariates are compared between risk groups in the matched sample. For a continuous covariate, the standardized difference is defined as

$$d = \frac{\overline{x}_{high-risk} - \overline{x}_{low-risk}}{\sqrt{\dfrac{s^2_{high-risk} + s^2_{low-risk}}{2}}}$$

where $\overline{x}_{high-risk}$ and $\overline{x}_{low-risk}$ denote the sample mean of the covariate in high-risk and low-risk subjects, and $s^2_{high-risk}$ and $s^2_{low-risk}$ denote the sample variance of the covariate in high-risk and low-risk subjects, respectively. For dichotomous variables, the standardized difference is defined as

$$d = \frac{\hat{p}_{high-risk} - \hat{p}_{low-risk}}{\sqrt{\dfrac{\hat{p}_{high-risk}\left(1 - \hat{p}_{high-risk}\right) + \hat{p}_{low-risk}\left(1 - \hat{p}_{low-risk}\right)}{2}}}$$

where $\hat{p}_{high-risk}$ and $\hat{p}_{low-risk}$ are the prevalence of the dichotomous variable in high-risk and low-risk subjects. The standardized difference is an effect size that compares the balance of variables measured in different units. Although there is still no universal agreement on the criterion of severe imbalance, a standardized difference that is less than 0.25 has been used to indicate negligible differences in baseline covariates between groups (Normand et al., 2001).

If the covariance balance has been achieved, we proceed to step 4: risk factor effect estimation by comparing the school discipline outcome direction between risk groups on the matched sample.

Demonstration

This section illustrates how to use MatchIt (Ho, Imai, King, & Stuart, 2011), one of the R packages, to implement the matching technique in school discipline disparity research. We first described the dataset used. Then we illustrate the implementation of the matching technique following the five steps discussed previously. We also show the R codes and output for the matching algorithm we use. Finally, we present the risk-factor effect estimated.

Research Question

For the past 5 years, there has been a growing debate regarding whether the presence of law enforcement in schools has the potential to increase students' risk for the receipt of overly punitive discipline that results in criminal justice contact. This concern has resulted in a number of non-profit organizations, activists, and prominent public figures calling for the replacement of law enforcement professionals in schools (e.g., school resource officers) with more school-based mental health professionals (e.g., school counselors, psychologists, school social workers). We use this demonstration to determine if the presence of one type of mental health professional differentially influences the discipline risk of girls from differing racial/ethnic backgrounds. Simply stated, our research question is whether the presence of more than two full-time social workers on high school campuses significantly reduced the relative risk of Black female students receiving single out-of-school suspension compared to their white female peers.

Data Sample

For demonstration purposes, we use two publicly available secondary datasets: the 2017- 2018 National Center for Education Statistics (NCES; https://nces. ed.gov/) and Office of Civil Rights Data collection (CRDC) datasets (https:// ocrdata.ed.gov/). The outcome variable for these demonstrative analyses is the risk ratio of Black female students who received a single out-of-school suspension compared to their white female peers during the 2017-2018 school year. The risk factor is whether more than two full-time social workers are present on the high school campus. The matching variables are as follows:

- School location based on the region of the United States schools are located [region], which we coded into four levels: South, West, Northeast, and Midwest
- School's Social Economic Status is measured by the free-reduced lunch rate, which is used as a proxy for school-level SES [ses_sch]. This variable was calculated by the percentage of free and reduced lunch students on each campus and coded into 4 levels: Low:>75%; Middle-Low: 50%-75%; Middle-High: 25%-50%; High: <25%
- School Size was measured by the total student enrollment for each campus [school_size]. For ease of interpretation, we coded this variable into four levels based on campus size: Level 1: <150 students; Level 2 151-499 students; Level 3: 500-999 students; Level 4: >999 students
- Total number of discipline incidents [n_discipline] was estimated as the sum of all types of discipline incidents on each campus
- The number of teachers within a campus was estimated by the total FTE (full-time equivalence) for teachers on each campus [SCH_FTETEACH_TOT]
- The racial demographics of each campus was calculated by the percentage of Black, white, and male students enrolled and is measured by the following variables:
  - percentage of Black students at school [per_bl];
  - percentage of white students at school [per_wh]
  - percentage of male students at school [per_male]

The Steps in Conducting Matching in R

Step 1. Install R and R studio.

Before we start, the R software and R studio are necessary to install. R software can be accessed at www.r-project.org, and Rstudio can be accessed at www. rstudio.com. Both softwares are open sourced and free.

Step 2. Install and load package.

After installing R and R studio, we install the following packages for data manipulation, matching, plotting, and robust standard error.

```
library(tidyverse)
library(MatchIt)
library(psych)
library(cobalt)
library(ggplot2)
library(lmtest)
library(sandwich)
library(boot)
```

Step 3. Prepare and load the data.

```
data <- readRDS(paste(data_path, "data_combined.rds", sep=""))
data_HS <- data %>%
  filter(School_Level== "High" & TOT_ENR_M+TOT_ENR_F >0 ) %>%
  mutate(SERVICES_SOC = ifelse(SCH_FTESERVICES_SOC > 2, 1, 0),
    school_size = ifelse((TOT_ENR_M+TOT_ENR_F) <150, 1,
                      ifelse((TOT_ENR_M+TOT_ENR_F) <450, 2,
                      ifelse((TOT_ENR_M+TOT_ENR_F) <1000, 3,
4)))) %>%
        mutate(RR_SINGOOS_F =
(SCH_DISCWODIS_SINGOOS_BL_F/SCH_ENR_BL_F)/(SCH_DISCWODIS_
SINGOOS_WH_F/SCH_ENR_WH_F))


outcome <- "RR_SINGOOS_F"
treatment <- "SERVICES_SOC"
data1 <- data_HS %>% select(region, ses_sch, bl_per, male_
per, wh_per,
                school_size, n_discipline, SCH_FTETEACH_TOT,
                !!as.name(outcome),!!as.name(treatment)) %>%
            filter(complete.cases(.) & !!as.name(outcome)> 0 &
            !!as.name(outcome) < 30)
```

Different types of data files can be loaded to the R environment, such as data files in CSV and Excel format. The readRDS function reads in an R object that is saved in RDS format. The tidyverse is a collection of R packages designed for data manipulation and data analysis. Functions such as filter, mutate and select are handy in creating new variables and filter the datasets.

Step 4. Perform matching and evaluate the results.

```
m.out1 <- matchit(RR_SINGOOS_F ~ SERVICES_SOC + region+ses_
sch + school_size
                        n_discipline + SCH_FTETEACH_TOT +
bl_per + male_per + wh_per, data = data1, caliper = 0.25)
```

The matching algorithm can be implemented using the matchit function, with the outcome variable on the left side of ~ and all covariates on the right side of ~ and connected with +.

```
plot_demo <- love.plot(m.out1, binary = "std",
                  thresholds = c(m = .25), abs = TRUE, line
                  = TRUE,
                  colors = c("red", "blue"),
                  shapes = c("triangle filled", "circle
                  filled"));
plot_demo
```

After matching, we examine the performance of the matching algorithm (see Figure 10.2). Using the plot below, we check the covariance balance before and after implementing the selected matching algorithm. The unadjusted line indicates the covariance difference between risk groups before matching, and the adjusted line shows the covariance balance after matching. The dotted line is the 0.25 cutoff point for the standardized difference.

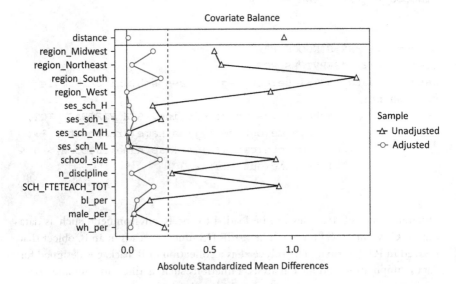

FIGURE 10.2   Absolute Standardized Mean Difference Comparison Before and After Matching

The graph show that the matching algorithm we selected performs well in reducing the covariance imbalance. More specifically, all covariance balances between risk groups are below 0.25 and indicate negligible differences after matching. Thus, we proceed with risk-factor effect estimation to assess if the presence of more than two full-time social workers significantly reduced the relative risk of Black female students receiving a single out-of-school suspension.

Step 5: Export matched data file for analyses

```
m.data1 <- match.data(m.out1, data = data1)
lm_fit_matching <- lm(as.formula(paste(outcome, "~",
paste(treatment,
     "region", "ses_sch", "school_size", "n_discipline",
"SCH_FTETEACH_TOT",
"bl_per","male_per","wh_per", sep=" + "), sep="")), data =
m.data1,
        weights = weights)

coeftest(lm_fit_matching, vcov. = vcovCL, cluster =
~subclass)[treatment,,
    drop=FALSE]


m.data1 %>%
  group_by(!!as.name(treatment)) %>%
            summarise(RR_mean = mean(!!as.name(outcome)))
```

After we extract the matched dataset, the risk factor effect estimation is relatively straightforward using linear regression (lm). The covariates used in matching were included in the linear regression to increase precision in the effect estimate, reduce the bias due to residual imbalance, and make the effect estimate "doubly robust." The cluster-robust standard error is used to account for pair membership

The regression analysis on the matched dataset suggest that more than two full-time social workers in high schools significantly reduce the relative risk of Black female students receiving a single out-of-school suspension, $B = -1.409$, $p = 0.008$. That is when high school girls come from similar school environments the effect of having at least two mental health professionals on the campus is greater for reducing Black girls' risk for out-of-school suspension than white girls.

Activity

The public-use CRDC that is used in the demonstration can be downloaded at https://ocrdata.ed.gov/resources/downloaddatafile. All R codes for data analysis and data preparation can be accessed from https://github.com/lucy7989/AIM-2021/. The readers can obtain the datasets and run the analyses provided in the demonstration to consider whether more than one full-time security staff onsite would negatively impact Black girls' discipline outcome compared to their white female peers. Following the R codes shown in the demonstration section, you should do matching and conduct risk factor effect estimation. What do these methods tell us about the data? How does this approach help us interrogate systemic racism Black girls (or your participants) are experiencing in schools? What should schools do differently to incorporate what you've learned and made a change?

Conclusion

For the last three decades, school discipline scholars have adopted a singular view to identify disparate discipline practices impacting students of color. The field's historical focus on examining racial/ethnic differences in discipline disparities without considering gender has resulted in Black girls over suspension to hide in plain sight. Movements to uncover the discipline disparities that Black girls face related to exclusionary discipline have resulted in a call for scholars to adopt an intersectional lens to understand discipline disparities, one that considers the intersection of both gender and race in discipline evaluation metrics. Unfortunately, the current standard of practice for assessing discipline disparities is not robust enough to fully capture the nuances that shape discipline outcomes at the individual (e.g., race, gender) or school contextual level.

> The field's historical focus on examining racial/ethnic differences in discipline disparities without considering gender has resulted in Black girls over suspension to hide in plain sight.

In this chapter, we offer matching, a commonly used statistical method as a viable option for the assessment of discipline disparities that has the potential to not only measure the intersecting identities that heighten marginalized students' risk for over discipline but also account for the systemic and structural factors that might underestimate the differential outcomes that marginalized students experience related to discipline as well if not adequately assessed and statistically modeled. Whereas no singular approach to the measurement of discipline disparities is free from limitations (see Curran, 2020; Osher et al., 2015), matching provides a sophisticated and empirically defensible method for addressing the measurement of discipline disparities from an intersectional lens while also accounting for structural properties of educational data (e.g., nested data structure) that has plagued discipline scholars and practitioners for decades. If the field moves toward the inclusion of matching as a standard of practice in the measurement of the disparate impact of school discipline for socially marginalized students, future researchers will need to develop tools and technologies to make this approach accessible to lay audiences, particularly educational stakeholders in district research and accountability offices charged with the evaluation of school districts' equity initiatives.

References

Annamma, S. A., Anyon, Y., Joseph, N. M., Farrar, J., Greer, E., Downing, B., & Simmons, J. (2019). Black girls and school discipline: The complexities of being over-represented and understudied. *Urban Education, 54*(2), 211–242.

Austin, P. C. (2011). An introduction to propensity score methods for reducing the effects of confounding in observational studies. *Multivariate Behavioral Research, 46*(3), 399–424. https://doi.org/10.1080/00273171.2011.568786

Blake, J. J., Butler, B. R., & Smith, D. (2015). Challenging middle class notions of femininity: The cause for black females' disproportionate suspension rates. In D. Losen (Ed.), *Closing the school discipline gap: Research to practice* (pp. 75–88). New York, NY: Teachers' Press..

Blake, J. J., Butler, B. R., Lewis, C. W., & Darensbourg, A. (2011). Unmasking the inequitable discipline experiences of urban black girls: Implications for urban educational stakeholders. *The Urban Review, 43*(1), 90–106.

Children's Defense Fund. (1975). *School suspensions: Are they helping children.* Cambridge, MA: Washington Research Project.

Crenshaw, K. (1989). Demarginalizing the intersection of race and sex: A black feminist critique of antidiscrimination doctrine, feminist theory and antiracist politics. *University of Chicago Law Forum, 140*, 139–167.

Crenshaw, K., Ocen, P., & Nanda, J. (2015). *Black girls matter: Pushed out, overpoliced, and underprotected.* Retrieved from http://www.atlanticphilanthropies.org/app/uploads/2015/09/BlackGirlsMatter_Report.pdf

Curran, F. C. (2020). A matter of measurement: How different ways of measuring racial gaps in school discipline can yield drastically different conclusions about racial disparities in discipline. *Educational Researcher, 49*(5), 382–387. https://doi.org/10.3102/0013189x20923348

Ho, D., Imai, K., King, G., & Stuart, E. A. (2011). MatchIt: Nonparametric preprocessing for parametric causal inference. *Journal of Statistical Software, 42*(8), 1–28. https://doi.org/10.18637/jss.v042.i08

Dehejia, R. H., & Wahba, S. (1999). Causal effects in nonexperimental studies: Reevaluating the evaluation of training programs. *Journal of the American Statistical Association, 94*(448), 1053–1062.

Dillon, S. (2010, September 13). Racial Disparity in School Suspensions. *The New York Times.*

Glazerman, S., Levy, D. M., & Myers, D. (2003). Nonexperimental versus experimental estimates of earnings impacts. *The Annals of the American Academy of Political and Social Science, 589*(1), 63–93.

Harper, S. R. (2015). Success in these schools? Visual counter narratives of young men of color and urban male high schools they attend. *Urban Education, 50*(2), 139–169. https://doi.org/10.1177/0042085915569738

Lewin, T. (2012). Black students face more discipline, data suggests. *The New York Times.*

Losen, D. J., & Gillespie, J. (2012). *Opportunities suspended: The disparate impact of disciplinary exclusion from school* (Report). Los Angeles, CA: The Civil Rights Project/Proyecto Derechos Civiles. Retrieved from http://civilrightsproject.ucla.edu/resources/projects/center-for-civil-rights-remedies/school-to-prison-folder/federal-reports/upcoming-ccrr-research

Marchbanks, M. P. III, Peguero, A. A., Varela, K. S., Blake, J. J., & Eason, J. M. (2018). School strictness and disproportionate minority contact: Investigating racial and ethnic disparities with the "school-to-prison pipeline". *Youth Violence and Juvenile Justice*, *16*(2), 241–259.

Mendoza, M., Blake, J. J., Marchbanks, M., & Ragan, K. (2020). Race, gender, disability and risk for juvenile justice contact. *The Journal of Special Education*, *53*(4), 226–235.

Morris, E. W., & Perry, B. L. (2017). Girls behaving badly? Race, gender, and subjective evaluation in the discipline of African American girls. *Sociology of Education*, *90*(2), 127–148.

Noltemeyer, A., & Mcloughlin, C. S. (2010). Patterns of exclusionary discipline by school typology, ethnicity, and their interaction. *Penn GSE Perspectives on Urban Education*, *7*(1), 27–40.

Normand, S. T., Landrum, M. B., Guadagnoli, E., Ayanian, J. Z., Ryan, T. J., Cleary, P. D., & McNeil, B. J. (2001). Validating recommendations for coronary angiography following acute myocardial infarction in the elderly: A matched analysis using propensity scores. *Journal of Clinical Epidemiology*, *54*(4), 387–398. https://doi.org/10.1016/s0895-4356(00)00321-8

Osher, D., Fisher, D., Amos, L., Katz, J., Dwyer, K., Duffey, T., & Colombi, G. D. (2015). *Addressing the root causes of disparities in school discipline: An educator's action planning guide*. Washington, DC: National Center on Safe Supportive Learning Environments.

Skiba, R. J., Arredondo, M. I., & Williams, N. T. (2014). More than a metaphor: The contribution of exclusionary discipline to a school-to-prison pipeline. *Equity & Excellence in Education*, *47*(4), 546–564.

Skiba, R. J., Horner, R. H., Chung, C. G., Rausch, M. K., May, S. L., & Tobin, T. (2011). Race is not neutral: A national investigation of African American and Latino disproportionality in school discipline. *School Psychology Review*, *40*(1), 85–107.

Skiba, R. J., Michael, R. S., Nardo, A. C., & Peterson, R. L. (2002). The color of discipline: Sources of racial and gender disproportionality in school punishment. *The Urban Review*, *34*(4), 317–342.

Skiba, R. J., Peterson, R. L., & Williams, T. (1997). Office referrals and suspension: Disciplinary intervention in middle schools. *Education and Treatment of Children*, 295–315. Retrieved from http://www.jstor.org/stable/42900491

Slate, J. R., Gray, P. L., & Jones, B. (2016). A clear lack of equity in disciplinary consequences for black girls in Texas: A statewide examination. *The Journal of Negro Education*, *85*(3), 250–260.

Smith, D., Ortiz, N. A., Blake, J. J., Marchbanks, M., Unni, A., & Peguero, A. A. (2020). Tipping point: Effect of the number of in-school suspensions on academic failure. *Contemporary School Psychology*, *25*(4), 466–475.

U.S. Department of Education. (2018). *New Release for 2018. 2015-16 Civil Rights Data Collection Data Highlights on School Climate and Safety*. Retrieved from https://www2.ed.gov/about/offices/list/ocr/docs/school-climate-and-safety.pdf

Wu, S. C., Pink, W. T., Crain, R. L., & Moles, O. (1982). Student suspension: A critical reappraisal. *The Urban Review*, *14*(4), 245–303.

11

DETECTING DIFFERENTIAL EFFECTS USING REGRESSION MIXTURE MODELS

Applications Using Mplus

Minjung Kim, Junyeong Yang

Note: For the answers to the activity, please see https://u.osu.edu/quallab/advanced-methods-institute/

Introduction

Quantitative research methods have been historically criticized by its tendency to totalize and homogenize the findings of data analysis by focusing on an *average* effect in general (Strunk & Hoover, 2019). Since the average effect represents the majority groups, it tends to overlook the marginalized groups. As discussed in other chapters of this book, one of the main goals of culturally responsive research is to bring those who have been marginalized to the center of research as co-constructors (Berryman, Soohoo, & Nevin, 2013). Thus, the culturally responsive methodology has been developed mostly under the qualitative research methodology framework, which focuses more on individual cases, than the quantitative research methodology framework, which drives the study results based on the larger population groups.

In addition, since quantitative data is generated by processing the human data into numbers in social science, some researchers have criticized that the quantitative data processing is dehumanizing the human data (Strunk & Hoover, 2019). Although it might be true that quantitative methods are totalizing, homogenizing, and dehumanizing in some ways, we should acknowledge that the quantitative research methods still have important roles in funding acquisition and policy making, especially in educational field. For example, Institute for Education Sciences, 2003) explicitly notes that "Well-designed and implemented randomized controlled trials are considered the *gold standard* for evaluating an intervention's effectiveness" (p. 1), which are under the quantitative methodology framework. Therefore, researchers need to be more attentive to use

DOI: 10.4324/9781003126621-14

the quantitative methods in a way to better position the marginalized groups as co-constructors of the research, rather than just excluding the quantitative methods from their options when conducting culturally responsive research.

In this chapter, we focus on the regression analysis, which is one of the most widely used quantitative analytical methods in social science research. Specifically, we focus on how we can use regression analysis for examining the potential heterogeneity in the effects of predictors on an outcome, instead of totalizing the effects across all populations. It is particularly useful for culturally responsive research, which has a great interest in discovering the heterogeneous groups that are often understudied.

Regression analysis is generally used to examine a linear relationship between a set of independent variables and an outcome variable. In a simple linear regression, the estimated parameter of the regression coefficient represents the *average* effect of predictor x on outcome y, which often disregards the potential heterogeneity in the effects. Adding a third variable z (e.g., birth gender, race, and ethnicity) with its multiplicative term with the predictor x (i.e., x*z) allows researchers to examine the differential effects of the predictor x depending on the third variable z. The multiplicative term is often called as a moderation or interaction in regression analysis. When there is a statistically significant moderation, we see that the strength or direction of the effect of a predictor variable on an outcome variable varies as a function of the values of the moderator (Marsh, Hau, Wen, Nagengast, & Morin, 2013). We will call this method as a *regression interaction approach* in this chapter.

Regression interaction approach uses a multiplicative term of the predictor x and third variable z (e.g., birth gender, race, and ethnicity) to examine the differential effect of x on y by z.

Another more recently developed approach that allows researchers to explore the effect heterogeneity is the regression mixture modeling (McLachlan & Peel, 2000). Regression mixture models have gained increasing attention and wider application to social science data as a means of detecting *latent* heterogeneity underlying a population. The word latent means that there is no designated third variable (moderator) in the analysis but identified based on the modeling technique. We introduce the regression mixture modeling to the readers in this chapter.

The structure of this chapter is as follows. We first describe the model formulation of the simple linear regression and the regression interaction approach. Next, we describe the regression mixture modeling compared to the regression interaction approach. The primary part of the chapter is for demonstrating the use of the regression mixture modeling using Mplus (Muthén & Muthén, 1998-2017). We aim to provide an easy-to-follow tutorial for novice users, who would probably not be comfortable or skilled for using the mixture modeling in general.

Regression Interaction Approach

We assume that a reader has a basic understanding of introductory statistics and regression analysis. If not, please see introductory references, such as Hahs-Vaughn and Lomax (2020) and Montgomery, Peck, and Vining (2012). For example, a simple linear regression equation can be written as:

$$y_i = \beta_0 + \beta_1 x_i + \varepsilon_i, \qquad\qquad \text{[Eq. 1]}$$

where

> y_i is the observed score of outcome y for individual i,
> β_0 is the intercept coefficient (i.e., the average value of y_i when x_i is equal to zero),
> β_1 is the slope coefficient (i.e., the change in y_i in every unit change in x_i),
> x_i is the observed score of predictor x for individual i, and
> ε_i is the deviation between the predicted score and the observed score for an individual i.

Here, β_1 is typically interpreted as the *overall* or *average* effect of x on y, which is criticized as the *totalized effect*.

We note that there are several assumptions made when using a regression analysis. First, a simple linear regression assumes that there is a linear relationship between outcome y and predictor x. Second, the random error part, ε_i, is normally distributed having a mean value of 0 and satisfied with homoscedasticity, which means that the variance is the same regardless of the value of x. Also, it should not be related to the predictor. If at least one of the above assumptions is violated, the relationship between x and y would be biased (Cohen, Cohen, West, & Aiken, 2003; Graybill, 1976; Van Horn et al., 2015).

In the regression interaction approach, we add another variable z to allow the differential effect of x depending on the value of z:

$$y_i = \beta_0 + \beta_1 * x_i + \beta_2 * z_i + \beta_3 * (x_i * z_i) + \varepsilon_i. \qquad\qquad \text{[Eq. 2]}$$

We can rearrange the regression equation of the interaction effect model based on the predictor x as below.

$$y_i = \beta_0 + \beta_2 * z_i + (\beta_1 + \beta_3 * z_i) * x_i + \varepsilon_i, \qquad\qquad \text{[Eq. 3]}$$

where

> β_0 is the average value of y_i when both x_i and z_i are equal to zero,
> β_1 is the slope coefficient of the predictor x_i conditional on the value of z_i,
> β_2 is the slope coefficient of the moderator z_i conditional on the value of x_i,
> β_3 is the coefficient of the interaction effect between x_i and z_i.

The interaction effect model also follows the above assumptions and, additionally, assumes that the effect of x on y is expected to be changed by β_3 as z increases by 1 unit.

In culturally responsive research, the moderator z is often a variable that represents different culture, such as, race/ethnicity related variables or gender identity variables.

For further illustration, we will use an example context of perceived discrimination and antisocial behavior. We suppose that a researcher wants to examine the effect of perceived discrimination (PDiscrim; x) on antisocial behavior (ASBehavior; y) and further examine if the effect is differed by birth gender (z). We rewrite the Equation 3 replacing the alphabetic notation with the variable names:

$$\text{ASBehavior}_i = \beta_0 + \beta_2 * \text{Gender}_i + (\beta_1 + \beta_3 * \text{Gender}_i) * \text{PDiscrim}_i + * \varepsilon_i. \quad \text{[Eq. 4]}$$

When the gender variable is coded as 0 for male and 1 for female, the Equation 3 can be rewritten for each gender group:

For male:

$$\text{ASBehavior}_i = \beta_0 + \beta_2 * 0 + (\beta_1 + \beta_3 * 0) * \text{PDiscrim}_i + \varepsilon_i, \quad \text{[Eq. 5]}$$

$$\text{ASBehavior}_i = \beta_0 + \beta_1 * \text{PDiscrim}_i + \varepsilon_i, \quad \text{[Eq. 6]}$$

where

β_0 is the intercept for male, which is the mean of antisocial behavior across all male students when they have zero value of perceived discrimination;
β_1 is the effect of perceived discrimination experiences on antisocial behavior for male students.

For female:

$$\text{ASBehavior}_i = \beta_0 + \beta_2 * 1 + (\beta_1 + \beta_3 * 1) * \text{PDiscrim}_i + \varepsilon_i, \quad \text{[Eq. 7]}$$

$$\text{ASBehavior}_i = (\beta_0 + \beta_2) + (\beta_1 + \beta_3) * \text{PDiscrim}_i + \varepsilon_i, \quad \text{[Eq. 8]}$$

where

$(\beta_0 + \beta_2)$ is the intercept for female, in which β_2 refers to the mean difference between the male and female students;

$(\beta_1 + \beta_3)$ is the effect of perceived discrimination experiences on antisocial behavior for female students, in which β_3 refers to the differential effects between the male and female students.

As this example shows, it is straightforward to examine the differential effects using the regression interaction approach when there is a clearly defined hypothesis to test. Here, the effect of perceived discrimination on antisocial behavior depends on the birth gender (likewise the effect of gender on antisocial behavior depends on the perceived discrimination as well) because there is an interaction term. That is, when the multiplicative term of x and z exists in the regression model, the coefficients of x and z are now conditional on each other.

Regression Mixture Modeling Approach

Regression mixture model is a novel statistical tool to detect *unobserved* subpopulations underlying the overall population based on the effect heterogeneity.

The regression mixture model, which is a type of finite mixture model (McLachlan & Peel, 2000), represents a novel statistical tool to detect latent subpopulations underlying the overall population. Regression mixture models follow several statistical assumptions comparable to those of regression interactions, including linearity, precise measurement of the predictors, independent observations, and normally distributed residuals (Van Horn et al., 2012; Van Horn et al., 2015). Beyond these similarities, regression mixture modeling has several unique features compared to the conventional regression interaction models (Van Horn et al., 2012; Van Horn et al., 2015). For example, it enables the detection of latent subpopulations only based on the differential regression effects without having to provide *a priori* hypotheses given the limited set of variables. Since the heterogeneous effects are based on the relationships between the predictor(s) and outcome, the model does not require the third variable (moderator) to be in place and, therefore, enables researchers to gain new insights into potential predictors as a means of understanding the differences in the effects.

Based on the understanding of the regression interaction approach, we describe the formulation of the regression mixture models. An equation for the simple linear regression mixture model where there is a single predictor x can be expressed as below:

$$y_{ik} = \beta_{0k} + \beta_{xk}x_{ik} + \varepsilon_{ik},$$

[Eq. 9]

where

y_{ik} is the observed score of outcome y for individual i classified into class k,

β_{0k} is the intercept coefficient for class k,

β_{xk} is the slope coefficient of the predictor x_{ik} for class k,

x_{ik} and ε_{ik} are the value of the predictor and random error for individual i in class k, respectively. Except for the subscript k, this equation is similar to the typical simple linear regression equation. Based on the number of latent classes, k, which is set by the user, all the model parameters (i.e., intercept, slope, and the residual error variance) are estimated. For example, if the user sets the model having two latent classes, then the two sets of parameters are estimated, one for each latent class.

Uniqueness of Regression Mixture Modeling Approach

In the regression mixture model, even if a researcher did not measure the moderator, z, it is possible to classify a specific class that has a different intercept and effect of x on y with others. If the moderator was perfectly measured without measurement error, and the effects of x on y for two groups (here, male and female) were clearly expected to be different based on the results of prior studies, the results of the regression mixture and moderation effect model would be very similar. In this case, the traditional moderation effect model can be applied more parsimoniously to examine the different effects of x on y in each group. However, if there is a measurement error in the moderator or there are no prior studies on what factors make the effect of x different on y differ, subpopulations with different effects of x on y could be examined through the regression mixture model rather than the moderation effect model. To sum up, the regression mixture can be applied in an exploratory way.

Illustration of Using the Regression Mixture Modeling

In this section, we illustrate the use of regression mixture modeling under the context of perceived discrimination and antisocial behavior. This section is written with an assumption that readers have prior knowledge of multiple regression with continuous outcomes. In this practice, the outcome Y is the antisocial behavior measure, the primary predictor X is the perceived discrimination measure, and acculturation and birth gender are used as latent class predictors (covariates) for the demonstration. We describe four steps for applying the regression mixture model: (1) establishing relationships between X and Y variables based on the theoretical background, (2) analyzing simple linear regression, (3) determining the optimal number of latent classes based on the simple linear regression model, and (4) examining the effect of covariate(s) on class memberships.

For the demonstration, we used Mplus 8.01 (Muthén & Muthén, 1998-2017), which is a statistical program for latent variable modeling. Since it is not feasible to cover all the features of Mplus in this chapter, we will focus on those commands that are specific to mixture modeling. Readers who are interested in more features of Mplus should refer to Muthén and Muthén (1998-2017). We have a short section below to introduce Mplus and the basic commands to analyze the example model for novice users. All the syntax and result outputs for the current demonstration are available at the online repository at The Ohio State University's QualLab (See https://u.osu.edu/quallab/advanced-methods-institute/).

The example data used in this section is artificially generated for the purpose of demonstration. Thus, the presented results should not be recognized as empirical research findings and extended for further discussion. We reviewed the relevant literature in perceived discrimination and antisocial behavior to mimic the realistic conditions and the effect sizes for simulating the data. We first briefly describe the context of the example variables.

Example Context

Outcome (Y)

Antisocial behavior is a concept including physical aggression, social aggression, and rule-breaking. Previous research has shown that antisocial behavior can be stimulated by the racial/ethnic discrimination experience (Brody et al., 2006). We used the Subtype of Antisocial Behavior (STAB; Burt & Donnellan, 2009) to simulate the data. In our example data, the STAB score has a mean of 50.46 with a standard deviation of 14.54, with higher score representing more severe antisocial behavior.

Predictor (X)

Perceived discrimination is a person's perception that he/she is not treated fairly due to his/her social status or group membership (Pascoe & Smart Richman, 2009). Previous research support that the perceived discrimination is positively associated with the antisocial behavior (Hartshorn, Whitbeck, & Hoyt, 2012; Taylor & Turner, 2002). We used the revised version of the Scale of Ethnic Experience (Malcarne, Chavira, Fernandez, & Liu, 2006) to simulate the scale of the measure. The mean of the perceived discrimination measure is 26.20 with a standard deviation of 2.43.

Latent Class Predictor (Covariates)

Acculturation can be conceptualized as a change that occurs while an individual adapts to another culture including cultural, social, and psychological change (Schwartz, Unger, Zamboanga, & Szapocznik, 2010). It is associated with perceived discrimination and depressive symptoms (Kam, Cleveland, & Hecht, 2010; Lorenzo-Blanco, Unger, Ritt-Olson, Soto, & Baezconde-Garbanati, 2011). We used the scales from the revised tool of the Short Acculturation Scale for Hispanic (Marin, Sabogal, Marin, Otero-Sabogal, & Perez-Stable, 1987) and the Bicultural Involvement Questionnaire-Revised (BIQ-R; Birman, 1998). The mean of the acculturation variable is 32.26 with a standard deviation of 2.26. The birth gender variable was created to be balanced (50% of male and 50% of female).

Example Data

Based on the example measures above, we simulated a dataset that is used for demonstrating the analysis of regression mixture model. The practice scenario assumes a situation in which a researcher is interested in the effects of perceived discrimination on antisocial behavior for international college students. Previous researches have shown the significant relationship between the discrimination experience and antisocial behaviors, and the relationship between those could be varied depending on the moderator, such as acculturation and gender identity (Finch, Kolody, & Vega, 2000; Gibbons et al., 2007; Jung, Hecht, & Wadsworth, 2007; Lorenzo-Blanco et al., 2011; Park, Schwartz, Lee, Kim, & Rodriguez, 2013). We generated a dataset with a sample size of 3,000 with four variables (i.e., antisocial behavior, perceived discrimination, acculturation, and birth gender).

Basic Mplus Commands for Mixture Modeling

Before we describe each step for analyzing the regression mixture model, we first briefly introduce the statistical program, Mplus 8.01, for basic commands. Figure 11.1 presents six commands that we use for the current demonstration.

First, `Title:` command is for naming the title of the syntax file. Second, `Data:` command is for importing the data file and directing the location of the file. If the syntax file is located in the same folder with the data file, the directory of the dataset can be omitted from this command. The example syntax in Figure 11.1 contains no file directory given the same reason. Third, `Variable:` command is for listing the names of the variables in the dataset. If some but not all variables are used for the data analysis, `usevariables` subcommand can be used for identifying which variables are used for the analysis. Next, `Analysis:`

```
TITLE: UNCONDITIONAL 1-CLASS
DATA: FILE IS rr_practice.csv;
VARIABLE: NAMES ARE y x m1 m2;
          USEVARIABLES y x;
          CLASS = c(1);
ANALYSIS: TYPE=MIXTURE;
MODEL: %OVERALL%
          y ON x;
          y;d
OUTPUT: STDYX;
```

FIGURE 11.1 Mplus Syntax for 1-Class (Traditional) Regression Model

command is required for identifying which type of analysis is used for estimating the model parameters. This is the key command for analyzing the current regression mixture model, with the subcommand of `Type=Mixture`. After providing all the information, users specify their model with `Model:` command. Finally, `Output:` command is an optional command to request for more information on the output file. In this example, `STDYX` is included to request for the standardized coefficients for the analysis results.

Step 1. Establishing Relationships between Variables Based on the Theoretical Background

When using any regression analysis, the first step is to establish a theoretical relationship between predictor(s) and an outcome. The same logic applies to using the regression mixture model. In this example, we have a hypothesis that perceived discrimination affects antisocial behavior (Hartshorn et al., 2012; Taylor & Turner, 2002).

Step 2. Analyzing the Simple Linear Regression Model

Based on the hypothesis at Step 1, we analyze the simple linear regression having antisocial behavior as an outcome y and perceived discrimination as a predictor x. Figure 11.1 shows the Mplus syntax for this simple regression model. In the `Model:` command, the regression model is specified with [*outcome*] `on` [*predictor*]. Here, "on" is the specific command to analyze the regression model. Since this model estimates a single set of model parameters (i.e., intercept, slope, and residual variance) for the entire sample, it is equivalent with the 1-class regression mixture model that defines the entire sample as one latent class.

Figure 11.2 presents the result output for the 1-class regression model. All the model parameters are statistically significant with p-value less than .05. The intercept and the slope coefficients are 33.416 and .651 with the standardized coefficients of 2.298 and .109, respectively. After confirming the small effect of perceived discrimination on antisocial behaviors, the researcher has decided to further explore the potential heterogeneity in the effect of perceived discrimination on antisocial behavior. Thus, the researcher proceeds with the next step for using the regression mixture model.

Step 3. Determine the Optimal Number of Latent Classes (Unconditional Model)

When using the regression mixture model, first, researchers need to determine the optimal number of latent classes based on their regression model in Step 2. In order to find the optimal number of latent classes (i.e., k in Equation 9), a series of regression mixture models is analyzed by increasing the number of latent classes, and then the analysis results are compared using model information criteria. For example, the single class model (i.e., regular regression model) in Step 2 is compared with the 2-class model and checked whether increasing the number of latent classes improves the model fit. Figure 11.3 presents the Mplus syntax to analyze the 2-class model.

```
MODEL RESULTS


Two-Tailed
                      Estimate      S.E.   Est./S.E.    P-Value
Latent Class 1
  Y           ON
    X               0.651        0.109      5.971       0.000
  Intercepts
    Y              33.416        2.833     11.796       0.000
  Residual Variances
    Y             208.937        5.772     36.198       0.000


STANDARDIZED MODEL RESULTS
STDYX Standardization


Two-Tailed
                      Estimate      S.E.   Est./S.E.    P-Value
Latent Class 1
  Y           ON
    X               0.109        0.018      6.020       0.000
  Intercepts
    Y               2.298        0.202     11.375       0.000
  Residual Variances
    Y               0.988        0.004    251.164       0.000
```

FIGURE 11.2 Mplus Partial Output for the Estimated Model Parameters for the 1-Class (Traditional) Regression Analysis

There are two changes made from the 1-class model to the 2-class model. First, in the Variable: command, the subcommand CLASS=C(1) is changed to CLASS=C(2) (see Figures 11.1 and 11.3, respectively). Here, the number in parentheses indicates the number of latent classes specified in the corresponding model. Next, the Model: command for the 2-class model is updated by adding the label %C#2% for allowing the second set of the model parameters to be estimated. In the same way, researcher can increase the number of latent classes to 3, 4, and above. The example syntax for the 3-class and 4-class models is available at the online repository (See https://u.osu.edu/quallab/advanced-methods-institute/).

Figure 11.4 presents the Mplus partial output for the 2-class regression mixture model results. For model comparisons of the regression mixtures, the Bayesian

```
TITLE: UNCONDITIONAL 2-CLASS
DATA: FILE IS rr_practice.csv;
VARIABLE: NAMES ARE y x m1 m2;
                    USEVARIABLES y x;
                    CLASS = c(2);
ANALYSIS: TYPE=MIXTURE;
MODEL: %OVERALL%
               y ON x;
               y;
               %C#2%
               y ON x;
               y;
OUTPUT: STDYX;
```

FIGURE 11.3 Mplus Syntax for the Unconditional 2-Class Regression Mixture Model

```
MODEL FIT INFORMATION

Number of Free Parameters                           7

Loglikelihood

        H0 Value                           -11528.268
        H0 Scaling Correction Factor          1.1748
          for MLR

Information Criteria

        Akaike (AIC)                        23070.536
        Bayesian (BIC)                      23112.581
        Sample-Size Adjusted BIC            23090.339
          (n* = (n + 2) / 24)
```

FIGURE 11.4 Mplus Partial Output for the Model Fit Information

TABLE 11.1 Model Information Criteria and the Class Proportion from the 1-Class to 4-Class Regression Mixture Models

	1-class	2-class	3-class	4-class
BIC	24563.75	23112.58	19346.76	19310.78
ABIC	24554.22	23090.34	19311.80	19263.12
% of Class 1	100.0%	27.7%	30.0%	30.0%
% of Class 2		72.3%	61.9%	7.3%
% of Class 3			8.1%	0.8%
% of Class 4				61.9%

Information Criterion (BIC; Schwarz, 1978) and the sample-size adjusted BIC (ABIC; Sclove, 1987) have shown good performance in the previous simulation studies (Kim, Vermunt, Bakk, Jaki, & Van Horn, 2016; Van Horn et al., 2012; Van Horn et al., 2015). For both BIC and ABIC, a smaller value implies the better fitting model. As shown in the result outputs for the 1-class and 2-class models, both BIC and ABIC are smaller for the 2-class model (BIC: 23112.58, ABIC: 23090.34) favoring the 2-class model over the 1-class model (BIC: 24563.75, ABIC: 24554.22).

Table 11.1 summarizes the BIC and ABIC values as well as the class proportions from the series of regression mixture models by increasing the number of latent classes. In this example, we have analyzed 1-class through 4-class models. The 3-class model shows the smallest value for both the BIC and ABIC, indicating that there are three distinctive classes based on the intercepts and the regression weights. For the 4-class model, even though the BIC and ABIC values are not very different from the ones for the 3-class model, the proportion of Class 3 is too small (0.8%) to classify it as one separate latent class. Therefore, the 3-class model was selected as the optimal unconditional model for the next step.

Table 11.2 presents the estimated model parameters for the 3-class model. As described in Equation 9, β_{0k}, β_{1k}, and σ_k^2 indicate the class-specific intercept, slope, and the residual variance. Based on the intercept and slope coefficient values for each class, we named Class 1, 2, and 3 as *Stable*, *Vulnerable*, and *Moderate* Class, respectively. As shown in Table 11.2, Stable Class had the lowest intercept value of the antisocial behavior ($\beta_{00} = 31.24$, $SE = 0.79$) and the non-significant effect of perceived discrimination on antisocial behaviors ($\beta_{10} = 0.04$, $SE = 0.03$). It means that people classified in this latent class tend to show relatively low antisocial behavior with no effect of the level of perceived discrimination. Vulnerable Class (Class 2) showed the highest intercept ($\beta_{01} = 48.58$, $SE = 2.35$) and slope ($\beta_{11} = 1.34$, $SE = 0.09$), indicating that they showed the highest average score of antisocial behavior with the most severe effect of perceived discrimination. Last, Moderate Class (Class 3) showed relatively moderate intercept ($\beta_{02} = 37.25$, $SE = 0.64$) and slope ($\beta_{12} = 0.68$, $SE = 0.02$) compared to other two latent classes. Based on the estimates from the unconditional model, we can draw a graph like Figure 11.5.

TABLE 11.2 Parameter Estimates and Standard Errors for the Unconditional 3-Class Regression Mixture Model

	Class 1: Stable (30.0%)		Class 2: Vulnerable (8.1%)		Class 3: Moderate (61.9%)	
	B	SE	B	SE	B	SE
Intercept (β_{0k})	31.24***	0.79	48.58***	2.35	37.25***	0.64
Perceived discrimination (β_{1k})	0.04	0.03	1.34***	0.09	0.68***	0.02
Residual variance (σ_k^2)	5.36***	0.25	7.62***	0.70	6.85***	0.21

Note.

*: $p < .05$;
**: $p < .01$;
***: $p < .001$.

Step 4. Predict Class Membership (Conditional Model)

The next step is to examine the relationship between the latent class predictors (covariates) and class membership. Through this step, we can determine which factors increase or decrease the membership probability of the corresponding latent class compared to the reference class. In the finite mixture modeling, a conditional model including covariates or distal outcomes can be estimated using one-step or three-step approaches. The one-step approach is a method to analyze structural parts including covariates or distal outcomes together with measurement parts simultaneously. However, the number of latent classes or characteristics for each latent class can be different from the unconditional model depending on covariate and distal outcomes when applying the one-step approach (Nylund-Gibson, Grimm, & Masyn, 2019).

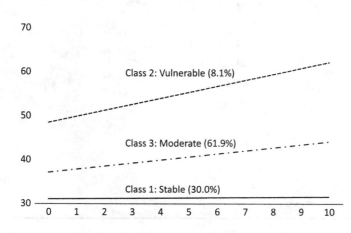

FIGURE 11.5 Regression Line for Each Latent Class from the Unconditional 3-Class Model

The three-step approach is a method that makes up for the shortcomings of the one-step approach. Each step is as follows. In the first step, it analyzes only the measurement part except for covariates and distal outcomes. In the second step, all individuals are assigned to each latent class. Last, in the third step, the structural parts including covariates or distal outcomes are analyzed after fixing the classification error derived from the first step (Asparouhov & Muthén, 2014; Bakk, Tekle, & Vermunt, 2013; Vermunt, 2010).

However, Kim et al. (2016) revealed that the effect of covariate was biased when the three-step approach was applied to the regression mixture model. They suggest an alternative approach: (1) determine the optimal number of classes by analyzing the unconditional model without covariates and (2) analyze the conditional model including covariates. They showed it perform better than the one- and three-step approaches. In this exercise, the alternative approach was applied following the suggestion of Kim et al. (2016). We already determined the optimal number of latent classes as three in the previous step. Thus, in this stage, the association between covariates and latent class membership was examined by analyzing the conditional model, the second step. The Mplus syntax for this step is presented in Figure 11.6.

```
TITLE: CONDITIONAL 3-CLASS
DATA: FILE IS rr_practice.csv;
VARIABLE: NAMES ARE y x m1 m2;
                USEVARIABLES y x m1 m2;
                CLASS = c(3);
ANALYSIS: TYPE=MIXTURE;
MODEL: %OVERALL%
            y ON x;
            y;
            y ON m1 m2;
            c ON m1 m2;
            %C#2%
            y ON x;
            y;
            %C#3%
            y ON x;
            y;
OUTPUT: STDYX;
```

FIGURE 11.6 Mplus Syntax for the Conditional (Step 2) 3-Class Regression Mixture Model

TABLE 11.3 Parameter Estimates for the Conditional 3-Class Model

	Class 1: Stable (30.0%)		Class 2: Vulnerable (8.1%)		Class 3: Moderate (61.9%)	
	B	SE	B	SE	B	SE
Intercept (β_{0k})	20.94***	.98	38.27***	2.37	27.09***	.89
Perceived discrimination (β_{1k})	.04	.03	1.35***	.08	.68***	.02
Acculturation (β_2)	.31***	.02	–	–	–	–
Birth gender (β_3)	.11	.09	–	–	–	–
Residual variance (σ_k^2)	4.87***	.22	7.31***	.72	6.33***	.20
Latent class predictor						
Acculturation (γ_1)	–	–	–.06*	.03	–.01	.02
Birth gender (γ_2)	–	–	–.13	.15	.01	.08

Note.

*: $p < .05$;
**: $p < .01$;
***: $p < .001$.

In comparison with the unconditional 3-class model syntax, names of covariates were added to the USEVARIABLES statement. Next, under the %OVERALL% label, a statement for estimating the direct covariate effects on the antisocial behaviors was added (Y on m1 m2), where m1 and m2 represent the acculturation and birth gender variables, respectively. Additionally, c on m1 m2 under the %OVERALL% label indicates the request to estimate the covariate effects on the class membership (c on m1 m2). Since the latent class variable is a nominal variable, the result of the covariate effects should be read as the multinominal logistic regression model. Table 11.3 presents the results of the conditional 3-class model.

Before interpreting the effects of covariates on class membership, it is necessary to examine whether the proportion or class-specific effect of each class in the conditional model is severely changed compared to the unconditional model. If severe changes occur, the covariate set or direct effects of covariates should be reconsidered because it might indicate that the sample classification is driven by the covariates (Kim et al., 2016) but not necessarily by the primary predictor of the interest. In this exercise, we have confirmed that there is no dramatic change in the overall pattern of the regression weights or the class proportions between the unconditional model (Table 11.2) and the conditional model (Table 11.3) although there is a slight decrease in the intercept coefficients.

In Table 11.3, along with the intercept and slope of perceived discrimination, the direct effects of acculturation (β_2) and birth gender (β_3) on antisocial behaviors are presented. The effect of acculturation on antisocial behaviors ($\beta_2 = 0.31$, $SE = 0.02$) was significant, which means that when acculturation increases by 1 unit, the antisocial behavior is also expected to be increased by 0.31, controlling for other variables. On the other hand, birth gender was not a statistically significant predictor.

The bottom of Table 11.3 shows the effects of covariates on the latent class membership when Stable Class is the reference group. When Vulnerable Class was the comparison group, only the coefficient of acculturation (γ_{11} = -0.06, *SE* = 0.03) was significant. This means that when acculturation increases, the likelihood of belonging to Stable Class, which is the reference group, is greater than that of Vulnerable Class, which is the comparison group. That is, a high level of acculturation increases the likelihood of belonging to a group maintaining a low level of antisocial behavior regardless of the perceived discrimination level. On the other hand, neither covariates significantly predicted the class membership probability between Stable Class and Moderate Class.

Concluding Remarks

In this chapter, we reviewed two quantitative methods to examine differential effects of predictors on an outcome in regression analysis – the regression interaction approach and the regression mixture modeling. Given that regression mixture modeling is relatively new and underutilized in social science research, especially under the culturally responsive research, we introduced the regression mixture modeling to the readers and provided the step-by-step tutorial to analyze the regression mixture models using Mplus. We provided key concepts, examples, and syntaxes for regression mixture in this chapter. For readers who want to apply this new method to their research, we strongly recommend doing the following activity to enhance one's understanding and practice the regression mixture.

Regression Mixture Activity

The activity scenario assumes a situation in which a researcher is interested in the effects of impulsivity on substance use for adolescents. We artificially generated a dataset with a sample size of 3,000, and all variables are assumed to be measured by valid tools. This activity requires you to follow the steps of regression mixture analysis using Mplus. Dataset and all the syntax for this activity are available at the online repository at The Ohio State University's QualLab.

1. **Fill out the blank of the below 2-class regression mixture model syntax.**
   Note. dataset: regression_mixture_activity.csv, y: substance use, x: impulsivity, m: parental depression

   TITLE: UNCONDITIONAL 2-CLASS
   DATA: FILE IS regression_mixture_activity.csv;
   VARIABLE: NAMES ARE y x m;

```
USEVARIABLES ARE (        )
CLASS = c(  );
ANALYSIS: TYPE = (              )
MODEL: %OVERALL%
(          )
y;
%C#2%
(        )
y;
OUTPUT: STDYX;
```

2. **Run a regression mixture model by increasing the number of latent classes one by one (from 2-class to 5-class model).**
3. **Is there a model that the best log-likelihood value was not produced?**
4. **Fill out the below table based on the results of question 3.**

	1-class	2-class	3-class	4-class	5-class
BIC					
ABIC					
% of Class 1					
% of Class 2					
% of Class 3					
% of Class 4					
% of Class 5					

5. **Determine the optimal number of latent classes by comparing BIC.**
6. **Name each latent class, considering the parameters (intercept and slope) of each class.**
   Note. Here, there is no correct answer. A researcher can assign any appropriate names that reveal well the characteristics of each latent class in mixture modeling.
7. **Draw a graph based on the intercepts and slopes for each latent class through Excel.**
8. **Run a conditional regression mixture model including parental depression (m) as a covariate.**
9. **Check whether the class proportion or class-specific effect of the conditional model changed severely compared to the unconditional model.**
10. **If there is a significant effect of parental depression on latent class membership, interpret it.**

For the answer sheet – see The Ohio State University QualLab website: https://u.osu.edu/quallab/advanced-methods-institute/

References

Asparouhov, T., & Muthén, B. (2014). Auxiliary variables in mixture modeling: Three-step approaches using mplus. *Structural Equation Modeling: A Multidisciplinary Journal*, *21*(3), 329–341. doi: https://doi.org/10.1080/10705511.2014.915181

Bakk, Z., Tekle, F. B., & Vermunt, J. K. (2013). Estimating the association between latent class membership and external variables using bias-adjusted three-step approaches. *Sociological Methodology*, *43*(1), 272–311. doi: https://doi.org/10.1177/0081175012470644

Berryman, M., Soohoo, S., & Nevin, A. (2013). *Culturally responsive methodology*. Bingley: Emerald Group Publishing Limited.

Birman, D. (1998). Biculturalism and perceived competence of latino immigrant adolescents. *American Journal of Community Psychology*, *26*(3), 335–354. doi: 10.1023/a:1022101219563

Brody, G. H., Chen, Y. F., Murry, V. M., Ge, X., Simons, R. L., Gibbons, F. X. … Cutrona, C. E. (2006). Perceived discrimination and the adjustment of African American youths: A five-year longitudinal analysis with contextual moderation effects. *Child Development*, *77*(5), 1170–1189. doi: 10.1111/j.1467-8624.2006.00927.x

Burt, S. A., & Donnellan, M. B. (2009). Development and validation of the subtypes of antisocial behavior questionnaire. *Aggressive Behavior: Official Journal of the International Society for Research on Aggression*, *35*(5), 376–398. doi: 10.1002/ab.20314.

Cohen, J., Cohen, P., West, S. G., & Aiken, L. S. (2003). *Applied multiple regression/correlation analysis for the behavioral sciences* (3rd ed.). New York, NY: Routledge. https://doi.org/10.4324/9780203774441

Finch, B. K., Kolody, B., & Vega, W. A. (2000). Perceived discrimination and depression among Mexican-origin adults in California. *Journal of Health and Social Behavior*, *41*(3), 295–313. doi: https://doi.org/10.2307/2676322

Gibbons, F. X., Yeh, H. C., Gerrard, M., Cleveland, M. J., Cutrona, C., Simons, R. L., & Brody, G. H. (2007). Early experience with racial discrimination and conduct disorder as predictors of subsequent drug use: A critical period hypothesis. *Drug and Alcohol Dependence*, *88*, S27–S37. doi: 10.1016/j.drugalcdep.2006.12.015

Graybill, F. A. (1976). *Theory and application of the linear model* (vol. 183). North Scituate, MA: Duxbury press.

Hartshorn, K., Whitbeck, L. B., & Hoyt, D. R. (2012). Exploring the relationships of perceived discrimination, anger, and aggression among North American indigenous adolescents. *Society and Mental Health*, *2*(1), 53–67. doi: 10.1177/2156869312441185.

Hahs-Vaughn, D. L., & Lomax, R. G. (2020). *An introduction to statistical concepts* (4th ed.). New York, NY: Routledge/Taylor & Francis Group.

Institute for Education Sciences. (2003, December). *Identifying and implementing educational practices supported by rigorous evidence: A user-friendly guide*. National Center for Education Evaluation and Regional Assistance. Retrieved from https://https://ies.ed.gov/ncee/pubs/evidence_based/randomized.asp_based/randomized.asp

Jung, E., Hecht, M. L., & Wadsworth, B. C. (2007). The role of identity in international students' psychological well-being in the United States: A model of depression level, identity gaps, discrimination, and acculturation. *International Journal of Intercultural Relations*, *31*(5), 605–624. doi: https://doi.org/10.1016/j.ijintrel.2007.04.001

Kam, J. A., Cleveland, M. J., & Hecht, M. L. (2010). Applying general strain theory to examine perceived discrimination's indirect relation to Mexican-heritage youth's alcohol, cigarette, and marijuana use. *Prevention Science*, *11*(4), 397–410. doi: 10.1007/s11121-010-0180-7

Kim, M., Vermunt, J., Bakk, Z., Jaki, T., & Van Horn, M. L. (2016). Modeling predictors of latent classes in regression mixture models. *Structural Equation Modeling: A Multidisciplinary Journal, 23*(4), 601–614. doi: 10.1080/10705511.2016.1158655

Lorenzo-Blanco, E. I., Unger, J. B., Ritt-Olson, A., Soto, D., & Baezconde-Garbanati, L. (2011). Acculturation, gender, depression, and cigarette smoking among US Hispanic youth: The mediating role of perceived discrimination. *Journal of Youth and Adolescence, 40*(11), 1519–1533. doi: 10.1007/s10964-011-9633-y

Malcarne, V. L., Chavira, D. A., Fernandez, S., & Liu, P. J. (2006). The scale of ethnic experience: Development and psychometric properties. *Journal of Personality Assessment, 86*(2), 150–161. doi: 10.1207/s15327752jpa8602_04

Marin, G., Sabogal, F., Marin, B. V., Otero-Sabogal, R., & Perez-Stable, E. J. (1987). Development of a short acculturation scale for hispanics. *Hispanic Journal of Behavioral Sciences, 9*(2), 183–205. doi: https://doi.org/10.1177/07399863870092005

Marsh, H. W., Hau, K.-T., Wen, Z., Nagengast, B., & Morin, A. J. S. (2013). Moderation. In T. D. Little (Ed.), *The Oxford handbook of quantitative methods: Statistical analysis* (pp. 361–386). Oxford: Oxford University Press.

McLachlan, G., & Peel, D. (2000). *Finite mixture models.* New York, NY: Wiley. doi: 10.1002/0471721182

Montgomery, D. C., Peck, E. A., & Vining, G. G. (2012). *Introduction to linear regression analysis* (5th ed.). New York: Wiley.

Muthén, L. K., & Muthén, B. O. (1998-2017). *Mplus user's guide* (8th ed.). Los Angeles, CA: Muthén & Muthén.

Nylund-Gibson, K., Grimm, R. P., & Masyn, K. E. (2019). Prediction from latent classes: A demonstration of different approaches to include distal outcomes in mixture models. *Structural Equation Modeling: A Multidisciplinary Journal, 26*(6), 967–985. doi: https://doi.org/10.1080/10705511.2019.1590146

Park, I. J., Schwartz, S. J., Lee, R. M., Kim, M., & Rodriguez, L. (2013). Perceived racial/ethnic discrimination and antisocial behaviors among Asian American college students testing the moderating roles of ethnic and American identity. *Cultural Diversity and Ethnic Minority Psychology, 19*(2), 166–176. doi: https://doi.org/10.1037/a0028640

Pascoe, E. A., & Smart Richman, L. (2009). Perceived discrimination and health: A meta-analytic review. *Psychological Bulletin, 135*(4), 531–554. doi: 10.1037/a0016059

Schwartz, S. J., Unger, J. B., Zamboanga, B. L., & Szapocznik, J. (2010). Rethinking the concept of acculturation: Implications for theory and research. *American Psychologist, 65*(4), 237–251. doi: 10.1037/a0019330

Schwarz, G. E. (1978). Estimating the dimension of a model. *Annals of Statistics, 6*(2), 461–464. doi: 10.1214/aos/1176344136

Sclove, S. L. (1987). Application of model-selection criteria to some problems in multivariate analysis. *Psychometrika, 52*, 333–343. https://doi.org/10.1007/BF02294360

Strunk, K. K., & Hoover, P. D. (2019). Quantitative methods for social justice and equity: Theoretical and practical considerations. In K. Strunk & L. Locke (Eds.), *Research methods for social justice and equity in education* (pp. 191–201). Cham: Palgrave Macmillan. https://doi.org/10.1007/978-3-030-05900-2_16

Taylor, J., & Turner, R. (2002). Perceived discrimination, social stress, and depression in the transition to adulthood: Racial contrasts. *Social Psychology Quarterly, 65*(3), 213–225. doi: 10.2307/3090120

Van Horn, M. L., Smith, J., Fagan, A. A., Jaki, T., Feaster, D. J., Masyn, K., & Howe, G. (2012). Not quite normal: Consequences of violating the assumption of normality in regression mixture models. *Structural Equation Modeling: A Multidisciplinary Journal*, *19*(2), 227–249. doi: 10.1080/10705511.2012.659622

Van Horn, M. L., Jaki, T., Masyn, K., Howe, G., Feaster, D. J., Lamont, A. E., & Kim, M. (2015). Evaluating differential effects using regression interactions and regression mixture models. *Educational and Psychological Measurement*, *75*(4), 677–714. doi: 10.1177/0013164414554931

Vermunt, J. K. (2010). Latent class modeling with covariates: Two improved three-step approaches. *Political Analysis*, *18*(4), 450–469. doi: https://doi.org/10.1093/pan/mpq025

12

THE UTILITY OF CRITICAL RACE MIXED METHODOLOGY

An Explanatory Sequential Example

Jessica T. DeCuir-Gunby, Whitney N. McCoy, Stephen M. Gibson

Mixed methods have grown in appeal as a research methodology and are frequently used to explore complex problems in education. Likewise, the popularity of critical race theory (CRT) in education research has exploded and has become the theoretical framework most commonly used to examine race-related issues within education (DeCuir-Gunby, Chapman, & Schutz, 2019). More recently, there has been a movement to combine the use of mixed methodology and CRT. The purpose of this chapter is twofold: (1) to explore the combining of mixed methodology and CRT through the explaining of Critical Race Mixed Methodology (CRMM); and (2) to explicate the utility of mixed methods approaches when there are problematic findings. In this chapter, we discuss how CRT is used to help frame an explanatory sequential mixed methods design (quant → QUAL), a design where quantitative data is initially collected followed by the qualitative data. Specifically, we focus on a research study examining African-American college students' experiences with racial identity, racial microaggressions, and belonging. The quantitative results from the study were not statistically significant, suggesting that racial identity does not mediate the relationship between racial microaggressions and sense of belonging. However, the qualitative findings revealed additional information that cannot be ascertained from the quantitative data alone. Specifically, focusing on the CRT tenets of centrality of racism, the challenge to dominant ideology, whiteness as property, and interest convergence, students discussed how their experiences with racial microaggressions impacted their racial identity and sense of belonging. In order to engage in this conversation, we begin by providing a discussion of CRT. We then provide a brief explanation of mixed methods research, focusing on explanatory sequential designs. Next, we explicate CRMM as well as provide an illustration of a CRMM study. We end the discussion by providing implications for using CRMM in higher education research.

DOI: 10.4324/9781003126621-15

Critical Race Theory as A Racial Framework

CRT is a counterlegal scholarship or racial framework that examines the relationships between race, racism, and power. Founded by Derrick Bell and many other scholars, CRT emerged in the 1970s as a way to challenge the law's complicity in upholding white supremacy as well as the slow progress of racial reform (Bell, 1995). According to Crenshaw et al., (1995), CRT has two main goals:

> The first is to understand how a regime of white supremacy and its subordination of people of color have been created and maintained in America, and in particular, to examine the relationship between that social structure and professed ideals such as 'the rule of law' and 'equal protection'. The second is a desire not merely to understand the vexed bond between law and racial power but to *change* it.
>
> *(p. xiii).*

CRT research can be largely categorized within 10 constructs or themes (DeCuir & Dixson, 2004; Ladson-Billings & Tate, 1995; Solórzano and Yosso, 2002; Tate, 1997). These constructs/themes include the following:

1. **Centrality of Race and Racism**—Focuses on the pervasiveness of racism in society.
2. **Challenge to Dominant Ideology**—Challenges the law's claims of neutrality, objectivity, and colorblindness.
3. **Centrality of Experiential Knowledge**—Centers on the experiences or counternarratives of people of color.
4. **Meritocracy Myth**—Confronts the beliefs that hard work and ability determines success.
5. **Whiteness as Property**—Examines the power of whiteness and white identity.
6. **Interest Convergence**—Explores how racial progress occurs when it benefits whites.
7. **Intersectionality**—Examines the intersection of subordinating identities such as race and gender.
8. **Interdisciplinarity**—Encourages the exploration of racism from various academic perspectives.
9. **Historical/Contextual Perspective**—Focuses on the importance of understanding the historical/contextual context.
10. **Commitment to Social Justice**—Embraces the goal of making change and providing equal opportunity.

CRT has been largely embraced by the field of education and most education subfields, including higher education (Lynn & Dixson, 2013). CRT research in higher education can be organized in the following categories: colorblind racism (e.g., analyses of language usage in policies), admissions policy analyses, and campus racial climate (e.g., faculty and student experiences) (Ledesma & Calderón, 2015; McCoy & Rodricks, 2015).

Our study can be categorized as a higher education campus racial climate study in that we examined African American students' experiences with racial microaggressions and their sense of belonging on campus. Researchers within higher education have explored the CRT constructs using various research methods, including mixed methods approaches.

Understanding Mixed Methods Research

How can you use CRT in your research? What CRT constructs are most relevant to your work?

Mixed methods research is "influenced by one's theoretical perspective, involves the collecting and analyzing of both quantitative and qualitative data within one study and, when applicable, is used to address issues of power." (Schutz, DeCuir-Gunby, & Williams-Johnson, 2016, p. 224). According to Hesse-Biber (2010), mixed methods research designs are either quantitative dominant, focusing on quantitative components while emphasizing the breadth of experiences, or are qualitative dominant and emphasize the qualitative elements while focusing on the depth of experiences. Generally, there are five basic mixed methods designs as described by Creswell and Plano Clark (2018): explanatory sequential (quantitative then qualitative data collected sequentially), exploratory sequential design (qualitative then quantitative data collected sequentially), concurrent parallel or convergent (data collected simultaneously), embedded (one method embedded in the other), and multiphase (alternating of quantitative and qualitative phases).

The design that we used for our study and one of the most commonly used designs in mixed methods research is the explanatory sequential design (Ivankova, Creswell, & Stick, 2006). In explanatory sequential designs, there are two major phases of a study. In the first phase of the study, quantitative data is collected first, followed by the second phase of the study where qualitative data is collected. The qualitative data is often used to explain or corroborate the findings from the quantitative data (Creswell & Plano Clark, 2018). In some cases, the qualitative data can also contradict the quantitative data (Greene, Caracelli, & Graham, 1989). Paradoxical findings are quite common in mixed methods research and can provide opportunities for future exploration. In addition, the quantitative component can also be used for purposive sampling for the qualitative component; the findings from the quantitative phase can dictate the groupings or sampling selection for the qualitative phase. It is important to point out that in most explanatory sequential designs, the quantitative data is analyzed before the qualitative phase can begin or is even conceptualized (e.g., determines the creation of interview questions). As such, explanatory sequential designs are often labor-intensive and time-consuming. These designs can be even more complicated when exploring issues of race within higher education.

> How can you use mixed methods research approaches in your work? How can an explanatory sequential design be used to address your research questions?

Exploring Critical Race Mixed Methodology

According to DeCuir-Gunby and Schutz (2019), CRMM is the combining of traditional mixed methods approaches with a CRT framework. It is a methodology used to examine issues of racial inequity. CRMM focuses on integrating race within all stages of the research process including the research goals/aims, research questions, inquiry worldview, instrumentation, data collection, data analysis, and validation/trustworthiness processes. In order to engage in CRMM, researchers must have an understanding of mixed methods research as well as CRT and how to effectively integrate them.

According to DeCuir-Gunby (2020), CRMM involves three major components. First, the research must center on race. Within higher education research, this often means focusing on individuals' or groups' racial experiences, exploring racial social structures, or examining racial policies. Second, the research must be grounded with a CRT framework specifically. There are many research studies that examine issues of race or use racial demographic variables. However, just studying race is not sufficient. There must be a connection to the CRT legal roots (Donnor & Ladson-Billings, 2017). Last, a goal of CRMM research is to challenge power structures and to help to create change. CRMM embodies the larger goal of CRT in terms of helping to address issues of equity.

The remainder of this chapter explicates CRMM through a real-world illustration of a research study. A CRMM sequential mixed method approach was used to explore the relationship between racial microaggressions, racial identity, and belonging of African-American college students. Phase one of the study focused on the quantitative aspect while phase two explored the qualitative component. A discussion is also provided regarding how the distinct findings can be integrated.

> How can a CRMM framework enhance your research? How does your research design adhere to the three requirements of a CRMM framework?

A CRMM Sequential Explanatory Mixed Methods Research Study: Racial Microaggressions, Racial Identity, and Belonging

Phase 1: Quantitative

Racial microaggressions are subtle slights and snubs based upon racial background and affiliation (Sue et al., 2007). Experiencing subtle, covert forms of racism is a common experience for African-American college students. Some studies have explored the impact of racial microaggressions on African-American students' outcomes such as academic involvement (Gomez, Khurshid, Freitag, & Lachuk, 2011), campus experiences (Harwood, Huntt, Mendenhall, & Lewis, 2012), and emotional and physical health (Yosso, Smith, Ceja, & Solórzano, 2009). Despite the growing research exploring African-American college students' experiences with racial microaggressions, truly understanding what occurs is a complicated process (Sue et al., 2007). Consequently, previous research has suggested racialized incidents, such as racial microaggressions, challenge African-American students' own racial affiliation (i.e., racial identity) and may impact African-American college students' sense of racial identity, belonging, or comfort on campus (Keels, Durkee, & Hope, 2017).

Research suggests that racial identity serves as a protective factor for African-American students (Sellers & Shelton, 2003). However, limited research has investigated the link between racial microaggressions, specifically microinsults (racial slights and insults) and microinvalidations (disregard about racial experiences), and African-American college students' sense of belonging with racial regard, including public regard (perception of how others view African-Americans) and private regard (personal feelings regarding being African-American), as mediating factors. Thus, the purpose of the current investigation was to explore the mediating factor racial regard plays in the relationship between African-American college students' experiences with racial microinsults and microinvalidations experiences and sense of belonging at predominantly white universities. We specifically explored the following research questions:

RQ1: *Does public regard mediate the relationship between racial microinsults and microinvalidations experiences and a sense of belonging for African-American college students?*

RQ2: *Does private regard mediates the relationship between racial microinsults and microinvalidations experiences and a sense of belonging for African-American college students?*

Methods

Participants. The sample consisted of 97 African-American college students with 75 self-identified women and 22 men attending Predominantly White Institutions (PWIs). Of the sample, 40% identified as graduate students, and 60% identified as undergraduate students. For the undergraduate student sample, 9%

identified as freshmen, 13% classified as sophomores, 14% identified as juniors, and 23% classified as seniors.

Data Collection

Participants were recruited anonymously to take a Qualtrics survey. Before taking the survey, respondents were asked to reflect on: (a) their experiences with racial microaggression in the last six months; (b) the extent of which they identify as a member of the African-American community; and (c) their thoughts and feelings about their college during the past three months. The survey consisted of several instruments including a demographics questionnaire (questions regarding personal characteristics), the assumptions of inferiority and the microinvalidation subscales of the Racial and Ethnic Microaggressions Scale (Nadal, 2011), the racial regard (public and private) subscales of the Multidimensional Inventory of Black Identity (Sellers, Smith, Shelton, Rowley, & Chavous, 1998, p. 18–39), and the relatedness (belonging) subscale of the Basic Psychological Needs at College Scale (Deci & Ryan, 2000).

Data Analysis Procedures

Using the Process (Hayes, 2012; Model #4) procedure in SPSS, hierarchical regression models, using a bootstrapping sample of 5,000, were conducted to examine if racial regard (e.g., public regard and private regard) mediated the relationship between racial microaggressions (e.g., microinsults and microinvalidations) and students' sense of belonging, resulting in two models. The series of regressions within the mediation model were calculated in the following sequence: (1) the independent variable predicting the dependent variable; (2) the independent variable predicting the mediator; and (3) the mediator predicting the dependent variable while controlling for the independent variable. Using the procedure outlined by Baron and Kenny (1986), the mediation evidence is confirmed under the following conditions: (a) the independent variable (microinsults or microinvalidations) significantly predicts the outcome variable (belonging); (b) the independent variable significantly predicts the mediator (public regard or private regard); and (c) the mediator significantly predicts the outcome variable, while the independent variable simultaneously no longer predicts the outcome variable.

Quantitative Findings

Public Regard as the Mediator. We hypothesized that public regard would mediate the relationship between both microinsults and microinvalidations and a sense of belonging. In regression model 1, microinsults/microinvalidations did not significantly predict a sense of belonging. Regression model 2, microinsults/microinvalidations did significantly predict public regard. In the final regression model 3, public regard did not significantly predict students' sense of belonging while controlling for microinsults/microinvalidations (see Figure 12.1)

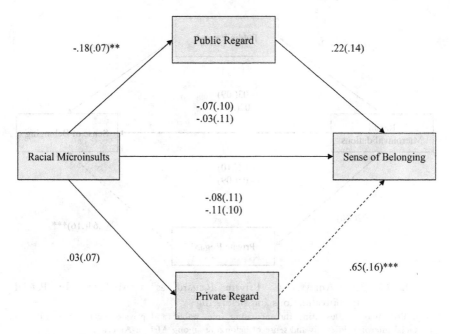

FIGURE 12.1 Path Analysis of Public Regard as a Mediator for Microinsults and
Belonging

Note. Path analysis illustrating the mediating roles public and private regard, in relation to racial
microinsults and sense of belonging among African-American college students. Statistically
significant (*p* < .05) direct effects are shown by solid lines. Non-significant direct effects are
shown by a dotted line. **p <. 01. ***p <. 001.

Private Regard as the Mediator. We hypothesized that private regard would
mediate the relationship between both microinsults and microinvalidations and
a sense of belonging. In regression model 1, microinsults/microinvalidations did
not significantly predict a sense of belonging. Regression model 2, microinsults/
microinvalidations did not significantly predict private regard. In the final regression model 3, private regard significantly predicts students' sense of belonging
while controlling for microinsults/microinvalidations (see Figure 12.2).

Phase 2: Qualitative

After the quantitative data was analyzed, although our findings were not statistically significant, we wanted to better understand how experiencing racial
microaggressions impacted students' racial identity and belonging on PWIs. The
following research questions guided the qualitative phase of the study:

1. What are African-American students' experiences with racial microaggressions in the PWI context?
2. How do racial microaggressions contribute to students' feelings of belonging
   in the PWI context?

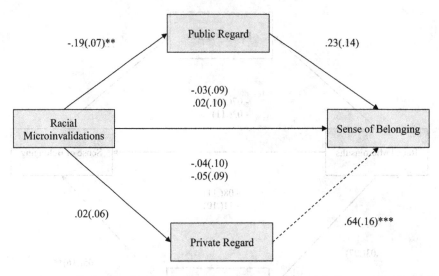

FIGURE 12.2 Path Analysis of Private Regard as a Mediator for Racial Microinvalidations and Belonging

Note. Path analysis illustrating the mediating roles public and private regard, in relation to racial microinvalidations and sense of belonging among African-American college students. Statistically significant (*p* < .05) direct effects are shown by solid lines. Non-significant direct effects are shown by a dotted line. **p <. 01. ***p <. 001.

Context/Participants

The qualitative phase consisted of fifteen participants (11 women and four men). Participants were full-time students enrolled in STEM, Education, or Psychology programs at the undergraduate (two senior-level students) or graduate levels (three masters and 10 doctoral students) from PWIs across the United States. Recruitment was based on convenience sampling.

Data Collection

Semi-structured interviews, or interviews that are conversational and informal in tone, allowed for the participants to provide open-responses while answering predetermined questions. These were conducted to elicit an understanding regarding the participant's experiences with racial microaggressions on campus and their feelings of belonging on their campuses. Interviews were conducted in neutral locations and lasted 30 minutes to an hour.

Data Analysis

Interviews were transcribed verbatim using a transcription service. Transcripts were reviewed, and changes were made to ensure accuracy. A codebook was created from theoretical and literature-based concepts, featuring primary and secondary codes, along with definitions and raw data examples from the narratives that each participant provided (Charmaz & Belgrave, 2012; DeCuir-Gunby, Marshall, & McCulloch, 2012; Strauss & Corbin, 1990). Codes were based upon concepts regarding racial microaggressions, student life on campus, campus/program perception, and campus racism. Using Dedoose 7.6.21, transcripts were uploaded and then coded using the codebook. The raw data was examined using open coding, while codes and concepts were connected using axial coding. The codes were then organized into larger themes (Merriam & Tisdell, 2015).

As the qualitative data was analyzed, to maintain credibility, codes, and themes were derived from peer-review articles within the field (Braun & Clarke, 2006). Also, thick, rich descriptions were given from the raw data to connect our claims to our analysis. Regarding trustworthiness, member checking was conducted with each participant. The research team worked to maintain inter-rater reliability of 85% or higher before coding the documents completely.

Qualitative Findings

African-American graduate students experienced various forms of racial microaggressions, although microinsults were experienced at a higher rate than the others. Within the context of microinsults, *ascription to intelligence* (questioning of one's intellect) was most often experienced. These experiences often impacted how the students felt about themselves as Black students and were examples of CRT's *centrality of racism* and *challenge to dominant ideology*. Wade, a second-year master's student studying nutrition, mentioned how his professors or other colleagues would talk about him being in the program: "Wow, you're doing really good to be an African American here on this campus. You're studying a white man's field. You're thriving in it."

Although most participants experienced microinsults, there were also microassaults that were within the campus community. These incidents and expressions affected how the students viewed the campus as a whole, clear examples of CRT's *challenge to dominant ideology*, *centrality of racism*, and *Whiteness as property*. Wade, a nutrition major, mentioned how students used a graffiti tunnel on campus:

> So, it was basically African Americans had written the "Dear White People" series across campus and they retaliated and went Dear Black People. And there were things in there like, you don't belong, Dear Black People, get over it. Dear Black People … just all types of craziness and … yeah. It was a mess for about two days. But, again, it was swept under the rug…they immediately went and tried to cover stuff up and change it and put the love messages and inspirational stuff.

Ultimately, experiencing racial microaggressions impacted their feelings of belonging. Participants often mentioned how their university had a mission of diversity and equity, but interactions with faculty members, students, and coursework made them feel disconnected, upset, or intimidated. Participants mentioned that diversity efforts on campus were not as strong, that equity was something the university needed to work on, and they thought the school would push diversity more. To the students, it seemed as if *interest convergence* allowed them to be recruited for university diversity efforts and *the challenge to dominant ideology* allowed departments to promote diversity yet ignore racial equity conversations. Wade said this about being the only Black man in his program and the diversity efforts in the program:

> I can't stand it. Because I think that it's false. I don't think they're trying to work on it. I know I won a diversity scholarship within my lab, and I mean, at first, I was excited about it, but then when I got here, I'm just like whoa. I kind of wish I chose another school, because I feel like I'm here just to add to that statistic, more so, you don't want my knowledge. You don't want my skill; you want my skin tone and to add to your labs.

The students' various experiences allowed us to see how *the centrality of racism* influenced African-American students at PWIs and continued to influence their racial identity during matriculation. Their stories also exhibited how colorblindness and *the challenge to dominant ideology* have allowed students, faculty, and staff to ignore or simply placate issues that African-American students faced on campus. Considering all of the racial barriers participants faced, they also noted how it contributed to their feelings of belongingness and subsequent desire to remain enrolled and make change on their campuses.

Integrating the Quantitative and Qualitative Findings

The current investigation's primary objective was to examine the relationships between racial microaggressions, racial identity, and belonging using CRMM. Consistent with CRMM, our study used a mixed methods design (explanatory sequential) and focused on issues surrounding race and racism, employed a CRT lens, and provided critiques for racial change within college campuses. For the quantitative phase, we examined the mediating role of racial regard in the association between racial microaggression experiences and a sense of belonging. Although our result yielded no significant mediation models, our findings still made some notable contributions to the existing literature on racial identity as a mediator and African-American college students' experiences with racial microaggressions and its impact on these students' sense of belonging. We found evidence of an indirect effect of private regard (e.g., positive feelings about African-Americans or being African-American) positively influencing students' sense of belonging when controlling for racial microaggressions (i.e., micro-insults and microinvalidations). The finding is consistent with previous litera-ture investigating the link between private regard attitudes and psychological adjustment (Rivas-Drake, 2012). Also, consistent with previous literature, when confronted with racial microaggressions, students reported lower levels of public regard (Sellers & Shelton, 2003). Overall, these microinsults and microinvalida-tions made African-American college students feel isolated and unsupported on their respective university campuses. These relationships were then corroborated and expanded by the qualitative findings in phase two of the study. Students experienced a variety of racial microaggressions which negatively impacted their racial identity and sense of belonging. Yet, the students remained committed to staying enrolled in their respective universities because they had positive racial identities. By using a CRT lens, specifically focusing on the centrality of racism, the challenge to dominant ideology, whiteness as property, and interest conver-gence, we were able to examine how racism influenced students' experiences within the PWI context.

Implications for Critical Race Mixed Methodology in Higher Education Research

There has been substantial discussion in higher education regarding race and race-related constructs, but less focus has been given on *how* to study race. A goal of this chapter was to explore methodological approaches to examine the study of race. Specifically, this chapter explored CRMM, the combin-ing of mixed methodology, and CRT through the explaining of a real-world research study. It examined how the qualitative findings can both corroborate and expand the quantitative findings, including how having qualitative data is useful when the quantitative data does not yield significant differences. From this discussion, there are several important implications that need to be con-sidered by the field.

First, although there has been a significant amount of research using CRT in the field of higher education, the research approaches need to be expanded. Most of the research, as mentioned earlier, focuses on policy analyses and campus climate issues, including the research presented in this chapter. More areas need to be explored including curriculum and pedagogy as well as teaching and learning. We need to learn how race is enacted within college classrooms. Also, we need to use all 10 of the CRT components as well as combinations of the components in our programs of research to examine sys-temic racism. Doing so will enable us to provide rich and nuanced analyses as well as enable us to better understand how race operates within the higher education context.

Second, much of the research in education is quantitative or even qualitative. The use of mixed methods approaches has been growing in education, includ-ing higher education. However, most CRT research is qualitative. The use of quantitative and mixed methods approaches in CRT is slowly growing (DeCuir-Gunby & Schutz, 2019). Yet much of the mixed methods and CRT research has been conducted within higher education (e.g. Covarrubias et al., 2018; Kouyoumdjian, Guzmán, Garcia, & Talavera-Bustillos, 2017; White, DeCuir-Gunby, & Kim, 2019). More research is needed focusing on CRT and mixed methods in general, including within higher education. In doing so, it is important to remember that mixed methods research can yield a variety of findings. Sometimes quantitative and qualitative findings can corroborate, expand upon, or even contradict each other. Whatever the case, mixed methods approaches allow for a richer examination of phenomena in higher education.

Last, there needs to be more advances in racial methodology, particularly in how to combine CRT and methodological approaches (DeCuir-Gunby & Schutz, 2019). This chapter focused on CRMM, a way to combine CRT and mixed methods research. However, this is just one of the many ways in which traditional methods can be expanded. As researchers study race, we should not be limited in the methodological approaches that are currently available because they may or may not be sufficient to meet our needs. We have to be innovative and continue to create new and intricate ways to examine race and racism in higher education.

Conclusion

Conducting race-related research in higher education can be challenging. In order to do so, it is necessary to understand racial constructs, racial frameworks, as well as racial methodologies. CRMM is a way of combining CRT, a racial framework, to explore racism and power. In conducting research using CRMM, researchers have an opportunity to expand traditional ways of conducting both mixed methods and CRT approaches. Yet more work is needed regarding CRMM as well as other racial methodologies within higher education. (See the following activity, Tables 12.1 and 12.2, to practice reimagining a traditional mixed methods research study into a CRMM study).

CRMM Activity

Using CRMM takes time because it requires researchers to re-envision and integrate CRT and mixed methods research. It is necessary to consider the various stages of the research process. This activity requires you to think about your current mixed methods research study and how you can re-imagine it as a CRMM study. Table 12.1 provides an example of a research study using a traditional mixed methods research approach and a CRMM approach. Each column represents a major component of a mixed methods research study. Note how the different components change when using CRMM. Table 12.2 is a blank template for you to practice reimagining your own traditional mixed methods research study into a CRMM study.

TABLE 12.1 Traditional Mixed Methods Approach Versus CRMM Approach Activity

	Research Questions/ Hypotheses/ Goals	Mixed Methods Design	Theories	Worldview	Sample/Context	Instrumentation	Analysis & Integration	Outcomes/Claims
Traditional Mixed Methods Approach	To understand how Black college students regulate their emotions when they experience racial situations.	Sequential explanatory mixed methods design	Emotions Emotion regulation	Constructivism (to understand how they construct their experiences)	Black college students. Quantitative sample (n=300). Qualitative sample will be chosen from the quantitative sample (n=30).	Emotion regulation scale Interviews (focus on emotions and emotion regulation)	Multiple regression or SEM Thematic Content analysis Joint displays Data triangulation	A better understanding of how students regulate their emotions in racial situations on campus. Implications will focus on emotions and emotion regulation on campus.
CRMM Approach	To understand Black college students' views about race and how they regulate their emotions when they experience racial situations.	Sequential explanatory mixed methods design	Emotions Emotion regulation Racialized emotions	Critical race theory • Whiteness as property • Centrality of racism • Intersectionality • Centrality of experiential knowledge	Black college students at PWIs. PWIs are important because of the history of racial hostility. Quantitative sample (n=300) Qualitative sample will be chosen from the quantitative sample (n=30).	Emotion regulation scale Racial ideology scale (necessary to understand view of race) Racial experiences scale (necessary to understand their experiences with race) Interviews (focus on race and emotions)	Multiple regression or SEM Narrative analysis Joint displays Data triangulation	A better understanding of how students experience racial situations on PWIs. A better understanding of how students regulate their emotions in racial situations on PWIs. Implications will focus on emotions and emotion regulation in the context of racial situations on PWIs.

TABLE 12.2 Traditional Mixed Methods Approach versus CRMM Approach Activity Template

	Research questions/ hypotheses/ Goals	Mixed methods design	Theories	Worldview	Sample/ context	Instrumentation	Analysis & integration	Outcomes/ claims
Traditional Mixed Methods Approach								
CRMM Approach								

Directions: This is a blank template for you to practice reimagining your own traditional mixed methods research study into a CRMM study. Think about your research ideas and fill in the blanks.

References

Baron, R. M., & Kenny, D. A. (1986). The moderator-mediator variable distinction in social psychological research: Conceptual, strategic, and statistical considerations. *Journal of Personality and Social Psychology, 51*(6), 1173.

Braun, V., & Clarke, V. (2006). Using thematic analysis in psychology. *Qualitative Research in Psychology, 3*(2), 77–101.

Charmaz, K., & Belgrave, L. (2012). Qualitative interviewing and grounded theory analysis. In J. Gubrium (Ed.), *The SAGE handbook of interview research: The complexity of the craft* (2nd ed., pp. 347–367). Thousand Oaks, CA: Sage.

Covarrubias, A., Nava, P. E., Lara, A., Burciaga, R., Vélez, V. N., & Solórzano, D. G. (2018). Critical race quantitative intersections: A testimonio analysis. *Race Ethnicity and Education, 21*(2), 253–273.

Creswell, J., & Plano Clark, V. (2018). *Designing and conducting mixed methods research* (3rd ed.). Thousand Oaks, CA: Sage.

Deci, E. L., & Ryan, R. M. (2000). The "what" and "why" of goal pursuits: Human needs and the self-determination of behavior. *Psychological Inquiry, 11*(4), 227–268.

DeCuir-Gunby, J. T. (2020). Using critical race mixed methodology to explore the experiences of African Americans in education. *Educational Psychologist, 55*, 244–255.

DeCuir-Gunby, J. T., Chapman, T. K., & Schutz, P. A. (Eds.) (2019). *Understanding critical race research methods and methodologies: Lessons from the field.* New York, NY: Routledge.

DeCuir-Gunby, J. T., Marshall, P., & McCulloch, A. (2012). Using mixed methods to analyze video data: A teacher professional development example. *Journal of Mixed Methods Research, 6*(3), 199–216.

DeCuir-Gunby, J. T., & Schutz, P. A. (2019). Critical race mixed methodology: Designing a research study combining critical race theory and mixed methods research. In J. T. DeCuir-Gunby, T. K. Chapman, & P. A. Schutz (Eds.), *Understanding critical race research methods and methodologies: Lessons from the field* (pp. 166–179). New York, NY: Routledge.

Donnor, J. K., & Ladson-Billings, G. (2017). Critical race theory and the postracial imaginary. In N. K. Denzin & Y. Lincoln (Eds.), *Handbook of qualitative research* (5th ed., pp. 195–213). Thousand Oaks, CA: Sage.

Gomez, M. L., Khurshid, A., Freitag, M. B., & Lachuk, A. J. (2011). Microaggressions in graduate students' lives: How they are encountered and their consequences. *Teaching and Teacher Education, 27*(8), 1189–1199.

Greene, J. C., Caracelli, V. J., & Graham, W. D. (1989). Toward a conceptual framework for mixed-method evaluation designs. *Educational Evaluation and Policy Analysis, 11*(3), 255–274.

Harwood, S. A., Huntt, M. B., Mendenhall, R., & Lewis, J. A. (2012). Racial microaggressions in the residence halls: Experiences of students of color at a predominantly white university. *Journal of Diversity in Higher Education, 5*(3), 159.

Hayes, A. F. (2012). PROCESS: A versatile computational tool for observed variable mediation, moderation, and conditional process modeling [White paper].

Hesse-Biber, S. (2010). Qualitative approaches to mixed methods practice. *Qualitative Inquiry, 16*(6), 455–468.

Ivankova, N. V., Creswell, J. W., & Stick, S. L. (2006). Using mixed methods sequential explanatory design: From theory to practice. *Field Methods, 18*(1), 3–20. https://doi.org/10.1177/1525822X05282260

Keels, M., Durkee, M., & Hope, E. (2017). The psychological and academic costs of school-based racial and ethnic microaggressions. *American Educational Research Journal, 54*(6), 1316–1344. doi: 10.3102/0002831217722120

Kouyoumdjian, C., Guzmán, B. L., Garcia, N. M., & Talavera-Bustillos, V. (2017). A community cultural wealth examination of sources of support and challenges among latino first-and second-generation college students at a Hispanic serving institution. *Journal of Hispanic Higher Education, 16*(1), 61–76.

Ledesma, M. C., & Calderón, D. (2015). Critical race theory in education: A review of past literature and a look to the future. *Qualitative Inquiry, 21*(3), 206–222.

Lynn, M., & Dixson, A. D. (Eds.). (2013). *Handbook of critical race theory in education.* London: Routledge.

Merriam, S. B., & Tisdell, E. J. (2015). *Qualitative research: A guide to design and implementation.* New York, NY: John Wiley & Sons.

McCoy, D. L., & Rodricks, D. J. (2015). *Critical race theory in higher education: 20 years of theoretical and research innovations: ASHE higher education report, volume 41, number 3.* New York, NY: John Wiley & Sons.

Nadal, K. (2011). The racial and ethnic microaggressions scale (REMS): Construction, reliability, and validity. *Journal of Counseling Psychology, 58*(4), 470–480.

Rivas-Drake, D. (2012). Ethnic identity and adjustment: The mediating role of sense of community. *Cultural Diversity and Ethnic Minority Psychology, 18*(2), 210.

Schutz, P. A., DeCuir-Gunby, J. T., & Williams-Johnson, M. R. (2016). Using multiple and mixed methods to investigate emotions in educational contexts. In M. Zembylas, & P. Schutz (Eds.), *Methodological advances in research on emotion and education* (pp. 217–229). New York, NY: Springer.

Sellers, R. M., & Shelton, J. N. (2003). The role of racial identity in perceived racial discrimination. *Journal of Personality and Social Psychology, 84*(5), 1079–1092. doi: 10.1037/0022-3514.84.5.1079

Sellers, R. M., Smith, M. A., Shelton, J. N., Rowley, S. A. J., & Chavous, T. M. (1998). Multidimensional model of racial identity: A reconceptualization of African American racial identity. *Personality and Social Psychology Review, 2*(1), 18-39.

Strauss, A., & Corbin, J. (1990). *Basics of qualitative research.* Thousand Oaks, CA: Sage publications.

Sue, D. W., Capodilupo, C. M., Torino, G. C., Bucceri, J. M., Holder, A. M. B., Nadal, K. L., & Esquilin, M. (2007). Racial microaggressions in everyday life: Implications for clinic practice. *American Psychologist, 62*, 271–286.

White, A. M., DeCuir-Gunby, J. T., & Kim, S. (2019). A mixed methods exploration of the relationships between the racial identity, science identity, science self-efficacy, and science achievement of African American students at HBCUs. *Contemporary Educational Psychology, 57*, 54–71.

Yosso, T., Smith, W., Ceja, M., & Solórzano, D., (2009) Critical race theory, racial microaggressions, and campus racial climate for Latina/o undergraduates. *Harvard Educational Review, 79*(4), 659–691. https://doi.org/10.17763/haer.79.4.m6867014157 m7071

13

ADVANCING CRITICAL RACE SPATIAL ANALYSIS

Implications for the Use of GIS in Educational Research

Verónica N. Vélez

At the Pan-African Congress in London, W. E. B. Du Bois (1990) reflected "how far differences of race – which show themselves chiefly in the color of the skin and the texture of the hair – will hereafter be made the basis of denying to over half of the world the right of sharing to utmost ability the opportunities and privileges of modern civilization" (para 1). These famous words uttered by Du Bois at the turn of the 20th century eerily echo what has come to pass – that the "color-line" indeed remains a permanent fixture in organizing and dividing the world. Du Bois theorized the "color-line" as a cartographic, geographic, and historical project that shapes and is shaped by white supremacy at multiple scales (Wilson, 2018; Battle-Baptiste & Rusert, 2018). One of the best examples of Du Bois' cartographic skill was his work, *The Georgia Negro: A Social Study,* in which he redraws the global map as two spheres, one half depicting Asia, Europe, Africa, and Australia, and the other depicting North and South America. He links both with a series of lines to mark routes of the slave trade from West Africa to Brazil, the US South, and Portugal, and used gradients of black and brown to note impacted regions. Finally, he added a star to bring attention to the state of Georgia. Du Bois' map – a rendition of his socio–spatial understanding of the world – aptly titled, "Black Atlantic World," was meant as a geohistorical visualization to underscore that Black life in Georgia could not be disarticulated from the global conditions that inform it. In essence, he employed cartography to display the "color-line" as a strategic structural response to those that would claim racial inequities were the result of personal failings (Wilson, 2018).

Fast forward to July 2020. The art of cartography is on full display at the annual Environmental Systems Research Institute's (ESRI) user conference. ESRI is one of the largest global manufacturers of geographic information systems (GIS); each year, their use of digital mapping technologies to produce high-tech spectacles of data never ceases to amaze. The 2020 annual conference was

DOI: 10.4324/9781003126621-16

equally spectacular, with an important addition – the launch of ESRI's racial equity initiative[1]. The timing of this launch was no accident. With daily storylines of the disparate impact of COVID-19 across racial groups and international uprisings calling for an end to anti-Black violence spurred by the police murder of George Floyd, ESRI was compelled to respond. Their tagline to customers, "address racial equity with location intelligence," was met with praise, excitement, and promise as ESRI positioned itself to join movements across the world to promote racial justice.

The parallels between Du Bois in 1900 and ESRI's 2020 user's conference are clear. Both understood the power of cartography, and the gaze associated with it. Both responded to the conditions of the moment, seeking to use maps to better understand these realities. And both insisted on sharing their visualizations on the world stage. *The difference?* Du Bois deeply understood the danger of employing maps as "rationale" or "scientific" artifacts to mask their use in justifying racial hierarchies. For Du Bois, the use of cartography had very specific political aims, anchored in a uniquely Black consciousness. Sharing his maps on the world stage was an act of Black self-determination that insisted racial oppression, and not natural aptitude, was the culprit of social inequities (Wilson, 2018). Engaging the world stage also provided Du Bois an opportunity to showcase how Blacks were not unmappable (McKittrick, 2006), and held critical cartographic insight to understand the spatiality of Black life and social life more broadly.

Inspired by Du Bois, Critical Race Spatial Analysis (CRSA; Vélez & Solórzano, 2017) was born out of a fascination with "the map" and its potential to engage a counter-*cartographic* narrative (Knigge & Cope, 2006) of everyday life, one built from spatial models of the world anchored in the lived experiences of Black, Indigenous, and People of Color (BIPOC). CRSA considers how GIS could be employed as a tool for analyzing race and racism in education. The journey to CRSA was driven by a desire to answer the following: *What types of education-related questions could GIS help us answer? What would it take to envision GIS as both a conceptual and methodological tool for critical race scholars and educators? Can GIS map-making be utilized for racial and social justice?*

Answering these questions led to several projects, each of which engaged GIS to foreground the relationship between the *social* and the *spatial* and make evident how power intervenes at this intersection to mediate educational (in)opportunities for BIPOC. From exploring the continued significance of geographic "color lines" in South Los Angeles for BIPOC students (Solórzano & Vélez, 2016), to the educational impact of racially restrictive covenants and redlining for Mexican American communities (Solórzano & Vélez, 2017), these projects made increasingly evident the potential of GIS to portray racialized, and arguably *racist*, histories, policies, and practices. Each endeavor deepened my commitment to refine GIS as *both* a conceptual and methodological tool in my work. This required, as core to my responsibility as a critical race scholar, that I wrestle with critiques put forth by other critical geographers and cartographers concerning the use of maps for white supremacist, patriarchal, and otherwise colonial aims. It wasn't enough to generate maps. GIS must be treated as an epistemological practice that requires attention to issues of positionality, power, knowledge construction, multiple subjectivities, and the politicized nature of representation.

> It wasn't enough to generate maps. GIS must be treated as an epistemological practice that requires attention to issues of positionality, power, knowledge construction, multiple subjectivities, and the politicized nature of representation.

This realization became most evident when I introduced GIS to a group of migrant mother activists mobilizing for educational change. Initially, the goal was to complete an assignment for a GIS course with the hope of producing a series of GIS maps that could be used by this group for their organizing efforts. What transpired in the process became the inspiration for CRSA and its ongoing developments. Refusing to limit their involvement to only the product of the map, the mothers insisted on driving an iterative process throughout the entire map-making exercise. Although exploratory spatial data analysis (ESDA)[2] was initially used, it was the mothers' intimate knowledge of the community and collaborative analysis in map-making that was key. By rooting the analytical capabilities of GIS in their experience, they drove an iterative inquiry that led to the building of a *counter*-cartographic narrative (Knigge & Cope, 2006) that spoke back to the post-racial discourse taking hold of educational reform in their local context. Each new map was only made possible because of the mothers' analysis of the previous one. Their experiential knowledge shaped decisions about the data, the analysis applied, and the aesthetics for each map, to make visible "color lines" that would otherwise go unnoticed. In the end, the mothers transformed the power of the maps to rest not in their "gee-whiz" displays of data, but in the weaving of a spatial narrative that linked their current efforts to historical struggles for racial justice in schools.

This chapter shares this methodological journey to CRSA, the details of which were provided at the Advanced Method Institute (AMI) convening in early Summer 2021. Shaped by the conversations at AMI, I offer new developments in CRSA that wrestle more explicitly with the computational methods upon which much of GIS relies. I conclude with implications for the continued use of GIS in educational research.

The Journey to Critical Race Spatial Analysis: The Case of Pasadena Unified

In 2007, I took my first GIS course taught by Dr. Leobardo Estrada at UCLA. At that time, I was a full-time grassroots organizer working with a group of migrant mother activists devoted to making change in schools and in US immigration policy. This group, located in my hometown of Pasadena, California, had been organizing for nearly two decades. They often shared their frustration at how school administrators would dismiss their concerns, citing that the mothers' evidence of harm was primarily anecdotal rather than a proven pattern of injury. One evening as we were strategizing for how to speak back to these dismissals, I shared GIS maps from UCLA's *Institute for Democracy, Education, and Access*[3] (IDEA). At that time, IDEA was just beginning to use GIS to expose the geography of educational (in)opportunity (e.g., access to materials and resources, access to quality teachers, access to advanced placement classes) in Los Angeles County. Their intention was to share GIS maps with a variety of stakeholders to increase dialog about the importance of geospatial configurations that link educational data with other social and economic data to understand the structural conditions that influence academic outcomes, particularly for BIPOC students.

Inspired by IDEA, the mothers discussed whether similar maps could be made to tell *their* truth about what was contributing to educational disparities in their community. Thankfully, Dr. Estrada agreed to reconfigure the final assignment to tailor my project to support the mothers. With his signoff, the mothers and I began to formulate questions that GIS could answer about our local context. We asked, *how does geography influence educational opportunity for Latinx students in Pasadena Unified? Is there a relationship between where Latinx students live and the type of resources they receive in schools? If so, what does this relationship reveal about the quality of schools in the Northwest neighborhood of Pasadena, an area that is predominantly Latinx?*

But before I could jump into GIS mapping, I first asked the mothers to define the boundaries of Pasadena's Northwest neighborhood. Demographic boundaries are not usually defined by those who reside in the communities that are being mapped. Given the widespread use of US Census data, geographic units (e.g., county and city limits, census tracts, zip codes) are preset for ease of categorizing and analyzing data. But it was important to the mothers (and me) that they draw the boundaries of the "Latinx neighborhood." Because most mainstream accounts of Pasadena tend to erase the prominence of the Latinx community, we wanted to ensure that the neighborhood was clearly marked by *those that reside in it*. Figure 13.1 demonstrates the Pasadena Unified School District (PUSD) boundary, along with the cities located in the San Gabriel Valley that comprise it. Figure 13.2 represents a map of the Latinx neighborhood – known as *Northwest Pasadena* – as drawn by the mothers.

The next step was to show demographically that this region was home to a thriving Latinx community and had been so for decades. I accessed decennial US Census data from 1940 – 2000 and mapped the density of Latinx residents by census tract for PUSD. The following maps (Figure 13.3) show that since 1940, Latinx residents have been growing within the Northwest section of the city. Thus, the mothers' knowledge of *where* the Latinx community resides was confirmed by demographic analyses that reveal that the densest Latinx neighborhood in PUSD indeed is, and always has been, the Northwest neighborhood.

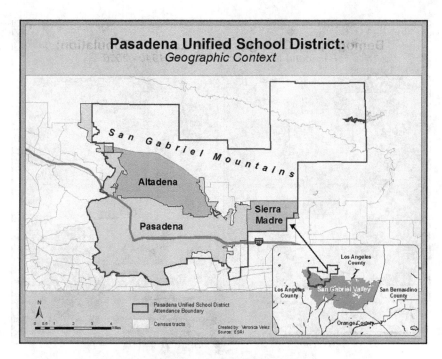

FIGURE 13.1 Pasadena Unified School District (PUSD)

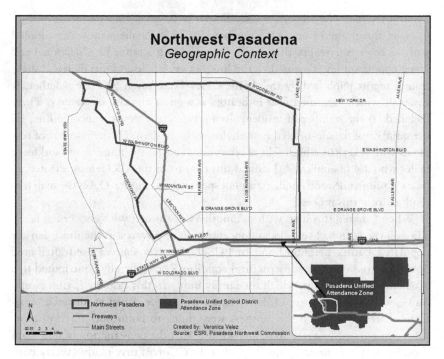

FIGURE 13.2 Northwest Pasadena

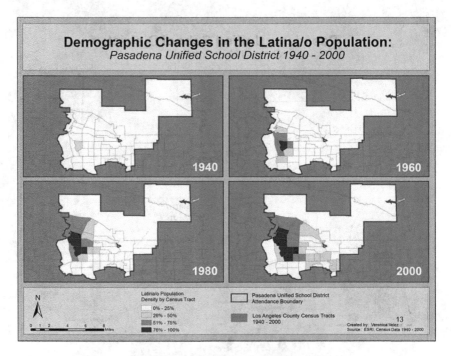

Demographic Changes in the Latina/o Population:
Pasadena Unified School District 1940 - 2000

FIGURE 13.3 Demographic Changes in the Latina/o Population

Next, the mothers wanted to show how Latinx in Pasadena must also contend with an economic reality that denies their children a range of educational and social opportunities. To visualize the link between race and social class, I drew from a report published by the Annie Casey Foundation (O'Hare, Mather, & E, 2003) which identified four indicators as a good measure of poverty. These included (1) the number of residents living below the poverty income line; (2) the number of female-headed households with children; (3) the number of residents with less than a high school education; and (4) the number of workforce males who are unemployed. I mined this data from the US Census, created an index through GIS, and conducted a hot spot analysis. Figure 13.4 is the map that resulted from this process.

When I shared this map with the mothers, I was met with concerned faces. Though the map had revealed a concentration of poverty in the most densely populated Latinx neighborhood in PUSD, the data sources used attributed poverty to individuals, not structural conditions, and thereby contributed to a problematic discourse in which the family unit – in this case the Latinx family unit – was the transmitter of deficiencies. In essence, I had produced a *topography of pathology*, which the mothers were quick to point out. Their critique was an important first step in demonstrating that the construction of GIS maps must be deeply attuned to the ways that data sources may inadvertently contribute to racist narratives. Without making clear *why* material realities, like

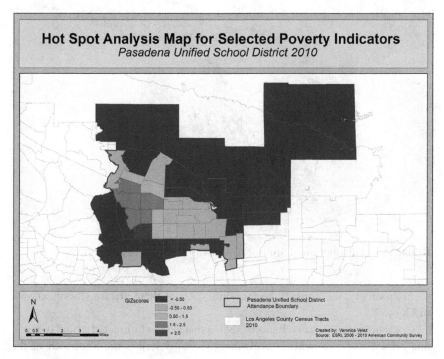

FIGURE 13.4   Hot Spot Analysis Map for Selected Poverty Indicators

poverty, exist *where* they do, maps can problematically conflate data correlations with causal patterns. Our computational approaches, thus, must problematize our sources of data and the portraits of deficiency that result when we fail to engage them critically.

We returned to the original questions guiding this project. The mothers set out to determine if there was a relationship between where Latinx students lived and the opportunities they received in schools. This required data about where Latinx students went to school in PUSD. I consulted with PUSD analysts who were using an early version of GIS to understand changes within the district. They shared the map in Figure 13.5, which demonstrates that across PUSD, schools were largely populated by students living in the Northwest neighborhood.

This map was interesting for two reasons. The first was that it challenged us to define "Latinx schools" in PUSD. A large proportion of Latinx students were essentially bussed from the Northwest neighborhood across the district. Thus, our attempt to unpack whether, and to what extent, a relationship existed between the Northwest neighborhood and its schools was thwarted. Second, it led us to ask – *where are all the white students?* Given the mothers' "ground-level" knowledge, it was clear that this map wasn't telling the whole story. To fill the cartographic void, they asked me to map the distribution of private schools alongside public schools within PUSD. Figure 13.6 represents this comparison.

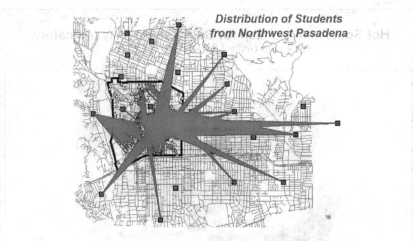

FIGURE 13.5 Distribution of Students from Northwestern Pasadena

Additionally, we mapped the founding dates of these private schools, shown in Figure 13.7.

Combined, these maps tell a story about what led to a bifurcated school system – one private and one public. Wollenberg (1976) describes the aftermath of the

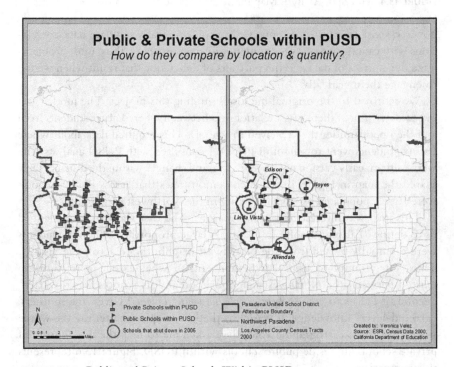

FIGURE 13.6 Public and Private Schools Within PUSD

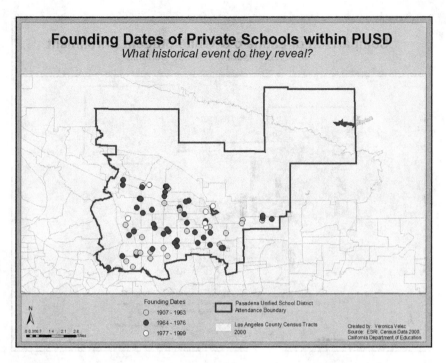

FIGURE 13.7 Founding Dates of Private Schools Within PUSD

landmark 1963 case of Jackson v. Pasadena, which gave Pasadena the distinction as the first non-Southern city ordered by the federal courts to desegregate its public school system. As it turns out, more than two-thirds of Pasadena's private schools were founded during the 5-year period during which Pasadena was undergoing desegregation through mandated busing. This discovery provided the argument and *visualization* the mothers needed to point to the "pattern of injury" affecting their children's education.

But we were left unsatisfied. We had not fully answered the questions that propelled this project. The mothers insisted that inequities were occurring *within* public schools, not just between them and private schools. They signaled to me that I needed to change my *scale*. Rather than look at the Northwest neighborhood as a point of reference for analysis, I needed to look at access to educational opportunities *within* schools. At that suggestion one of the mothers offered the idea of looking at gifted and talented education programs, also known as GATE. These were specialized programs within PUSD public schools that benefited from the most well-resourced classrooms taught by the most qualified teachers. One of the mothers had been struggling for years to access the program for her child. We decided to look at each of the elementary schools in which the mothers had children enrolled at the time. We first mapped the overall distribution of white and Latinx students at each of these schools (Figure 13.8), and then mapped the distribution of white and Latinx students in GATE programs within these schools (Figure 13.9).

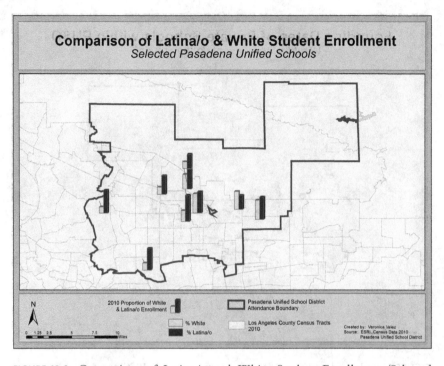

FIGURE 13.8   Comparison of Latina/o and White Student Enrollment (Selected Pasadena Unified Schools)

The comparison of these maps indicated that Latinx students, despite being a majority with PUSD, were being locked out of the few highly resourced programs within public schools. Thus, while Latinx students may walk into a diverse school building, the opportunities (or lack thereof) they were experiencing inside were largely determined by race and ethnicity.

At the conclusion of this project, the mothers decided to hold a community forum where they invited elected officials and shared these maps to the public. Though their stories of struggle as mother activists did not require substantiation through GIS, they nonetheless found utility in the maps to generate dialogue, curiosity, and, in some case, rage at the state of schooling for Latinx students in PUSD. In the months that followed pressure mounted and PUSD had to account for how it identified students for its GATE programs. Though a small victory, this project reveals the potential of GIS as a political visual literacy tool (Tate, 2008), that when rooted and guided by the experiences of BIPOC, can mobilize efforts toward change.

Critical Race Spatial Analysis: Advancing Conceptual and Methodological Applications

Inspired by this project, I began to lay the groundwork for a theoretical and methodological approach that utilizes GIS to investigate educational research

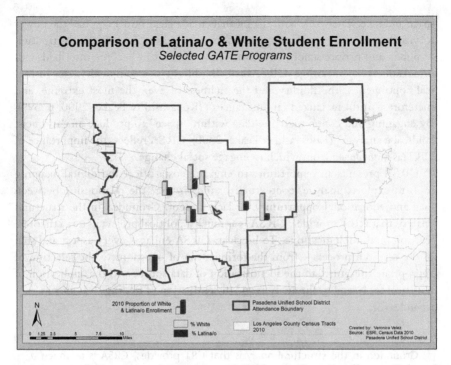

Comparison of Latina/o & White Student Enrollment
Selected GATE Programs

FIGURE 13.9 Comparison of Latina/o and White Student Enrollment (Selected GATE Programs)

questions on schools and space, particularly the role of race and racism in shaping these spaces. Together with my mentor, Dr. Daniel Solórzano, we introduced an initial working definition of *CRSA* (Vélez & Solórzano, 2017):

> Critical race spatial analysis (CRSA) is an explanatory framework and methodological approach that accounts for the role of race, racism, and white supremacy in examining geographic and social spaces and that works toward identifying and challenging racism and white supremacy within these spaces as part of a larger goal of identifying and challenging all forms of subordination. CRSA goes beyond description to spatially examine how structural and institutional factors influence and shape racial dynamics and the power associated with those dynamics over time. Within educational research, CRSA is particularly interested in how structural and institutional factors divide, constrict, and construct space to impact the educational experiences and opportunities available to students based on race.
>
> *(p.20)*

Anchored in Critical Race Theory (CRT; for a definition and citations see DeCuir-Gunby, et al.'s, chapter in this same volume), CRSA argues that GIS has specific epistemological and ontological implications for conducting research on space and race. The work with the mothers made clear how maps had the power to visualize the ways in which specific spatial markers, such as the distribution of public and private school attendance in a region, can become inscribed with important racial meaning. CRSA can "highlight the complexity, the historical contingency, the fluidity and the richness of even the most extreme, and therefore painful racialized circumstances" (Kobayashi & Peake, 2000, p. 399). By engaging and contextualizing data within "space" to produce an "antiracist landscape analysis" (Kobayashi & Peake, 2000), CRSA reflects the importance of CRT as a *standpoint* from which to engage social change.

CRSA presents an opportunity to engage geostatistical and digital mapping tools to explore, analyze, contextualize, and *visualize* the relationship between race and educational opportunity, or lack thereof. Grounded in the structural analysis that CRT provides, CRSA is as much a political project as it is a theoretical and methodological one. To be clear, CRSA engages every aspect and step of the research process – from the formulation of questions to the selection of appropriate literature, to the identification of data sources, to the application of statistical tools, and to the analysis and dissemination of findings – as an anti-racist endeavor.

Grounded in the structural analysis that CRT provides, CRSA is as much a political project as it is a theoretical and methodological one. To be clear, CRSA engages every aspect and step of the research process – from the formulation of questions to the selection of appropriate literature, to the identification of data sources, to the application of statistical tools, and to the analysis and dissemination of findings – as an anti-racist endeavor.

The implications of grounding CRSA within an explicit commitment to end racism in all its forms require on ongoing reflexivity on how power intervenes at every step of the research process, iteratively asking: *how is power being challenged at this stage of geospatial inquiry and analysis?* CRT calls on researchers to draw on subaltern experiences to consider how we might "speak back" to mainstream discourses that erroneously frame BIPOC as inherently deficient and shift the gaze away from racist institutional policies and practices. Although critical race scholarship considers a wide range of methodological tools to accomplish this task, it focuses largely on the use of *counter-storytelling*. Rooted in the belief that the experiences of BIPOC are critical and valid sources of evidence, counter-stories serve as "a tool for exposing, analyzing, and challenging the majoritarian stories of racial privilege" (Solórzano & Yosso, 2002, p. 31).

Though the creation of counterstories has largely been a qualitative effort within critical race scholarship, CRSA considers how statistical and computational approaches can be deployed to center the "voice" of BIPOC in much the same fashion as their qualitative counterparts. CRSA also considers how best to approach geographic visualizations that integrate subjectivity and positionality.

Toward this end, CRSA cites the practices of critical, feminist, and postcolonial cartographers, who argue that GIS can be renegotiated as a discursive tactic to create *counter-maps* (Kwan, 2002a) or what Crampton and Krygier (2005) refer to as *subversive cartographies* that challenge dominant representations of the world. Kwan (2002a) refuses to accept the "technological determinism" of associating GIS with a particular positivist epistemology, asserting that the very subjectivities and agency of GIS users can help illuminate the meaningful aspects of everyday life. Used critically, GIS has the capacity to create cartographic narratives that establish connections between large-scale phenomena and the everyday lives of people.

Kwan (2002a, 2002b) challenges GIS users to complement their quantitative data with other contextual information and using primary sources from individuals to complement secondary sources that can often overgeneralize. Kwan (2002b) also suggests that GIS users need to practice reflexivity when using GIS methods by considering: (a) what we want to "produce" through maps; (b) the actual image of the map to examine the possible exclusions, silences, and marginalizing power of our representations; and (c) the audience to whom we hope to convey our representations as a way of thinking ahead about how our maps may be contested and renegotiated by different people.

Inspired by this body of geographic and cartographic scholarship, and the Pasadena project led by the mothers, CRSA:

1. **Analyzes and visualizes the color-line, refusing causal understandings of racial inequities that promote culturally deficit portraits. Rather, CRSA seeks to explore and expose the structural conditions of racial injustice *multiscalarly* and its material impact on the daily lives of BIPOC students, their families, and their communities.**

    CRSA foregrounds the color-line analytically and visually, exploring the breadth and depth of white supremacy's influence in determining who will occupy space along(side) the color-line, and the opportunities – educational and otherwise – that are then afforded as a result. The visibility of color-lines, particularly through GIS mapping, can be dependent on scale. Du Bois (1903) reminds us of this. In describing southern communities in the United States at the turn of the 20th century, he highlights the intricacy of form and shape the color-line assumes as it separates, divides, and shapes the experiences of individuals based on their proximity to "the line." He writes, "I know some towns where a straight line drawn through the middle of the main street separates nine-tenths of the whites from nine-tenths of the blacks. In other towns, the older settlement of whites has been encircled by a broad band of blacks; in still other cases, little settlements or nuclei of blacks have sprung up amid surrounding whites" (Du Bois, 1903, pp. 106–107).

The intricacy of the color-line may require different vantage points to visualize and analyze. At times, a "bird's eye" view is appropriate. Other times, a close-up analysis at a lower scale makes visible color-lines embedded within spaces that may not look like a line at all, such as in the Pasadena case where the "line" wasn't necessarily drawn *between* schools that served different ethno-racial populations of students, but *within* schools.

2. **Challenges race-neutral representations of space by insisting on data sources, data mining, statistical techniques, and data visualization tools that make evident how race, racism, and white supremacy have been deployed to impact educational (in)opportunity for BIPOC students, their families, and their communities. This includes reconsidering spatial features and their underlying quantification, such as *distance*, *density*, *scale*, and *"hot spots,"* to name a few, as socio-spatial indicators of policies and practices that serve white interests.**

   In her groundbreaking work on educational journey mapping, Annamma (2017) argues that space can be understood as *topographical* (e.g., forms and features of land surfaces), *physical* (e.g., urban planning and design of cities), and *political* (e.g., policies guiding the use of space to serve particular interests), all of which influence how we experience the relationship between race, space, and education. Thus, no space is "race-neutral." Methodologies employed to study space must first recognize the depth to which space is informed by particularly histories, social and political processes, and the forces affecting those processes. For example, in the Pasadena case study, the mothers demonstrated that the density of private schools compared to public schools in PUSD was no coincidence. Rather, it was the result of white flight by families who refused to integrate their children with BIPOC students.

3. **"Ground-truths" each step of the research process in the spatial wisdom of BIPOC as necessary to the development of counter-cartographic narratives.**

   Ground-truthing is traditionally understood as a process whereby GIS technicians are sent to gather data in the field that either complement or dispute airborne remote-sensing data collected by aerial photography, satellite sidescan radar, or infrared images. From this data, maps are then verified and updated. To align with critical race efforts in education, CRSA asks – *what would happen if maps were ground-truthed by [BIPOC communities]? What if these ground-truthers, "employ[ed] their expertise as community members, to define and verify neighborhood boundaries, color-lines, the use of certain spaces, and the perception of those spaces?"* (Vélez & Solórzano, 2017, p. 22). Ground-truthing, (re) imagined in this fashion, relies on critical community expertise to measure an entire system of resource distribution and its impact on a region. Additionally, while research guided by CRSA may primarily be interested in understanding how white supremacy mediates educational (in)opportunity, it must consider BIPOC experiences as sources of strength. This challenges us to consider the types of data we use to generate GIS maps.

4. **Centers a transformative solution by investing in and reimagining spatial and quantitative research tools that work for racial justice and expanding the reach and use of these tools to eliminate subordination in and beyond the academy.**

CRSA is also deeply committed to advancing a social and racial justice agenda. To do this, CRSA must reckon with the ways that GIS maps, along with the data and computational tools used to generate them, can flatten, homogenize, and/or distort the experiences of BIPOC individuals – thereby contributing to geospatial portraits that harm rather than support efforts toward racial justice. This was evident in the Pasadena case study where my attempt to produce an intersectional "hot spot" map ended up perpetuating a culturally deficit portrait of Latinx families.

I am especially inspired by the work of William Tate (2008), who frames GIS as a visual political literacy project. He cites the work of Myron Orfield (2002) in *American Metropolitics*, who argues that GIS, when used critically, can increase dialogue among interdependent institutions and community actors about the geospatial configuration of social, political, and economic realities. I agree with both Tate (2008) and Orfield (2002) that GIS, particularly as employed through CRSA, can be the methodological engine to jump-start and support community mobilization, as evidenced by how the mothers used GIS to shift how students were identified for GATE programs.

5. **Utilizes the interdisciplinary knowledge base of critical race studies in education (ethnic studies, women's studies, sociology, history, humanities, and the law) as well as visual sociology, critical geography, and radical/tactical cartography to inform praxis.**

CRSA works between and beyond disciplinary boundaries, drawing on multiple approaches to listen to and learn from those knowledge otherwise silenced by popular discourse and academic research. In addition to the more traditional disciplinary anchors in CRT, CRSA also draws on visual sociology, critical geography, and tactical cartography. The work of Katherine McKittrick (2006), for example, underscores the important addition of critical and feminist geography to the interdisciplinary knowledge base that informs CRSA. Though she draws from the cannons in the field of geography, she pushes spatial theorizing to consider what happens when "… we pursue the links between practices of domination and [B]lack women's experience in places" (McKittrick, 2006, p. xii). For McKittrick (2006), understanding where race takes place is important, but such analyses can leave out the subjectivities, imaginations, and stories of those at the margins.

6. **Emphasizes GIS maps as a point of departure for analyzing the socio-spatial relationship between race and space and refusing to allow maps to speak for themselves.**

Lastly, CRSA emphasizes that GIS maps are not the end, but rather the point of departure for analyzing the socio-spatial relationship between race, space, and education. Maps can't always tell you why things happen in space. They must be situated within a critical analysis that recognizes the importance of the relationship between people, places, and power. Moreover, CRSA is committed to building *counter-cartographic narratives*, in much the same way that CRT is committed to *counterstorytelling*. By contextualizing maps through counternarratives, we address the concern that GIS, and the computational approaches it relies on, can be "used in ways that rigidify power structures while simultaneously *masking* – through the legitimizing strength of 'science' – the possibility of multiple versions of reality or 'truth,' socially constructed knowledges, and other sources of subjectivity that are inherent in all social research" (Knigge & Cope, 2006, p. 2022).

In sum, CRSA requires that we consider how these tenets factor into each step of constructing GIS maps – from identifying and mining data, determining boundaries, drawing from local expertise, engaging in spatial analysis, and producing a cartographic narrative. And as demonstrated by the Pasadena case study, CRSA demands that we engage an iterative process of reflexivity, where the mapmaker is constantly assessing their approach to map-making, deeply attuned to their own epistemological anchors that shape the research process. The following activity provides a helpful guide for those interested in applying CRSA to educational inquiry with GIS.

Activity: Considerations for Applying CRSA in Educational Research with GIS

Before jumping into the geospatial analyses and visualizations that GIS provides, CRSA requires that we consider how our inquiry is first rooted in a CRT analysis of the relationship between race and space. Thus, before moving forward, understanding CRT is key, both as a conceptual framework and as a methodological approach. This will also help determine whether GIS is the appropriate tool for a project. It may be the case that other methodological approaches are better suited. Digital mapping is only *one way* to approach the study of space. As stressed above, GIS is an enticing technology that can push us prematurely into mapping before we consider the questions and theoretical anchors guiding our work. CRSA encourages us not to bypass key steps early in the research process where, arguably, a critical reckoning with power is *most* needed to inform how we approach our research design.

With CRT as a theoretical anchor and having determined GIS as an appropriate methodological approach, CRSA can then be *mapped* onto the research process. The following table aligns CRSA-informed questions with the different stages of GIS map-making. Though not exhaustive, these questions serve as an important initial inquiry for applying CRSA:

TABLE 13.1 CRSA-Informed Questions and Stages of GIS Map-Making.

GIS Map-Making	CRSA Guiding Questions
Identifying and Mining Data	1. *How can my data sources inadvertently perpetuate culturally deficit portraits of BIPOC students, families, and communities?* 2. *If my data is limited to individually derived variables (e.g., US Census), how do I refuse causal understandings that blame BIPOC for material realities produced by structural conditions?*
Determining Boundaries and Spatial Features	1. *How are spatial features such as distance, density, scale, and "hot spots," measures of racial (in)equity?* 2. *How do the boundaries and spatial features I choose to map reflect the consequential geographies (Soja, 2010) of policies and practices that have and continue to serve white interests?*
Engaging with Stakeholders	1. *How will I integrate the subjectivity and positionality of BIPOC students, families, and communities into GIS?* 2. *How will I rely on BIPOC expertise at each step of the map-making process?*
Conducting Spatial Analysis	1. *How do spatial features (e.g., scale) impact the form, shape, and visibility of color-lines, particularly within and connected to schooling?* 2. *How do patterns of spatial concentration reveal the enduring organizing effects of white supremacy?*
Producing a (Counter) Cartographic Narrative	1. *How am I committed to racial justice throughout the map-making process?* 2. *How do I deploy maps that refuse to "speak for themselves"?*

Mapping Forward

I end this chapter in the same way I began – *inspired by Du Bois*. As Wilson (2018) points out, Du Bois utilized cartography to "… spatialize the scale and scope of the [B]lack diaspora from the local to the global" (p. 41). His data visualizations shatter the invisible shell of neutrality that often covers maps. His body of cartographic work demonstrates that maps don't reflect facts as much as they reflect a particular consciousness of approaching and organizing space. As the Pasadena case study makes evident, it was the mothers' intimate knowledge of the community and collaborative analysis in the process of map-making that was key. They demonstrated how the spaces that define our lives are not arbitrary, but rather concrete manifestations of the complexity of social life. Informed by their cartographic insights and spatial wisdom, CRSA contends with the epistemological underpinnings in our methodological decisions as we consider GIS in educational research, particularly inquiry on

> Maps don't reflect facts as much as they reflect a particular consciousness of approaching and organizing space. As the Pasadena case study makes evident, it was the mothers' intimate knowledge of the community and collaborative analysis in the process of map-making that was key.

race and space. These types of considerations will animate CRSA as a conceptual and methodological approach for understanding, theorizing, and *mapping* answers to the most pressing questions in educational research today and into the future.

Notes

1 For more on ESRI's racial equity initiative, see: https://www.esri.com/en-us/racial-equity/overview
2 Exploratory Spatial Data Analysis (ESDA) is the first stage of understanding phenomena distribution in space. GIS maps are neither restricted to presenting conclusions nor the only way of querying data but are interactively combined with theoretical explanations and statistical analysis in an incremental manner (Anselin, 1998; Steinberg & Steinberg, 2015).
3 https://www.idea.gseis.ucla.edu/

References

Annamma, S. A. (2017). Mapping consequential geographies in the carceral state: Education journey mapping as a qualitative method with girls of color with dis/abilities. *Qualitative Inquiry, 24*(1), 1–15. https://doi.org/10.1177/1077800417728962

Anselin, L. (1998). GIS research infrastructure for spatial analysis of real estate markets. *Journal of Housing Research, 9*(1), 113–133. https://doi.org/10.1080/10835547.1998.12091930

Battle-Baptiste, W., & Rusert, B. (Eds.). (2018). *WEB Du Bois's data portraits: Visualizing Black America*. San Francisco, CA: Chronicle Books.

Crampton, J. W., & Krygier, J. (2005). An introduction to critical cartography. *ACME: An International E-Journal for Critical Geographies, 4*(1), 11–33. https://acme-journal.org/index.php/acme/article/view/723

Du Bois, W. E. B. (1990). To the nations of the world. Pan-African Congress. London. Speech retrieved from: https://www.blackpast.org/african-american-history/1900-w-e-b-du-bois-nations-world/

Du Bois, W. E. B. (1903). *Souls of Black folk*. New York, NY: W.W. Norton and Company.

Knigge, L., & Cope, M. (2006). Grounded visualization: Integrating the analysis of qualitative and quantitative data through grounded theory and visualization. *Environment and Planning, 38*, 2021–2037. https://doi.org/10.1068/a37327

Kobayashi, A., & Peake, L. (2000). Racism out of place: Thoughts on whiteness and an antiracist geography in the new millennium. *Annals of the Association of American Geographers, 90*(2), 392–403. https://doi.org/10.1111/0004-5608.00202

Kwan, M. (2002a). Feminist visualization: Re-envisioning GIS as a method in feminist geographic research. *Annals of the Association of American Geographers, 92*(4), 645–661. https://doi.org/10.1111/1467-8306.00309

Kwan, M. (2002b). Is GIS for women? Reflection on the critical discourse in the 1990s. *Gender, Place and Culture, 9*(3), 271–279. https://dusk.geo.orst.edu/wis/feministGIS2.pdf

McKittrick, K. (2006). *Demonic grounds: Black women and the cartographies of struggle*. Minneapolis, MN: University of Minnesota Press.

O'Hare, W., Mather, M., & E, A. Casey Foundation, Baltimore, MD, & Population Reference Bureau, Inc. (2003). The growing number of kids in severely distressed neighborhoods evidence from the 2000 census: A kids count/PRB report on census 2000. *Educational Resources Information Center (ERIC).* Retrieved from https://files. eric.ed.gov/fulltext/ED481477.pdf

Orfield, M. (2002). *American Metropolitics: The new suburban reality.* Washington, DC: Brookings Institution Press.

Soja, E. W. (2010). *Seeking spatial justice.* Minneapolis, MN: University of Minnesota Press.

Solórzano, D., & Vélez, V. (2016). Using critical race spatial analysis to examine the Duboisian color-line along the Alameda corridor in Southern California. *Whittier Law Review, 37,* 423–438.

Solórzano, D., & Vélez, V. (2017). Using critical race spatial analysis to examine redlining in Southern California communities of color—Circa 1939. In D. Morrison, S. A. Annamma, & D. Jackson (Eds.), *Critical race spatial analysis: Mapping to understand and address educational inequity* (pp. 91–108). Sterling, VA: Stylus.

Steinberg, S. L., & Steinberg, S. J. (2015). *GIS research methods.* Redlands, CA: Esri Press.

Tate, W. F. IV (2008). "Geography of opportunity": Poverty, place, and educational outcomes. *Educational Researcher, 37*(7), 397–411. https://doi.org/10.3102/0013189X08326409

Vélez, V., & Solórzano, D. G. (2017). Critical race spatial analysis: Conceptualizing GIS as a tool for critical race research in education. In D. Morrison, S. A. Annamma, & D. Jackson (Eds.), *Critical race spatial analysis: Mapping to understand and address educational inequity* (pp. 8–31). Sterling, VA: Stylus.

Wilson, M. (2018). The cartography of WEB Du Bois's color line. In W. Battle-Baptiste & B. Rusert (Eds.), *W.E.B Du Bois's data portraits: Visualizing Black America* (pp. 37–43). San Francisco, CA: Chronicle Books.

Wollenberg, C. (1976). *All deliberate speed: segregation and exclusion in California schools, 1855–1975.* Berkeley, CA: University of California Press.

SECTION IV

The Future of Culturally Responsive Research

Transformative intellectuals are truly counterhegemonic. They not only theorize about activism, but live in solidarity with marginalized, oppressed groups and work alongside them for transformation of unjust material conditions (p. 13).

~ *Colette N. Cann and Eric J. DeMeulenaere* ~

Cann, C. N., & DeMeulenare, E. J. (2020). *The activist academic: Engaged scholarship for resistance, hope and social change.* Gorham, ME: Myers Education Press.

DOI: 10.4324/9781003126621-17

14

THE FUTURE

Advancing Innovations of Culturally Sustaining Research and Researchers

e alexander, Penny A. Pasque

This volume's chapters take up ways in which culturally responsive research transforms the research process itself, providing examples and activities to support your praxes as readers. In chapter 1, we define "culturally responsive research" based on existing literature and introduce each chapter's contribution to this volume. In this summative chapter, we reflect on common themes throughout the chapters as we strive to expand existing conceptualizations of culturally responsive research.

First, we offer themes presented throughout the volume as they pertain to engaging in culturally responsive research, which is our way of talking "with you" – the reader – about lessons learned and important takeaways. We explore theorizing methods, including transformation, expansion, and specificity. Importantly, theory is not abandoned after the "review of literature" section but utilized throughout the design and dissemination of researchers' projects. Second, we reflect on culturally responsive qualitative innovations of researcher liminality, self-work as community work, and resistance of white supremacy of dominant approaches. Next, we share culturally responsive quantitative and mixed-methods innovations of research principles and research practices. From here, the chapter advances current ontoepistemic conceptualizations of *doing* transformative culturally responsive research. We provide tangible takeaways for readers that include attention to (a) the political nature of scholarship, (b) the importance of researcher accountability, and (c) culturally responsive research as an existential reflection on academia. We then conclude with considerations and recommendations.

The chapter ends with "A Call to Action" closing activity, to support you in thinking about your own development and practice as culturally responsive researchers. We mean this to be but one point in time that connects the historical with contemporary – knowing (and hoping) that further advances in culturally

DOI: 10.4324/9781003126621-18

responsive research will continue to be taken up in service to expanding its reach, impacts, innovations, and potentials for use in praxis.

Common Themes

What is abundantly clear through the contributions to this volume is the necessity of culturally responsive scholars and scholarship to acknowledge the humanity of all parties involved with research, as foundational to knowledge construction. This includes the reflexivity and positionality of you as a culturally responsive researcher, which is always an iterative and changing process. It also includes engaging the humanity of participants or co-conspirators in designing research project questions and their components (i.e., methodology, collection, analysis, "quality"), disseminating findings, and collaborating with scholars who continue to push your thinking.

Our chapter authors who use qualitative methods tell their stories as parents, children, community members and leaders, creatives, activists, etc. – all aspects of themselves that inform how they engage with research. They share these parts of themselves with us through poetry, letters to loved ones, journal entries, rap lyrics, and many more representations. By doing so, they invite us as readers – and participants in their scholarship – into their emotions, histories, localities, and realities. The authors also acknowledge their humanity by writing their biases and human limits into their scholarship as both topics of exploration and signposts to support the future possibilities of their work. In doing so, *they engage in research as alchemy* that includes current topics of interests, other people, location, emotions, histories, themselves, and other aspects of existence – transforming it into possibilities and imaginations for future projects.

Our colleagues who use quantitative and mixed methods invite us to complicate research through more time and attention to the manners in which we define, construct, and operationalize metrics and constructs in our studies – *as not to perpetuate the very harms that we aim to disrupt as members of the academy.* The authors do so by developing new designs and analytical approaches, using literature and theory to inform both, taking time to adjust and recalibrate their approaches as needed, and carrying out their studies in iterative manners to achieve their aims.

Taken together, the quantitative, qualitative, mixed methods, and philosophical chapters in this book suggest a possibility for, or necessity in, crossing borders of "quantitative" and "qualitative" approaches in service to culturally responsive research. There is much to be learned across boundaries that are not always mutually exclusive.

Theorizing Methods: Transformation, Expansion, and Specificity

Hurtado, Lather, and Thompson introduce us to the concept of culturally responsive research methods as a duty that we have as scholars – to our studies, our studies' participants, studies' contexts, and ourselves. Upon reflection, they also identify three overlapping mandates of this duty: transformation, expansion, and specificity. These mandates serve to expand academia's knowledge constructions beyond conventions of whiteness, maleness, elitism, and other power structures that position all other ways of being as having no place in scholarship.

Foremost, culturally responsive research must *transform* the research process itself. Transformation extends beyond how data is collected and analyzed, to include how projects are: re/de/constructed through use of creativity and exploration; carried out at each stage; concluded; engaged with peoples beyond the study itself; and engaged by researchers both internally (e.g., reflexivity) and externally (e.g., interactions with others). As part of this work, Hurtado, Lather, and Thompson invite us to design research that behaves in certain ways if it is to be culturally responsive. It should combat epistemic injustice by redefining concepts that commonly guide studies – in support of creating a more just world, and with the understanding that colonialism and anti-Blackness undergird the logics that drive academia's "conventions" of research practice.

We can actualize transformations of research practices by (a) prioritizing listening to and learning from the study process itself and (b) positioning participants as experts whose knowledge directs studies' data sources, findings, and dissemination. These are simple yet powerful ways that we might attend to closing power differentials in our research; doing so is particularly important in uplifting small populations that "conventional" research methods render invisible, especially where we hold more social privileges than people in those groups. Engaging minoritized groups of people in our scholarship as fellow experts also supports relationship-building with participant communities. Last, as a foundation for transforming research methods, our colleagues in Section I of this volume invite us to practice self-exploration as a required part of study design. In doing so, we should seek to understand (a) our motivations for undertaking our chosen projects, (b) contexts in which we do so, and (c) obligations we have to participants, ourselves, and other stakeholders.

This understanding of our research blends into the second mandate for culturally responsive research that our colleagues offer: *specificity*. Thompson directly names that a study cannot and should not be disentangled from its contexts, the cultures of researchers and participants, and communities that it creates/dissolves/illuminates/welcomes to form as part of its process. He, along with Hurtado and Lather, require said specificity when tending to issues of justice – as *not* to avoid or erase contexts, cultures, and communities throughout study processes. Doing so also helps identify research obstacles (e.g., there are no "limitations" outside of positivist research), where broad applications of methods might fail to bring issues to light with groups rendered invisible by research "conventions." Perhaps unsurprisingly: all the volume's contributors intrinsically practice this mandate – and, hence, uplift specificity in research design for its merits regarding both rigor and research morality as Thompson discusses them.

Transformation and specificity of culturally responsive research also usher in its third mandate as identified by Hurtado, Lather, and Thompson; *expansion* in both scholarly design and praxiology, with the understanding that they are neither mutually exclusive nor ever finished. Our colleagues highlight that "good" scholarship is incomplete on its own: it should be evolving and dialogical such that it invites more exploration of and discussion about the topic at hand – rather than quelling it through illusions of finality. It also prompts more people – fellow researchers, community members, and other stakeholders – to *act* on it as the next step in praxis. Said differently, *a culturally responsive project brings more voices and actions into its fold at its conclusion, which serves as a springboard into successive projects as part of the topic's broader saga of inquiry* (e.g., additional studies, policy changes, community programs and development).

Expansion is also intrinsic to culturally responsive research design. As this volume's contributors illuminate, the methods that we use in this type of scholarship must move away from conceptualizing knowledge and its representations as distinctively qualitative or quantitative, or empirical or theoretical – to honor them all more holistically, wherever and however they exist. This expansion normalizes acknowledging and engaging more sources and forms of information as part of a single study to provide fuller contexts for its topic(s), finding(s), and implication(s) while inviting more voices into its design. The expansion also embraces the multiple lived realities of researchers and participants: we all move through life constructing knowledge without nominal boundaries of "qualitative," "quantitative," "empirical," "theoretical," etc. As researchers, we can also remove boundaries to invite "everyday" knowledge of the communities in which we study to epistemically innovate our scholarship. Said differently, *we can advance our scholarship by expanding how we think about "data" – which requires us to tap into our full personhoods and human connections with others.* This realization highlights (a) how society can advance academia, (b) the necessity of positioning participants as experts, and (c) the importance of expanding research through praxis. It also suggests that culturally responsive research is, at its core, a practice of our humanity.

Qualitative Approaches to Innovation

As experts in qualitative approaches, our colleagues in Section II of the volume use stories to offer insights about what is important in advancing culturally responsive research. Their first set of insights highlights the liminal positioning of researchers as occupying multiple spaces and roles simultaneously. Their second set of insights emphasizes the necessity of researchers to engage in self-work as part of community work, which is inherent to culturally responsive research. The third set of insights reminds us that such scholarship – in its obligations, operationalizations, and forms – should serve to resist the white supremacy of academia's scholarly "conventions" as it redefines and reimagines possibilities for future scholarship.

Liminality of the Researcher

In Section II of this volume, Alexander, Bhattacharya, and Wong emphasize the importance of situating the inquirer in both their projects and the world, as part of scholarship; as such, they offer us intimate looks into who they are throughout their chapters. Alexander and Bhattacharya name embodied theorization through their relationality to others (on which we elaborate in the next section), situating their theorizations through their experiences, and treating themselves as sites of understanding the sociocultural contexts in which their works take place. Both they and Wong also illustrate great vulnerability as part of their scholarship: Alexander shows us intimate moments he has with his father as a child; Bhattacharya recounts seeing death and despair in India during the ongoing COVID-19 pandemic; Wong bares his emotions through his rap lyrics and spoken word, and in his contemplation about the role of joy in his scholarship.

In examining their relationality to others, our colleagues in Section II of this volume explore themselves (and those who participate in their inquires) as beings who inhabit multiple and liminal epistemic positions and modalities at once – inquirers, subjects in their inquiries, and humans. As such, their positions as scholars place them in a constant state of becoming that requires them to maintain fluidity – in their projects, and in interpersonal relationships and cultural settings. While researchers who have trained using "conventional" approaches may find such fluidity and subjectivity daunting, our colleagues engage in practices that support bringing their entire selves into their projects: advocacy, creativity, cultural practice, emotion, bearing witness to others, etc. These practices of the Self support the idea that people are, as Wong describes, constituted based on ever-shifting conditions of their environments. Such fluidity allows us to have imagination – not only about expanding knowledge in the academy, but about possibilities for how we exist in connection with our pasts, loved ones, emotions, places of significance, aspirations, mistakes, shortcomings, etc. This subjectivity requires us to be aware of how our ontoepistemic approaches are informed by ever-shifting compositions of our surroundings and discourses that exist therein.

Self-Work as Community Work

Our colleagues with expertise in qualitative approaches also suggest that exploring and reimagining the self are intrinsic practices for culturally responsive scholarship. As community work, we do not do our research alone, nor do we do it only for ourselves. It is important to treat scholarship as a dialogue with the communities, cultures, and groups in which it occurs. Such dialogue includes bearing witness to each other, supporting each other's journeys of knowledge construction/s, and tending to shifts among all involved parties who have more and less agency than us throughout inquiry processes. Bhattacharya and Wong point out the importance of scholars (a) understanding their connections to others as also being connections to power and privilege, and therefore (b) coming to all sites of inquiry with humility to support being in community with all parties. When you/we/scholars can do this, you/we/they are more likely to cross borders or boundaries – allowing everyone involved in a project to coexist through a shared humanity. Said humility supports bringing others into our realities and invites them to share their realities in return.

Foregrounding the universality of human experiences as part of inquiry creates space for both researchers and study participants to interrogate power structures, including sociopolitical and sociocultural constructs, that inform the "conventions" of academia. It also provides opportunities for all parties involved to collaborate in world-building. Alexander does so through embodying his performances and asking students to think through their own autoethnographic constructs. Bhattacharya does so through witnessing the formation of COVID response groups among community members in India, and in speaking to them about their efforts amid government failures to meet their needs. Duran and Jones encourage researchers to tend to the intersectionality of participants' and researchers' own multiple identities. Wong does so through participating in the hip-hop community, as simultaneously scholar and subject in that social environment. Our colleagues illustrate how they invite others, including us as readers, to world-build with them through their subjectivities. They are whole people as they engage in culturally responsive work; we can and should be, too.

Resistance of White Supremacy of Dominant Approaches

The contributors to this volume are all members of western academia; those in Section II almost inevitably interrogate it as a primary site at which they explore their constitutions, and the constitutions of people with whom they sit in community as scholars. More specifically, our colleagues name academia's "conventions" as colonialist, racist, and violent – due to dominant research conventions' lack of ontoepistemic space for peoples who are not white or not western. Here, it is important to name that all our colleagues in Section II who interrogate the academy's conventions belong to groups that those conventions exclude – as do the individuals they discuss in their chapters with whom they sit in community. Alexander and Wong characterize these non-white and non-western bodies as sites where hegemonic knowledge regimes are exercised (e.g., projecting deficit-centered narratives about Black men onto them). They and Bhattacharya go on to identify ways that academia exercises those regimes through its ontoepsitemic conventions:

1. Conceptualizing humanity through lenses of whiteness (e.g., temporality, knowledge binaries), which then inform knowledge and research development through those lenses;
2. Presuming that western research practices are correct, just, incapable of harming anyone, and able to accommodate all knowledge that exists and/or "matters"; and
3. Privileging or normalizing objectivity, impersonality, power imbalances, and the researcher as a foreign abstracter of knowledge from others.

Whether intentionally or unintentionally, implicitly or explicitly, our col-leagues conduct culturally responsive research as political/politicized acts that directly respond to these regimes. They do so – conceptually and in practice – by expanding where knowledge exists and lives, and by challenging the academy for its investment in hegemonic notions of how knowledge is valid. Wong also names this type of research as dispelling hegemonic goals of "integrating" non-white subjects (including researchers) into white ontoepistemic environments and frames.

Alexander, Bhattacharya, Duran and Jones, and Wong take up their scholar-ship through a number of approaches and principles. Foremost, they all empha-size the importance of honoring specificity in knowledge and refocusing one's work to directly address its intended audiences. Alexander, Bhattacharya, and Wong do so through exploring and expanding knowledge where it lives and shares meaning with(in) its environments – namely, as Black boyhood and man-hood, postcolonial embodiment, and Black-affirming and anti-colonial ways of knowing. Duran and Jones, and Wong emphasize the importance of acknowl-edging the historicity and genealogy of liberatory approaches, to position schol-ars' uses in each project; they also advise researchers to ground their work in specific traditions of those approaches to serve more intentional purposes.

As with our contributors to Section I, those to Section II also characterize research as "*doing*" that invites others to take on additional action through their own inquiries. Their calls to action highlight (a) theory-building through a con-stellation of knowledge sources in specific environments, and (b) exploring con-structions of liberatory futures that center lives of the most marginalized groups. Duran and Jones also advise scholars to allow participants to show up holistically in projects through how they are recruited, provide information, and have their data analyzed and shared. Participatory action research (PAR) is one way to sup-port this centering, and it provides more opportunities to improve participants' lives through scholarship. As a mixed-methods study, Vélez's work in Section III is a shining example of PAR and its potential.

Quantitative and Mixed-Methods Innovations

As experts in quantitative and mixed-methods approaches, our colleagues in Section III of the volume offer guiding principles and research practices to sup-port expanding culturally responsive scholarship. Overall, they emphasize the need for making analyses more complex. Those whose projects incorporate the-ory also use frameworks to inform their computations.

Research Principles

Kim and Yang – and Blake, Chen, Pearson, Ruffin, and Jackson – acknowledge that traditional practices for statistical analyses, such as using only one model for exploring a social phenomenon, erase the nuances of how people live out said

phenomena in relation to equity – due to their simplicity, linearity, and homoge-
nization of groups. These characteristics of "conventional" quantitative methods
pose risks of disregarding outcomes for smaller populations in statistics, and/or
nuances in results – especially where inequities impact a small part of a population in group-specific manners. Almost as a direct response to these limitations:
DeCuir-Gunby, McCoy, and Gibson – and Johnson and Jabbari – recommend
interrogating systems and structures that inform disparities in traditional statistical analyses, placing analytical attention on causes of phenomena rather than on
individuals who experience them. Such an interrogation would engage two concepts that offer starting places in innovation: (1) contemplating "technologies" of
knowledge and (2) utilizing critical frames as a technology in methods that have
traditionally been absent of it (as phrased by Johnson and Jabbari).

Beyond expanding approaches to analysis, Vélez provides us recommendations
for utilization of data sources, collection and mining methods, and approaches
to dissemination that serve to highlight specificities of the focus populations in
a study – an important callback to mandates of our colleagues in Section I and
practices of our colleagues in Section II. As a mixed methodologist, Vélez also
offers two tips in the marronage of methods across nominal boundaries. First, she
demonstrates using qualitative methods to illuminate the substantive significance
of a phenomenon that statistical analysis finds to be insignificant, while providing context for statistical findings; doing so helps to address erasures that Kim
and Yang, and Blake and colleagues acknowledge. Second, Vélez does not privilege quantitative or computational findings as complete enough to stand alone
as the findings for a study – treating them as starting points for deeper analyses;
this is another callback to mandates of our colleagues in Section I and practices of
our colleagues in Section II. Finally, as with our colleagues in Sections I and II,
Vélez and other contributors to Section III call for scholars to sit in community
with study participants, as co-constructors of research design.

Research Practices

As illustrations of their principles, our colleagues who conduct quantitative
and mixed-methods research offer us many approaches for being more culturally responsive. In statistics, these include using advanced or unique modeling, computations, and data preparation to both center voices of minoritized
groups and account for nuances of topics being studied. They note that such
modeling requires more intentionality and effort to find the best fitting adjustments. DeCuir-Gunby et al. also name how utilizing more unique and complex
approaches for analysis support the identification of nuances, outliers, and individual conditions that are overlooked in traditional computations – and, in doing
so, challenges dominant narratives that frame minoritized groups as inherently
deficient in comparison to statistical majorities.

Kim and Yang, and Blake, et al., recommend matching, regression interaction,
and mixture modeling, or adjusting weights of variables and reorganizing nested

data, to highlight populations and/or phenomena of interest that may receive little attention otherwise. Authors of both chapters warn of perpetuating erasures of marginalized groups, and phenomena that uniquely impact them, when such adjustments are not made in models. Kim and Yang note that doing so would account for differential statistical effects for those populations and phenomena.

DeCuir-Gunby and colleagues, and Johnson and Jabbari operationalize concepts from theories, and/or literature about a social phenomenon, to define and weight their models' variables, predictors, modifiers, covariates, and levels of analysis. This research process was significant to account for phenomena that occur intentionally (e.g., student placement in certain schools) – as compared to traditional statistical methods that assume conditions to be random across a large population. These approaches to modeling also meant that researchers were required to elaborate on their operationalization at each step of analysis, in relation to their supporting theories and literature. In this way, theory is not abandoned when it comes to methods of analysis but is centered throughout the research project.

Vélez collaborated with her project's participants to define and refine its outcomes and scope, as foundational to her approach in doing mixed-method culturally responsive work. Reflective of that approach, Vélez's project grew to be praxis that was experiential, archival, participatory, communal, iterative, and context-specific – incapsulating most of the practices that her colleagues in Sections II and III engaged. Notably, her work with participants embodied the mandates that our colleagues in Section I identified: it transformed the research process for the project itself over time; it was specific to the contexts and communities in which it occurred; it invited others to expand on its findings through praxeology. Vélez was successful in doing culturally responsive research because she pushed beyond nominal borders of "qualitative," "quantitative," "empirical," and "theoretical" – and did so as a practice of her humanity.

Looking Forward: Doing Culturally Responsive Research

The contributors to this volume have gifted us with frameworks, approaches, and action items that illuminate possible steps in how we might grow in doing culturally responsive work. Many of their gifts also conflict with academia's research "conventions." In closing this volume, we review major takeaways and summarize tensions that you/readers might consider as you/we embark on engaging with or expanding practices of being culturally responsive. We also offer recommendations and questions to support readers in thinking about this practice and expansion.

Major Takeaways

Foremost, *culturally responsive scholars must understand their research as political in nature.* Contributors to Section II explain the necessity of doing so as part of resisting academia's white supremacy. Contributors to Section III do so regarding one's chosen methods in support of social change, and in one's intentions for exploring, analyzing, contextualizing, and presenting findings in the manners that they choose. One example of doing so is interrogating how systems and structures inform disparities through traditional approaches. Another is repurposing methods that have historically been culturally unresponsive, to identify systemic problems that findings conventionally present as individuals' unfavorable behaviors or characteristics (i.e., not blaming them for social problems they experience, when systemic oppression causes those problems).

This reframing of methods places accountability on research practices themselves to not perpetuate harm toward marginalized groups. By interrogating research approaches themselves, the contributors to this volume suggest that conventional methods uphold systemic oppression through questions they ask and seek to answer, and through their approaches to seeking answers. In contrast, *culturally responsive methods ask and seek to answer questions that deconstruct dominant narratives about populations and topics of focus, using approaches that disrupt or transform conventions in service to oppressed groups.* As examples, Bhattacharya does this through her decolonizing autoethnography of culture in the era of COVID-19, and Vélez illustrates doing so by using GIS and census data to challenge "a topography of pathology."

Second, *culturally responsive scholars must lean into the experimentality of knowledge construction*; central to experimentation are the needs, perspectives, social locations, and desired outcomes of study participants. Experimentality also comes with a spirit of scholarly expansion: the conclusion of each project invites others to start new ones, in support of bringing more voices and ontoepistemic understandings of people and phenomena into larger discourses.

Qualitative methods in this volume that embraced experimentality included PAR practices, developing studies one step at a time while consulting with primary stakeholders (read: participants or co-conspirators), and conducting follow-up data collection and analysis to better understand observed social phenomena. Quantitative methods that did so included designing models to highlight outliers that represent marginalized groups, adjusting models to center minoritized groups as numerical minorities, and integrating theory and literature into design and analyses. Mixed methods that did so included using computational findings as starting points for qualitative analyses that could illuminate substantive significances of statistically insignificant phenomena.

Third, and as part of experimentation, *culturally responsive researchers should account for their subject positions in their projects*; positions include interrogating how power is being exercised and/or shared amongst all project stakeholders at each project step. Because this type of culturally responsive research centers study participants, and because scholars ideally sit *in* community with their study participants as co-creators, it is important that researchers understand themselves internally and in relation to others. Sometimes, scholar positionalities are simultaneously as researcher and study participant. Regardless of methods used, they are always simultaneously a researcher and a person whose humanity influences how they engage their work – through project design, implementation, dissemination, and praxeology. This fact reminds us why self-work is also community work at all points in culturally responsive research.

Existential Reflections on Academia

Culturally responsive approaches as political stances – in both concept and practice – pose existential threats to dominant mythologies of western academia and its ontoepistemic traditions as universally applicable, substantively reliable, relatable, and empowering to all. It is important to remember that our profession's contemporary conventions are borne from the Scientific Method, Renaissance, and Enlightenment – all knowledge movements that originally took place in Europe. These movements were revolutionary moments and tools that supported individual Europeans in drawing conclusions for themselves about the world around them – a departure from monarchs and clergy thinking for them. The movements were also the origins of positivism, which has become part of academia's research "conventions" and is reified by western onto-epistemology. Given this sociohistory, we make several assertions:

1. The academy's "conventions" are in fact culturally responsive research approaches that are specific to contexts and communities of Europe, making them Eurocentric by definition.
2. Western imperialism has created a global schema wherein European ways of knowing are exported to other regions (e.g., what are commonly referred to as the Americas, Australia, South Africa, etc.) through apparatuses of power and influence – including academia.
3. Hence, academia must evolve to treat Eurocentric approaches to knowledge construction as one set of possibilities – rather than as a universal "convention" for all scholarship.

Academia is a site of (re)producing Eurocentric knowledge approaches: if we follow their conventions, we will be trained to privilege them as "correct" or "superior" in doing scholarship. However, their specificity dictates that they cannot be ontoepistemically responsive to cultures, communities, and contexts that do not have European roots. As we work to (literally) decolonize our ontoepistemic practices, we should not presume that non-Europeans do not have their own knowledge conventions and tools, or that those conventions and tools are any less valid than those with European roots. To do so would be enacting Eurocentrism, if not western and white supremacy in a racialized and colonized world. Yet, academia does just that: it privileges drawing from European ways of knowing as "default" approaches for engaging in knowledge practices. These truths are precisely why practices of culturally responsive research are political. The call for expansion of research methods invites scholars to move away from a presupposition of Eurocentric realities and sensibilities with regard to ontoepis-temic practices. It also invites them to challenge the knowledge oppression of western frames that have been hegemonically impressed upon all research in the academy without regard for cultures, communities, or contexts of the parties involved in projects. To be culturally responsive is to do anti-oppression work.

That work, however, conflicts with how the academy functions as our workplace. Its European sensibilities privilege scholars who subscribe to them: awarding them more funding, accepting their work more often to esteemed pub-lications, offering them more opportunities to share their work as a public good, and so on. Researchers in fields of study that systematically rely on ontoepsitemic practices from Europe (e.g., those often referred to as "natural sciences") may not see either these practices' hegemonic nature, or benefits in expanding practices to be more culturally responsive. Resistance to expanding may even be heightened if their scholarship practices have consistently brought them success! We call on academics in such fields – or those who have adverse reactions to expanding cul-turally responsive approaches at all – to interrogate their investment in western and white supremacy. They can do so by exploring how they participate in, pro-mote, protect, and privilege Eurocentric ontoepistemic practices in their work duties and research practices.

Considerations and Recommendations

Colleagues who use quantitative methods have unique challenges in doing cul-turally responsive research because their approaches are often most closely aligned with academia's "conventions." The intention of traditional statistical analyses is presumed objectivity in service to findings that are theoretically universal; it stands in opposition to the specificity of cultural responsiveness that this volume's contributors have highlighted as essential. Importantly, contributors in Section III suggest that culturally responsive statistics should interrogate traditional mod-els for their role in pathologizing marginalized groups and/or individuals from those groups based on results from analyses, in support of research specificity. Hence, statisticians who strive to take up these charges may face a challenge of being too different from peers in their field who prefer "conventional" analyses: their philosophies about and purposes for doing statistics might be diametrically opposed. Going against the grain of one's field might threaten opportunities for research support, publishing, and sharing work as a public good. It might also create strain on statistician's professional relationships, and/or pose threats to promotion and tenure.

Because the volume's contributors uplift being in community with stake-holders as part of culturally responsive research, colleagues who use qualitative methods have challenges that call back to previous generations of fieldwork. Regardless of research method, at the fore is the importance of protecting study participants with regard to safety, boundaries, power dynamics, and informed consent. Because qualitative research is so (inter)personal, researchers who do it must be particularly aware of safety. While research boards and "human sub-jects" training programs specify stipulations for the most pressing priorities in protecting participants, they name others as being context-specific and left to researchers to ascertain based on judgment. Still, these entities err on the side of caution where participants likely will not.

Participants are more apt to be authentic when in community with research-ers and may then show parts of themselves to researchers that they might not have if they were not as comfortable. Thus, scholars have to determine: how much personal information to share and receive; in which community settings or activities to participate, and to what degree; what degree of discomfort or pos-sible danger is appropriate; and what degrees of transparency, authenticity, and liminality are appropriate. They must do all this while prioritizing participants' wellbeing in decision-making, balancing adherence to academe's research ethics and being steered by the community in which they are doing their work. Where scholars' liminality is more significant in a project, they must also be mindful not to do too much navel-gazing unless doing so supports them in being culturally responsive.

Across approaches, scholars who aim to do culturally responsive research face a challenge of positioning scholarship in their fields with regard to proving its "quality" – a term often used in faculty annual reports and by journal reviewers. Unlike "conventional" research designs, culturally responsive designs do not have a template on which they can rely as a "shorthand" to demonstrate their rigor. During review for publication, for example, the specificity of projects may challenge peers in evaluating designs that are iterative, emergent, collaborative with participants, and/or different from "conventions" of their field. These are opportunities for researchers to educate peers on cultural responsiveness through detailing how they ensure rigor in their projects. Explanations might be about how literature or theories inform designs, evolutions in designs over the course of projects, PAR, and so on. They might also speak to the roles of researcher liminality, personhood, culture, or context for topics that need explanations. For example, a statistician might explain why they weighted variables a cer-tain way based on literature, and how they interpreted literature based on their personhood.

Scholars might also choose to use their projects as sites for exploring interplays of "conventional" and culturally responsive conceptualizations of research prac-tices regarding rigor and ethics. Here, we welcome researchers to work through complications of defining validity, generalizability, reliability, trustworthiness, objectivity, subjectivity, boundaries, power dynamics, protection from harm, and others based on the considerations we have discussed.

Additionally, we encourage culturally responsive scholars to embrace their identity as such in support of both expanding said approaches and promoting their work among colleagues in their fields. As we each develop and evolve, we shape and shift stories about who we are as scholars and what we seek to accomplish through our work. Our stories include our choices about topics we address, frameworks and literature from which we borrow, methods for data collection and analysis we prioritize, relationships we form with participants and/ in their communities, follow-up work we do, and so on. These stories can and should become part of our portfolios, if not shape them, to illustrate how culturally responsive work is intentional and larger than ourselves. Projects that are founded in them are not "passion projects" or "experiments" – they are practices of anti-oppression that are integral to the work of the academy, in serving the global social good.

We can claim a space as culturally responsive researchers, in support of our longevity in the academic workplace, through our dossiers. As with projects, dossiers should bring attention to manners in which we transform and expand knowledge in the world while foregrounding how the specificity of cultures, contexts, and communities informs what we do. We should also speak to how our personhoods and participant relationships support our work, and uplift our fights against hegemonic counting and gatekeeping mechanisms in order to improve academia for all stakeholders in research (including participants).

Last, we should continue to seek out opportunities for growth and networking that will support our journeys of becoming more culturally responsive. These include participating in local, regional, national, and international associations, collectives, and conferences (such as the Advanced Methods Institute). With regard to publications, opportunities also include submitting our work to those that embrace our approaches, "special issue" calls from those that typically prioritize "conventional" approaches, and even those that prioritize "conventional" approaches with the intention of disrupting their investments in western and white supremacy. As a cornerstone of culturally responsive research, scholars should also invest in engagement with stakeholders beyond the academy. Doing so includes active participation in activism and advocacy efforts, providing and/or creating access to goods, services, and spheres of influence, and sharing your work in popular publications and public forums to solicit broader engagement.

We leave you with questions that you might work to answer as you prepare to embark on or advance in developing research that is culturally responsive.

A Call to Action: Closing Activity
Questions for Consideration

1. How do/can your research projects:

    a. Transform the methods you use to challenge "convention?"
    b. Invite others to engage with your research through additional studies and community actions?
    c. Specify the communities, cultures, and their contexts as part of their research design?

2. How do/can you engage your liminality as a person, researcher, and member of your study populations (where applicable) as an important part of your research in community *with* participants?

3. How do/can your approaches challenge dominant concepts about where knowledge exists, how to gather and analyze it, how to engage with research participants, and researcher positionality in scholarship?

4. Have you experienced the challenges we discussed as part of doing culturally responsive research? How did you navigate them? How could you (have) navigate(d) them?

5. How does/can your research agenda illustrate your scholarly identity as being culturally responsive?

6. How does/can your dossier illustrate your scholarly identity as being culturally responsive more broadly?

7. What is your research dissemination action plan: how will you connect with

   a. Other scholars and researchers?
   b. Journals, other publications, conferences, etc.?
   c. Practitioners?
   d. Community members?

INDEX